STUDY GUIDE on DICKENS'

A CHRISTMAS CAROL

MADE SUPER SUPER EASY

TEXT EXPLAINED IN GREAT DETAIL

ACHIEVE TOP GRADES
A MUST FOR ALL STUDENTS

EVELYN SAMUEL on Dickens

Dickens' A Christmas Carol
Made Super Super Easy
First Edition Published by Evelyn Samuel
Copyright © 2020 Evelyn Samuel

EveMadeSuperEasyBooks
www.EveSuperEasyBooks.com
EveSuperEasyBooks@gmail.com

DEDICATED TO

My late sister Mavis, you will always be treasured and never forgotten

REVIEWS

★★★★★ **The only book you need for A Christmas Carol**
Reviewed 1 June 2021
My son, who is in year 11, has used this book and no other in order to further his knowledge of A Christmas Carol. This guide puts other, more popular study guides to shame, as not only does it have detailed scene summaries and quotation analysis, but also a wide range of possible questions from numerous exam boards and even model answers. An absolute gem of a book!

★★★★★ **Amazing**
Reviewed 20 February 2022
This book is amazing and has helped me and provided me with all the knowledge that I need about a Christmas Carol. It has helped me understand the book and has made it easier

★★★★★ **Very easy to understand**
Reviewed 3 June 2021
The book is amazing my soon found it very easy, thank you so much for the support.

★★★★★ **Such a good buy – very helpful book**
Reviewed 18 February 2021
The book is so helpful as basically all in one. Probably the only book you need to learn Christmas Carol. It gives context, expands on each character whilst also highlighting the txt and expanding it on the right-hand side. It's a very easy book to understand.

★★★★★ **Fantastic resource!**
Reviewed 25 August 2021
Easy to follow guide. The kids absolutely love it! Definitely recommending this to my friends and family.

★★★★★ **A Christmas Carol Made Super Super Easy by Evelyn Samuel**
Reviewed 30 May 2021
I absolutely loved the revision guide and it really helped me with my work during this very difficult time. I would highly recommend buying this book for other GCSE students.

★★★★★ **English**
Reviewed 19 October 2021
Great revision guide.

PREFACE

To all students reading my study guide A Christmas Carol Made Super Super Easy. I do hope that my wealth of information will assist you to achieve the highest possible grades. I have formulated a unique structure where detailed explanations are next to the text to make it super super easy for you to connect and understand the book, and to revise without the need to resort to more than one book.

Each Stave is defined by a Summary followed by in-depth explanations which is highlighted with relevant important quotes. It identifies connotated meaning, imagery, symbolism, and linguistic devices. The context identifies the rationale behind the book, so that although Dickens wrote the book as a fantasy Ghost story, the novel essentially revolves around and relates to social issues in the Victorian age, exactly as Dickens intended.

A set of short questions are added to **Stave1** through to **Stave 5**, the answers to which can be easily found in my text. A detailed explanation of each main character in the book is provided so that the fabric of their relationships can be better understood. The social themes authenticate the human interactions portrayed in the book - the gulf between rich and poor. Typical exam questions are included to give some idea of the scope sought by the Exam Boards. Further details can be found in the Specification published by the Exam Boards on their websites.

Finally, sample essays are provided to give you some idea of the standard expected by the Exam Boards.

Good Luck with your studies and your exam results.

FOREWARD

What a super super easy way to study and understand Dickens' 'A Christmas Carol'. No need to match text with explanation when both are next to each other.

I really enjoyed looking left at the text and right at the explanation. The structure and content of this fantastic book is a solid base to get to grip with this wonderful, emotional, fantasy where Jacob Marley the deceased partner of Ebenezer Scrooge, seeks to save him from the heavy chains of iniquity by sending three Spirits, each Spirit taking Scrooge on a journey of truth.

I can definitely recommend this study guide to all students, and hope they gain as much insight, as I did, into Dickens' 'A Christmas Carol'.

Teacher of English

**BOOKS PUBLISHED IN THE SERIES
MADE SUPER SUPER EASY**

Shakespeare's
MACBETH
ROMEO AND JULIET
OTHELLO
HAMLET

Priestley's
AN INSPECTOR CALLS

Dickens'
A CHRISTMAS CAROL

_____

**SOON TO FOLLOW IN THE SERIES
MADE SUPER SUPER EASY**

Shakespeare's
THE TEMPEST
TWELFTH NIGHT
A MIDSUMMER'S NIGHT DREAM
THE MERCHANT OF VENICE

www.EveSuperEasyBooks.com
EveSuperEasyBooks@gmail.com

CONTENTS

THEMES   130

EXAM STYLE QUESTIONS   179

AUTHOR   200

AUTHOR

Charles Dickens published 'A Christmas Carol' in 1843, and although one of many books written by him on the theme of Victorian life, is perhaps his most popular piece of fiction, much loved by readers for its warmth and hope that deep inside every person is a generosity without bounds that can defeat the evils of greed, avarice, and selfishness.

His main aim was to expose the exploitation of the underprivileged class prevalent in Victorian society.

NOVELLA

A Christmas Carol is the story of Ebenezer Scrooge, a wealthy old miser who is set in his way with no love for anything except for the making of money. He is confronted by the Ghost of his former business partner Jacob Marley who out of concern for his mortal soul, has arranged for three Spirits in turn to visit Scrooge.

The First Spirit takes Scrooge on a journey through his past life. The Second through his present life. Finally, the Third into the future, where Scrooge's old ways lead to unhappiness. Whereas carol singers, charity collectors, relatives, are shunned by Scrooge, and Bob Cratchit underpaid and overworked, redemption turns Scrooge into a new person set in new ways to help those less fortunate than himself. Scrooge becomes a second father to Tiny Tim, the crippled son of Bob Cratchit.

CONTEXT

Right at the outset we have to understand what prompted Charles Dickens to write the novel 'A Christmas Carol'. His ideas for writing this novel stemmed from harrowing accounts that arose from his childhood.

He was born in an affluent middle-class family in 1812. Unfortunately, his father was heavily in debt and had to go to a debtor's prison. Sadly, he was forced to leave school at the age of 12 to work in a factory. He witnessed firsthand the struggles and the miseries experienced by the poor whilst working in the factory and he highlighted the terrible plight of the poor socialist class in Victorian Britain. He wanted to fire up people's consciousness and hoped that through his writings the Capitalist class will become more socially aware of the underlying problems of the poor and assume social responsibility for them.

He became an ardent supporter and campaigned fervently for social reforms especially child labour. He was bitterly opposed to the Capitalist classes shoddy treatment of the poverty-stricken Socialist under-class and he voiced this by writing in a bitter tone. This prompted him to expose the avaricious nature of the Victorian Capitalist class. The characters in 'A Christmas Carol' reflects the relationship between poverty and crime. Many innocent people had to resort to criminal behaviour out of desperation.

To create social awareness, Dickens had carefully and meticulously crafted his characters. Each character is reflective of the social situation in Victorian Times. For example, Scrooge is portrayed as a caricature of a typical Capitalist class avaricious business owner who exploit the poor. On the other hand, the Cratchits perfectly represent the poor poverty-stricken Socialist class.

CHARACTERS

EBENEZER SCROOGE	businessman
JACOB MARLEY	deceased business partner of Scrooge

[Spirits]

FIRST SPIRIT	ghost of Christmas Past
SECOND SPIRIT	ghost of Christmas Present
IGNORANCE	boy representing Doom
WANT	girl representing Poverty
LAST SPIRIT	ghost of Christmas Yet to Come

[Cratchit Family]

BOB CRATCHIT	clerk to Scrooge
TINY TIM	crippled son of Bob Cratchit
MARTHA	second eldest daughter of Bob Cratchit
PETER	son of Bob Cratchit
BELINDA	eldest daughter of Bob Cratchit

[Scrooge Family]

FAN	sister of Scrooge
FRED	nephew to Scrooge
FRED's WIFE	niece to Scrooge

[Others]

TOPPER	friend of Fred
ALI BABA	woodsman
ROBIN CURSOE	green and yellow tail parrot
FEZZIWIG	employer of Scrooge
DICK WILKINS	apprentice friend
BELLE	fiancée of Scrooge
OLD JOE	Beetling Shop Owner
CHARWOMAN	house cleaner
LAUNDRESS	Mrs Dilber, linen washer and ironer
UNDERTAKER	scavenger of personal belongings of the dead
CAROLINE	in debt to Scrooge

ENTRANCES

STAVE 1	STAVE 2	STAVE 3	STAVE 4	STAVE 5
OFFICE	**LODGINGS**	**LODGINGS**	**EXCHANGE**	**LODGINGS**
Scrooge	Scrooge	Scrooge	Scrooge	Scrooge
Cratchit	First Spirit	Second Spirit	Last Spirit	Boy
Nephew Fred			Businessmen	Poulterer
Charity Workers				
Carol Singers				
LODGINGS	**SCHOOL**	**MARKET**	**STREET**	**STREET**
Scrooge	Scrooge	Scrooge	Scrooge	Charity Worker
Ghost Marley	First Spirit	Second Spirit	Last Spirit	Church goes
	Boy Scrooge	Shopkeepers	Two Persons	Passers by
	Sister Fan	Shoppers		
	School Master			
	WAREHOUSE	**CRATCHIT's**	**BEETLING**	**FRED's HOUSE**
	Scrooge	Scrooge	Scrooge	Scrooge
	First Spirit	Second Spirit	Last Spirit	Nephew Fred
	Fezziwig	Mrs Cratchit	Old Joe	Scrooge's Niece
	Young Scrooge	Belinda	Charwoman	Topper
	Dick Wilkins	Master Peter	Laundress	Invited Guests
	Invited Guests	Martha	Undertaker man	
		Bob Cratchit		
		Tiny Tim		
	PARK BENCH	**MOOR**	**DARK ROOM**	**OFFICE**
	Scrooge	Scrooge	Scrooge	Scrooge
	First Spirit	Second Spirit	Last Spirit	Bob Cratchit
	Young Scrooge	Miners	Dead Man	
	Fiancee Belle			
	BELLE's	**LIGHTHOUSE**	**CAROLINE's**	
	Scrooge	Scrooge	Scrooge	
	First Spirit	Second Spirit	Last Spirit	
	Belle & Child	Lighthouse Men	Caroline	
	Husband		Husband	
	LODGINGS	**SHIP**	**CRATCHIT's**	
	Scrooge	Scrooge	Scrooge	
	First Spirit	Second Spirit	Last Spirit	
		Ship's Crew	Cratchit Family	
			Bob Cratchit	
			Tiny Tim	
		FRED's HOUSE	**OFFICE**	
		Scrooge	Scrooge	
		Second Spirit	Dead Man	
		Nephew Fred		
		Scrooge's Niece		
		Niece's Sisters		
		Topper		
		Invited Guests		
		OPEN SPACE	**CHURCHYARD**	
		Scrooge	Scrooge	
		Second Spirit	Last Spirit	
		Boy Ignorance		
		Girl Want		
		Last Spirit		

TIMELINE

Events take place over **TWO** days: - **Christmas Eve** and **Christmas Day**.
On Christmas Eve, Marley's Ghost tells Scrooge of three visits by different Spirits on three consecutive nights. The first Spirit at 1AM, the second Spirit at 1AM the next night, and the last Spirit at 12AM on the final night. However, Scrooge wakes on Christmas Day – the Spirits have done it all in one night! Scrooge still has Christmas Day to redeem himself and save Tiny Tim.

STAVE 1	Office	Scrooge berates his Clerk Bob Cratchit, Nephew Fred, Charity collectors, Carol Singers for celebrating Christmas
	Lodgings	Marley's Ghost informs Scrooge of visitations by Spirits
STAVE 2	Lodgings	First Spirit visits Scrooge to take him into his past
	School	Scrooge observes his unhappy childhood whereas a boy he is consoled by his sister Fan
	Warehouse	Scrooge observes his apprenticeship at Fezziwig
	Park Bench	Fiancée Belle rejects young Scrooge as a suitor because of his love for nothing but money
	Belle's	Scrooge sees how happy Belle is with her children
	Lodgings	Scrooge traps the Spirit under an extinguisher-cap
STAVE 3	Lodgings	Second Spirit visits Scrooge to take him on a journey to see how others celebrated Christmas in the present
	Market	Scrooge sees the joy felt by ordinary people at Christmas
	Cratchit's	Bob arrives home with Tiny Tim on his shoulder, to enjoy Mrs Cratchit's wonderful Christmas dinner
	Moor	Scrooge observes Miners celebrating Christmas
	Lighthouse	Scrooge observes Light-Keepers celebrating Christmas
	Ship	Scrooge observes ship's crew celebrating Christmas
	Fred's House	Nephew Fred tries to defend Scrooge
	Open Space	Ageing Spirit reveals Boy Ignorance and Girl Want, and then encounters the Last Spirit
STAVE 4	Merchants	Businessmen discuss Scrooge's demise
	Street	Two by-standers on the street discuss Scrooge's demise
	Beetling	Shopkeeper Old Joe trades with Charwomen, Laundress and Undertaker to buy dead man's possessions
	Dark Room	Scrooge views dead man who he believes might be him
	Caroline's	Scrooge views Caroline family and their joy on hearing of the dead of Scrooge
	Cratchit's	Bob sits by deceased Tiny Tim and cannot be consoled
	Office	Scrooge observes a different person sitting in his office
	Churchyard	Scrooge is shown his grave. Distraught Scrooge pledges to honour Christmas. Spirit melts into bedpost.
STAVE 5	Lodgings	Scrooge calls street boy to get Poulterer to bring Turkey and then take it to the Cratchits
	Street	Scrooge greets pedestrians, guarantees money to Charity
	Fred's House	Nephew Fred welcomes Scrooge to his Christmas dinner
	Office	Scrooge berates Bob for lateness, then reveals his plan to help the Cratchit family and in particular Tiny Tim

SYNOPSIS

A Christmas Carol is a short, entertaining story written for both young and old, delivering a heartfelt message about the joy of self-redemption when guided by others. In this case, a ghost Jacob Marley heralding the arrival of Three Spirits, each Spirit taking Ebenezer Scrooge on a journey of truth to change his miserly and uncaring ways.

Stave One of the Book introduces the reader to Ebenezer Scrooge whose sole focus is to make money by whatever means. His long-suffering clerk, Bob Cratchit works long hours in cold conditions because Scrooge won't pay for coal. In the afternoon on Christmas Eve, Scrooge's nephew Fred arrives to invite him to Christmas dinner but is treated very badly by Scrooge. Next the two charity collectors, and then a carol singer, are both refused money. Later, having left the office, and arriving at his lodgings, strange events happen. The front door knocker changed into the face of Jacob Marley, his now deceased and former business partner, and later in his bedroom, a clanging noise heralded the arrival of the ghostly form of Marley bound in heavy chains, there to warn Scrooge of the visitations by Three Spirits sent to teach him a lesson of love and charity.

Stave Two, at twelve midnight, the Ghost of Christmas Past appears, sent to take Scrooge on a journey through his unhappy childhood. Scrooge as a boy is seen alone in a schoolroom, and later during another Christmas, with his sister Fan. The journey continues with Scrooge now a young man, at a Christmas party of his first employer Fezziwig where Scrooge enjoys partaking in the merriment. But later, on a park bench, he is rejected by his fiancée Belle for his love of money followed by the heartache of seeing her later in life happily married with children.

Stave Three, at one in the morning on Christmas Day, the Ghost of Christmas Present appears. Both visit a busy street as preparations are made for Christmas celebrations, where humour and happiness abound. Then they visit the Cratchit family as they prepare lunch, where Scrooge learns that crippled Tiny Tim the son of Bob Cratchit will not survive unless the future is changed. As darkness is falling, they watch a series of visions showing how miners and sailors spend Christmas. Next, they arrive at Fred's house where a party is about to begin and learn that he is pitied. At a quarter to Midnight on Christmas Eve, the Ghost began to age, and from beneath his robes emerged a boy called Ignorance and a girl called Want. The Ghost warns Scrooge to beware of Ignorance, and then vanishes.

Stave Four, the clock strikes twelve midnight, it's Christmas Day, the Ghost of Christmas Yet to Come glides ominously towards Scrooge to take him into the future to witness conversations among businessmen about a man who has just died. No one cares, and no respect is paid, as Scrooge is witness to the selling of the dead man's bed-curtains, shirt, and possessions at a shop.

They journey to the dead man's room, where Scrooge refuses to look at the dead man face, fearing that it is he. Scrooge witnesses a couple who are relieved that they will not have to repay their debt owed to the dead man. They continue their journey to the Cratchit's house to learn of the untimely, but not unexpected death of Tiny Tim. Bob and the family are grief-stricken. Scrooge is now in a somber mood. Finally, the Ghost and Scrooge stand in front of a neglected tombstone overgrown with weeds, on which is engraved the name EBENEZER SCROOGE. Shocked, Scrooge vows to change his ways. The Ghost then disappears.

Stave Five, Scrooge wakes to discover that all the visitations have taken place over one night. He opens his bedroom window, asks a boy to buy the biggest Turkey and pays for a cab to take the boy and the Turkey to Bob Cratchit's house. He then greets people on the street; gives a generous donation to the charity collector whom he had refused earlier; goes to church; and arrives at Fred's house wary to enter, but is greeted with such love and affection. The next day, Scrooge surprises Bob, raises his wage, and promises to help his family and, most importantly, Tiny Tim who does not die early, and who has a second father in Scrooge. Scrooge is redeemed, is not a lover solely of money, and is known as a man who keeps Christmas. Dickens end the A Christmas Carol with Tiny Tim's prayer "God bless Us, Every One"

SETTING

Dickens book 'A Christmas Carol' is set in the Victorian age when the British Empire was beginning to emerge, and the population growth in cities such as London fueled its development. Unfortunately, no provision was made for social issues, so many people found themselves competing for lack of resources, resulting in squalor and poverty for those without means. Even Dickens's father found himself in a debtor's prison. Dickens used London to expose the type of environment where squalor and poverty were prevalent as it contained a high proportion of the population at the time; this was where jobs were more likely available.

The London locations used in the story are:

SCROOGE's Office	SCROOGE's House	SCROOGE's Grave
FRED's House	CRATCHIT's House	JOE's Shop
CAROLINE's House	The STREET	The CHURCH
The DARK ROOM	The MARKET	The EXCHANGE

The other locations used in the story are:

SCROOGE's School	BELLE's House	FEZZIWIG's Warehouse
The MOOR	The LIGHTHOUSE	The SHIP

FORM

A Christmas Carol is a work of narrative prose fiction, longer than a short story but shorter than a novel, typically of no more than 120 pages or 40,000 words. Dickens refers to each section as a Stave not a Chapter to imply that the book has a musical form built in, to be read aloud as a rhythm, much as carols are sung aloud.

STRUCTURE

A Christmas Carol is a typical novella where unlike a novel with several reversal of character in the development of the storyline, this has one reversal: the redemption of Scrooge. Marley is the character who sets the story in motion. Each Ghost develops the action or creates a rising action. Eventually, this leads to the climax when Scrooge is confronted by the gravestone, an epiphany, the moment that Scrooge see the world in a new way, the moment when he knows that he needs to change and to reform if he is to get any happiness from his life. Only by helping others will this happen. Stave Five, is the path of falling action, where Scrooge has changed, and ensues that Tiny Tim will not die prematurely.

LANGUAGE

Dickens creates a lively narrative filled with linguistic techniques, and based his characters on his observations of real people and the places they inhabited and worked in.

The narrative language device is used with great effect by Dickens to inform the reader and bring the characters and the places to live. This gives an insight into Scrooge's thoughts and feelings throughout the story and creates realism.

The character language device is used to great effect to define who each person is and their associated occupation. For example, the name Cratchit identifies with someone who scratches out a living and survives only through mutual support, acting as a crutch for others.

The imagery language device is used create rich descriptive scenes. Dickens make use of this device through the story, stimulating the readers imagination. For example,

'Upon it's coming in, the dying flame leaped up, as though it cried, 'I know him! Marley's Ghost! and fell again.'

The simile language device is used to compare different things so as to gain a greater understanding of one of them. Dickens uses it to great effect. For example, when describing solitude, the simile is 'solitary as an oyster', implying no friends in Scrooge's case.

The personification language device is used to give human attributes or feelings to an inanimate object. An example, would be
'not a knocker, but Marley's face'.

The knocker is now endowed with human form.

The pathetic fallacy language device is used to give objects and events human emotions and traits. Dickens makes good use of this device to introduce human emotions into potatoes who

'knocked loudly at the saucepan-lid to be let out and pealed'.

The weather is another use by Dickens of pathetic fallacy:

'cold, piping for the blood to dance to'.

The sentence style language device is used to keep the flow going when there are many clauses and phrases connected together in a sentence: use of the 'and' rather than 'comma'. Short sentences are used to create a sense of emotion.

The adjective language device is often used by Dickens to create humour by modifying nouns in such a way as to make the noun seem ridiculous. For example,

'Oh! But he was tight-fisted hand at the grindstone, Scrooge! a squeezing, wrenching, grasping, scraping, clutching, covetous old sinner!'

We can assume that Dickens spits out these many adjectives to show his bitterness and anger towards the capitalist class. Hence writing in a very bitter tone. The extended image of the sinner made more effective by the adjectives revealing Scrooge's terrible character.

TEXT AND EXPLANATION

The Dickensian text is written in the left column, and the explanation and interpretation, in the right column.

Important quotes and phrases in the text are highlighted and reproduced in the explanation column for discussion, on the same page. Consequently, there is no need to turn pages!

A summary of each Stave precedes the text and explanation to give an overall perspective of the events in the story.

The writer is talking directly to us and he wants us to connect and identify with his poignant message of social responsibility. We learn that Jacob Marley is dead, and we are introduced to Ebenezer Scrooge who is an avaricious, cold-hearted miser. He was 'tight-fisted 'and left his clerk Bob Cratchit very cold and refused to give him adequate heating. Dickens deliberately chose a very jovial time of the year - Christmas Eve - for his setting. This perfect setting creates a very festive, joyful atmosphere, a season of giving, sharing, love and generosity. We are appalled at Scrooge's shoddy treatment of his visitors, like his cheerful nephew,

"A merry Christmas, Uncle!"

and Scrooge rudely replied,

"Humbug!"

Even when the two charity collectors approached him for a donation, he again enquired whether,

"Are there no prisons?"

He is also cold and ruthless towards the carol singer as well and he,

'Seized the ruler with such energy of action that the singer fled in terror.'

That night, the Ghost of Jacob Marley - his dead business partner - visits Scrooge. Marley warns him that his mean ways and lack of social responsibility will lead to his doom.

Marley also tells Scrooge that three ghosts will visit him and show him the error of his ways.

End of SUMMARY on STAVE one

Marley was dead: to begin with. There is no doubt whatever about that. The register of his burial was signed by the clergyman, the clerk, the undertaker, and the chief mourner. Scrooge signed it: and Scrooge's name was good upon 'Change, for anything he chose to put his hand to.

Old Marley was as dead as a door-nail

Mind! I don't mean to say that I know, of my own knowledge, what there is particularly dead about a door-nail. I might have been inclined, myself, to regard a coffin-nail as the deadest piece of ironmongery in the trade. But the wisdom of our ancestors is in the simile; and my unhallowed hands shall not disturb it, or the Country's done for. You will therefore permit me to repeat, emphatically, that Marley was as dead as a door-nail.

Scrooge knew he was dead? Of course he did. How could it be otherwise? Scrooge and he were partners for I don't know how many years. Scrooge was his sole executor, his sole administrator, his sole assign, his sole residuary legatee, his sole friend, and sole mourner. And even Scrooge was not so dreadfully cut up by the sad event, but that he was an excellent man of business on the very day of the funeral, and solemnised it with an undoubted bargain.

The mention of Marley's funeral brings me back to the point I started from. There is no doubt that Marley was dead. This must be distinctly understood, or nothing wonderful can come of the story I am going to relate. If we were not perfectly convinced that Hamlet's Father died before the play began, there would be nothing more remarkable in his taking a stroll at night, in an easterly wind, upon his own ramparts, than there would be in any other middle-aged gentleman rashly turning out after dark in a breezy spot—say Saint Paul's Churchyard for instance—literally to astonish his son's weak mind.

Stave 1 starts with a very direct matter-of-fact sentence.

'Marley was dead to begin with'

It's a very poignant start heralding a sort of warning. Dickens places much emphasis on the fact that Marley is dead which foreshadows his appearance to Scrooge later in the novel. The narrator's direct address to us forces us to listen to him and he further makes use of a simile,

'Old Marley was a dead as a door-nail'

ensuring that the reader has established the fact that Marley was dead. Ironically, Dickens uses a repeated repetition of the adjective 'sole' to describe Marley's loneliness, "sole administrator", "sole assign" and he later describes Scrooge as being,

"solitary as an oyster"

Dickens gives us a first glimpse of Scrooge's cold, detached character, shown towards the death of Marley,

'not so dreadfully cut up by the sad event'

Scrooge's shocking behaviour even extends to Marley's funeral when he continued to do business,

'an excellent man of business on the very day of the funeral'

Marley's Funeral Procession to Churchyard

Scrooge never painted out Old Marley's name. There it stood, years afterwards, above the warehouse door: Scrooge and Marley. The firm was known as Scrooge and Marley. Sometimes people new to the business called Scrooge Scrooge, and sometimes Marley, but he answered to both names. It was all the same to him.

Warehouse Sign still with Marley's name

Oh! But he was a tight-fisted hand at the grindstone, Scrooge! a squeezing,
wrenching, grasping, scraping, clutching, covetous, old sinner! Hard and sharp as flint, from which no steel had ever struck out generous fire; secret, and self-contained, and solitary as an oyster.

Scrooge 'solitary as an oyster'

Dickens writes with a mocking tone by using the adjective 'excellent', and he highlights Scrooge's greed for money and lack of social responsibility.

Dickens gives us a vivid, visual picture with his detailed description of Scrooge.

'tight-fisted hand at the grindstone'

'Tight-fisted' relating to his meanness whilst the physical properties of a grindstone is hard and cold which can be attributed to Scrooge's character. Note how Dickens' anger is expressed by the use of the exclamation mark when he spits out the name 'Scrooge!', which is filled with bitterness for the cold Capitalist classes and their avaricious nature. Dickens goes on by using a string of unflattering verbs,

'squeezing, wrenching, grasping, scraping, clutching, covetous, old sinner!'

Once again, Dickens uses an exclamation mark to show his fury and his use of many harsh verbs - squeezing, wrenching, grasping, scraping, and clutching can denote his rising anger towards Scrooge's selfish behaviour.

Dickens also describes Scrooge's ruthlessness with a simile,

'Hard and sharp as flint'

Dickens uses very strong, harsh words to describe Scrooge's terrible, greedy nature. The simile here to describe Scrooge's ruthless character suggests he is hard and harsh, and he is compared to flint which is sharp and poky. The noun 'steel' is also cold and hard used by Dickens to describe Scrooge's personality.

Dickens use of the alliteration,

'self-contained and solitary'

bluntly attacks his isolated and reserved lifestyle. The imagery of the oyster is an example of his isolation and loneliness,

"solitary as an oyster"

The rough exterior of the oyster can be associated with Scrooge's rough, unkind behaviour to other people.

The cold within him froze his old features, nipped his pointed nose, shrivelled his cheek, stiffened his gait; made his eyes red, his thin lips blue; and spoke out shrewdly in his grating voice. A frosty rime was on his head, and on his eyebrows, and his wiry chin. He carried his own low temperature always about with him; he iced his office in the dog-days; and didn't thaw it one degree at Christmas.

Scrooge in his Office

Scrooge in his cold office

Dickens also confirms that Scrooge's greed and selfishness isolated him like the lonely pearl living inside an oyster, with no family of friends.

Dickens gives vent to his fury and frustration towards the Capitalist class by presenting Scrooge in a very negative light, so that we will take note of the consequences of our selfish behaviour. He uses cold imagery to highlight the extent of Scrooge's cold, ugly, selfish behaviour.

'cold within him froze'
'carried his own low temperature'

Dickens negatively describes and mocks Scrooge's changing physical features,

'nipped his pointed nose,
shrivelled his cheeks,
stiffened his gait'

insinuating that his ugly mean character is having a negative impact on his physical features.

Dickens even attacks him using colour imagery,

'made his eyes red, his thin lips blue'

suggesting that even his appearance is odd, considering his ugly personality which is matching his ugly character.

Dickens also mockingly picks on his

'grating voice'

and he describes, once again his cold character by using cold imagery, 'frosty-rime.'

'a frosty rime on his head, and on his eyebrows, and his wiry chin'

Dickens ensured that just like his cold unappealing appearance, his surroundings matched, because

'he iced his office'

and refused to pay for heating.

External heat and cold had little influence on Scrooge. No warmth could warm, no wintry weather chill him. No wind that blew was bitterer than he, no falling snow was more intent upon its purpose, no pelting rain less open to entreaty. Foul weather didn't know where to have him. The heaviest rain, and snow, and hail, and sleet, could boast of the advantage over him in only one respect. They often "came down" handsomely, and Scrooge never did.

Nobody ever stopped Scrooge in the street

Nobody ever stopped him in the street to say, with gladsome looks, "My dear Scrooge, how are you? When will you come to see me?" No beggars implored him to bestow a trifle, no children asked him what it was o'clock, no man or woman ever once in all his life inquired the way to such and such a place, of Scrooge. Even the blind men's dogs appeared to know him; and when they saw him coming on, would tug their owners into doorways and up courts; and then would wag their tails as though they said, "No eye at all is better than an evil eye, dark master!"

But what did Scrooge care! It was the very thing he liked. To edge his way along the crowded paths of life, warning all human sympathy to keep its distance, was what the knowing ones call 'nuts' to Scrooge.

Once upon a time—of all the good days in the year, on Christmas Eve—old Scrooge sat busy in his counting-house. It was cold, bleak, biting weather: foggy withal: and he could hear the people in the court outside, go wheezing up and down, beating their hands upon their breasts, and stamping their feet upon the pavement stones to warm them.

and refused to pay for heating. Dickens's bitterly describe Scrooge's wretched personality and the use of pathetic fallacy,

'and snow, hail, and sleet'

further enhances his cold, uncharitable, greedy nature and the constant repetition of the negative,

'no'

tells us of his stern, rigid character. Scrooge was only interested in money, and he did not communicate socially with people.

Dickens said that he

'carried his own low temperature'

'nobody ever stopped him in the street'

and extended a cordiality towards him

"When will you come and see me?"

Even the dogs would tug their owners away. Scrooge was referred to as,

'dark master'

Once again, Dickens is very forthright in his harsh criticism of Scrooge by using dark imagery to refer to him - highlighting for the reader his dark evil side.

The use of the rhetorical question,

"But what did Scrooge care!"

Dickens wanted to shock the reader about Scrooge's terrible behaviour towards the poor and life in general. He was contented to keep his distance from people.

Scrooge is portrayed as being greedy because instead of blending in with the Christmas buzz, he was busy in his counting-house counting his money.

Dicken's uses pathetic fallacy,

'It was cold, bleak, biting weather: foggy withal."

The city clocks had only just gone three, but it was quite dark already—it had not been light all day—and candles were flaring in the windows of the neighbouring offices, like ruddy smears upon the palpable brown air. The fog came pouring in at every chink and keyhole, and was so dense without, that although the court was of the narrowest, the houses opposite were mere phantoms. To see the dingy cloud come drooping down, obscuring everything, one might have thought that Nature lived hard by, and was brewing on a large scale.

The door of Scrooge's counting-house was open that he might keep his eye upon his clerk, who in a dismal little cell beyond, a sort of tank, was copying letters. Scrooge had a very small fire, but the clerk's fire was so very much smaller that it looked like one coal. But he couldn't replenish it, for Scrooge kept the coal-box in his own room; and so surely as the clerk came in with the shovel, the master predicted that it would be necessary for them to part. Wherefore the clerk put on his white comforter, and tried to warm himself at the candle; in which effort, not being a man of a strong imagination, he failed.

"A merry Christmas, uncle! God save you!" cried a cheerful voice. It was the voice of Scrooge's nephew, who came upon him so quickly that this was the first intimation he had of his approach.
"Bah!" said Scrooge, "Humbug!"

He had so heated himself with rapid walking in the fog and frost, this nephew of Scrooge's, that he was all in a glow; his face was ruddy and handsome; his eyes sparkled, and his breath smoked again.

"Christmas a humbug, uncle!" said Scrooge's nephew. "You don't mean that, I am sure?"

"I do," said Scrooge. "Merry Christmas! What right have you to be merry? What reason have you to be merry? You're poor enough."

"Come, then," returned the nephew gaily. "What right have you to be dismal? What reason have you to be morose? You're rich enough."

Dickens once again highlights the situation of the poor who couldn't afford warm clothes and shoes because they had to stamp their feet on the pavement to keep warm. The sufferings of the poor Socialist class in Victorian Britain embittered Dickens and he fought passionately to improve the great divide between the rich Capitalist class and the poor Socialist class.

We are told that Scrooge's clerk sat rooted to his desk in a

'dismal little cell'

suggesting imprisonment

Bob warms himself at the candle

Scrooge's nephew bursts in, all cheerful and happy.

One can juxtapose Fred's warm personality to Scrooge's cold, indifferent character. He even changes the atmosphere in Scrooge's cold, dingy office. He creates a warm ambience in there,

'he was all in a glow.'

Scrooge's nephew challenges him after Scrooge's shock response to Christmas,

"What right have you to be merry?"

Followed by

"You're poor enough."

Scrooge pours contempt on the poor which is evident here.

Scrooge having no better answer ready on the spur of the moment, said,

"Bah!" again; and followed it up with "Humbug."
"Don't be cross, uncle!" said the nephew.
"What else can I be," returned the uncle, "when I live in such a world of fools as this? Merry Christmas! Out upon merry Christmas! What's Christmas time to you but a time for paying bills without money; a time for finding yourself a year older, but not an hour richer; a time for balancing your books and having every item in 'em through a round dozen of months presented dead against you? If I could work my will," said Scrooge indignantly, "every idiot who goes about with 'Merry Christmas 'on his lips, should be boiled with his own pudding, and buried with a stake of holly through his heart. He should!"

"Uncle!" pleaded the nephew.
"Nephew!" returned the uncle sternly, "keep Christmas in your own way, and let me keep it in mine."
"Keep it!" repeated Scrooge's nephew. "But you don't keep it."
"Let me leave it alone, then," said Scrooge. "Much good may it do you! Much good it has ever done you!"

"There are many things from which I might have derived good, by which I have not profited, I dare say," returned the nephew. "Christmas among the rest. But I am sure I have always thought of Christmas time, when it has come round—apart from the veneration due to its sacred name and origin, if anything belonging to it can be apart from that—as a good time; a kind, forgiving, charitable, pleasant time; the only time I know of, in the long calendar of the year, when men and women seem by one consent to open their shut-up hearts freely, and to think of people below them as if they really were fellow-passengers to the grave, and not another race of creatures bound on other journeys. And therefore, uncle, though it has never put a scrap of gold or silver in my pocket, I believe that it has done me good, and will do me good; and I say, God bless it!"

The terrible attitude of the Capitalist class towards the poor Socialist class angered Dickens and he was determined to teach them a lesson to see the error of their ways. Scrooge hates Christmas, thinking its rather foolish,

"I live in such a world of fools."

We literally see Scrooge's lack of heart here. Christmas is a time of cheer and excitement, but he is rude and bitter because his only concern is to make money. Dickens highlights Scrooge's bitterness for Christmas by giving us a graphic, violent imagery about idiots who goes about with,

"Merry Christmas, on his lips, should be boiled with his own pudding and buried with a stake of holly through the heart."

Scrooge's nephew extolling Christmas

His nephew expresses his joyous view of Christmas as,

"a kind, forgiving, charitable, pleasant time."

Scrooge's nephew reflects Dickens own experience of Christmas when he was young. He loved and enjoyed Christmas festivities.

Hence, Dickens is very clear in his message about how the poor should be treated during this time - that people should,

"open their shut-up hearts freely, and to think of people below them."

Dickens also hints at our mortality,
"fellow-passengers to the grave"

The clerk in the tank involuntarily applauded. Becoming immediately sensible of the impropriety, he poked the fire, and extinguished the last frail spark for ever.

"Let me hear another sound from you," said Scrooge, "and you'll keep your Christmas by losing your situation! You're quite a powerful speaker, sir," he added, turning to his nephew.
 "I wonder you don't go into Parliament."
"Don't be angry, uncle. Come! Dine with us to-morrow."

Scrooge said that he would see him—yes, indeed he did. He went the whole length of the expression, and said that he would see him in that extremity first.

"But why?" cried Scrooge's nephew. "Why?"
"Why did you get married?" said Scrooge.
"Because I fell in love."

"Because you fell in love!" growled Scrooge, as if that were the only one thing in the world more ridiculous than a merry Christmas. "Good afternoon!"

"Nay, uncle, but you never came to see me before that happened. Why give it as a reason for not coming now?"
"Good afternoon," said Scrooge.
"I want nothing from you; I ask nothing of you; why cannot we be friends?"
"Good afternoon," said Scrooge.

"I am sorry, with all my heart, to find you so resolute. We have never had any quarrel, to which I have been a party. But I have made the trial in homage to Christmas, and I'll keep my Christmas humour to the last. So A Merry Christmas, uncle!"
"Good afternoon!" said Scrooge.
"And A Happy New Year!"
"Good afternoon!" said Scrooge.

"Nay, uncle, but you never came to see me before that happened. Why give it as a reason for not coming now?"
"Good afternoon," said Scrooge.
"I want nothing from you; I ask nothing of you; why cannot we be friends?"
"Good afternoon," said Scrooge.

This foreshadows when the ghost reveals Scrooge's grave to him later on in the story.

Bob Cratchit angered Scrooge with his response for applauding Scrooge's nephew's outright bravery. But to the shock of the reader Scrooge threatens to fire him,

"and you'll keep your Christmas by losing your situation!"

Scrooge hates the fact that his nephew got married for love and not money. The animal imagery, 'growled'

"Because you fell in love, growled Scrooge."

suggests Scrooge's animalistic tendencies, his aggressive nature is evident here and his condemnation of love and marriage foreshadows the ghosts 'visits and its revelation of Scrooge's younger days when he ignored marriage and chose money above love.

Scrooge threaten to fire Bob his clerk

"I am sorry, with all my heart, to find you so resolute. We have never had any quarrel, to which I have been a party. But I have made the trial in homage to Christmas, and I'll keep my Christmas humour to the last. So A Merry Christmas, uncle!"
"Good afternoon!" said Scrooge.
"And A Happy New Year!"

"Nay, uncle, but you never came to see me before that happened. Why give it as a reason for not coming now?"
"Good afternoon," said Scrooge.
"I want nothing from you; I ask nothing of you; why cannot we be friends?"
"Good afternoon," said Scrooge.
"I am sorry, with all my heart, to find you so resolute. We have never had any quarrel, to which I have been a party. But I have made the trial in homage to Christmas, and I'll keep my Christmas humour to the last. So A Merry Christmas, uncle!"
"Good afternoon!" said Scrooge.
"And A Happy New Year!"
"Good afternoon!" said Scrooge.

His nephew left the room without an angry word, notwithstanding. He stopped at the outer door to bestow the greetings of the season on the clerk, who, cold as he was, was warmer than Scrooge; for he returned them cordially.
"There's another fellow," muttered Scrooge; who overheard him: "my clerk, with fifteen shillings a week, and a wife and family, talking about a merry Christmas. I'll retire to Bedlam."

This lunatic, in letting Scrooge's nephew out, had let two other people in. They were portly gentlemen, pleasant to behold, and now stood, with their hats off, in Scrooge's office. They had books and papers in their hands, and bowed to him.
"Scrooge and Marley's, I believe," said one of the gentlemen, referring to his list. "Have I the pleasure of addressing Mr. Scrooge, or Mr. Marley?"

"Mr. Marley has been dead these seven years," Scrooge replied. "He died seven years ago, this very night."

Dickens use of sensory imagery draws a contrast to the bitter-toned Scrooge to that of his clerk,

'who, cold as he was, was warmer than Scrooge'

Dickens emphasise the fact that despite his clerk being poor and cold, he was more loving than Scrooge. He gave off a warmth and love in keeping with the Christmas spirit, but Scrooge looks down upon his difficult life,

"with fifteen shillings a-week, a wife and family"

It certainly was for they had been two kindred spirits. At the ominous word "liberality," Scrooge frowned, and shook his head, and handed the credentials back.

"We have no doubt his liberality is well represented by his surviving partner," said the gentleman, presenting his credentials.

"At this festive season of the year, Mr. Scrooge," said the gentleman, taking up a pen, "it is more than usually desirable that we should make some slight provision for the poor and destitute, who suffer greatly at the present time.

Many thousands are in want of common necessaries; hundreds of thousands are in want of common comforts, sir."
"Are there no prisons?" asked Scrooge.
"Plenty of prisons," said the gentleman, laying down the pen again.
"And the Union workhouses?" demanded Scrooge. "Are they still in operation?"
They are. Still," returned the gentleman, "I wish I could say they were not."
"The Treadmill and the Poor Law are in full vigour, then?" said Scrooge.

"Both very busy, sir."
"Oh! I was afraid, from what you said at first, that something had occurred to stop them in their useful course," said Scrooge. "I'm very glad to hear it."
"Under the impression that they scarcely furnish Christian cheer of mind or body to the multitude," returned the gentleman, "a few of us are endeavouring to raise a fund to buy the Poor some meat and drink, and means of warmth. We choose this time, because it is a time, of all others, when Want is keenly felt, and Abundance rejoices. What shall I put you down for?"
"Nothing!" Scrooge replied.
"You wish to be anonymous?"
"I wish to be left alone," said Scrooge. "Since you ask me what I wish, gentlemen, that is my answer. I don't make merry myself at Christmas and I can't afford to make idle people merry. I help to support the establishments I have mentioned—they cost enough; and those who are badly off must go there."

Next to come under Scrooge's line of fire are two charity collectors who are collecting donations for the,

'poor and
destitute who suffer greatly at the present time'

The TWO Charity gentleman

Scrooge very rudely asks him,

"Are there no prisons?"

When the parishes raised the taxes to support the poor, the Poor Law became unpopular with the new middle-class taxpayers, hence in 1834 the Poor Law Amendment Act was passed. Scrooge enquiries,

"The treadmill and the Poor Law are in full vigour then?"

The treadmill was a cruel means of punishment which prisoners had to walk for several hours a day. Dickens father was imprisoned for not paying his debt. This first-hand experience is one of the reasons which motivated Dickens to write this novel.

Dickens uses a prison imagery to refer to the workhouses because his biggest problem was the workhouses which housed the poor people. They were known to be cruel and demeaning and people were afraid of going to the workhouse and Dickens wanted this to be changed to provide for the poor.

"Many can't go there; and many would rather die."

"If they would rather die," said Scrooge, "they had better do it, and decrease the surplus population. Besides—excuse me—I don't know that."

"But you might know it," observed the gentleman.

"It's not my business," Scrooge returned. "It's enough for a man to understand his own business, and not to interfere with other people's. Mine occupies me constantly. Good afternoon, gentlemen!"

Seeing clearly that it would be useless to pursue their point, the gentlemen withdrew. Scrooge resumed his labours with an improved opinion of himself, and in a more facetious temper than was usual with him.

Meanwhile the fog and darkness thickened so, that people ran about with flaring links, proffering their services to go before horses in carriages, and conduct them on their way. The ancient tower of a church, whose gruff old bell was always peeping slily down at Scrooge out of a Gothic window in the wall, became invisible, and struck the hours and quarters in the clouds, with tremulous vibrations afterwards as if its teeth were chattering in its frozen head up there.

The cold became intense. In the main street, at the corner of the court, some labourers were repairing the gas-pipes, and had lighted a great fire in a brazier, round which a party of ragged men and boys were gathered: warming their hands and winking their eyes before the blaze in rapture. The water-plug being left in solitude, its overflowings sullenly congealed, and turned to misanthropic ice. The brightness of the shops where holly sprigs and berries crackled in the lamp heat of the windows, made pale faces ruddy as they passed. Poulterers 'and grocers 'trades became a splendid joke: a glorious pageant, with which it was next to impossible to believe that such dull principles as bargain and sale had anything to do.

"Many can't go there, and many would rather die"

The prison imagery here can denote how the poor Socialist class in Victorian Britain were imprisoned by poverty. Scrooge was hard-hearted and he refused to contribute and believes that the tax he pays is enough to provide for the poor.

Scrooge referred to the people as 'idle 'and made a rather terrible statement that will shock a modern audience,

"If they would rather die, they had better do it, and decrease the surplus population"

Scrooge's hardened heart is visible here. Scrooge is echoing Thomas Malthus 'theory that there will be food shortages and poverty, and there will be hunger, and Dickens was totally against this theory.

Dickens shows us with much regret Scrooge's lack of social responsibility and selfishness,

"It's enough for a man to understand his own business, and not to interfere with other people's"

The use of the pathetic fallacy here,

"the fog and darkness thickened"

can be an example of Scrooge's dark, alien character and the fog can be associated with his 'blindness' being unable to see the suffering of the poor in the same way as you can't see through fog.

The symbolism of the bell is important here and Dickens personifies the bell giving it human qualities,

"gruff old bell was always peeping slily down at Scrooge"

One can connote that the bell is looking mockingly down upon Scrooge for his ugly behaviour towards the poor.

Dickens gives us a visual picture of Scrooge's surroundings. The jolly Christmas atmosphere filling the air,

"The brightness of the shops where holly sprigs and berries crackled"

The Lord Mayor, in the stronghold of the mighty Mansion House, gave orders to his fifty cooks and butlers to keep Christmas as a Lord Mayor's household should; and even the little tailor, whom he had fined five shillings on the previous Monday for being drunk and bloodthirsty in the streets, stirred up to-morrow's pudding in his garret, while his lean wife and the baby sallied out to buy the beef.

Foggier yet, and colder. Piercing, searching, biting cold. If the good Saint Dunstan had but nipped the Evil Spirit's nose with a touch of such weather as that, instead of using his familiar weapons, then indeed he would have roared to lusty purpose. The owner of one scant young nose, gnawed and mumbled by the hungry cold as bones are gnawed by dogs, stooped down at Scrooge's keyhole to regale him with a Christmas carol: but at the first sound of

"God bless you, merry gentleman!
May nothing you dismay!"

Scrooge seized the ruler with such energy of action, that the singer fled in terror, leaving the keyhole to the fog and even more congenial frost.

Unfortunately, most people worked on Christmas Day, especially the poor. But the Lord Mayor gave orders to his fifty cooks and butlers to keep Christmas as a Lord Mayor's household should. Here Dickens is mocking the rich for their careless, wasteful living yet the poor are cold and hungry at Christmas time.

Carol singers celebrating Christmas

Dickens 'mention of the indulgent lifestyles and extravagance of the rich Capitalist class indicates how frustrated he was at the lack of generosity and kindness among the rich in Victorian society. A total lack of kindness towards the poor, especially when Scrooge threatened the young carol singer with a ruler

Scrooge seized the ruler with such energy of action, that the singer fled in terror

Scrooge with the ruler to frighten the singer

TEXT Stave 1	EXPLANATION
At length the hour of shutting up the counting-house arrived. With an ill-will Scrooge dismounted from his stool, and tacitly admitted the fact to the expectant clerk in the Tank, who instantly snuffed his candle out, and put on his hat.	His last attack was on his clerk, and he accuses his clerk of being a pickpocket,
"You'll want all day to-morrow, I suppose?" said Scrooge.	"A poor excuse for picking a man's pocket every twenty-fifth of December"
"If quite convenient, sir."	
"It's not convenient," said Scrooge, "and it's not fair. If I was to stop half- a-crown for it, you'd think yourself ill-used, I'll be bound?"	Scrooge is furious that he has to give his clerk the day off on Christmas Day and pay him and he walked out with a 'growl 'once again suggesting his animalistic behaviour.
The clerk smiled faintly.	
"And yet," said Scrooge, "you don't think me ill-used, when I pay a day's wages for no work."	
The clerk observed that it was only once a year.	Dickens highlights for us how Scrooge's love for money had left him a very lonely man living in isolation. Remember the imagery of the pearl,
"A poor excuse for picking a man's pocket every twenty-fifth of December!" said Scrooge, buttoning his great-coat to the chin. "But I suppose you must have the whole day. Be here all the earlier next morning!"	"solitary as an oyster"

At length the hour of shutting up the counting-house arrived. With an ill-will Scrooge dismounted from his stool, and tacitly admitted the fact to the expectant clerk in the Tank, who instantly snuffed his candle out, and put on his hat.
"You'll want all day to-morrow, I suppose?" said Scrooge.
"If quite convenient, sir."
"It's not convenient," said Scrooge, "and it's not fair. If I was to stop half- a-crown for it, you'd think yourself ill-used, I'll be bound?"
The clerk smiled faintly.
"And yet," said Scrooge, "you don't think me ill-used, when I pay a day's wages for no work."
The clerk observed that it was only once a year.
"A poor excuse for picking a man's pocket every twenty-fifth of December!" said Scrooge, buttoning his great-coat to the chin. "But I suppose you must have the whole day. Be here all the earlier next morning!"

The clerk promised that he would; and Scrooge walked out with a growl. The office was closed in a twinkling, and the clerk, with the long ends of his white comforter dangling below his waist (for he boasted no great-coat), went down a slide on Cornhill, at the end of a lane of boys, twenty times, in honour of its being Christmas Eve, and then ran home to Camden Town as hard as he could pelt, to play at blindman's-buff.

Scrooge took his melancholy dinner in his usual melancholy tavern; and having read all the newspapers and beguiled the rest of the evening with his banker's-book, went home to bed. He lived in chambers which had once belonged to his deceased partner. They were a gloomy suite of rooms, in a lowering pile of building up a yard, where it had so little business to be, that one could scarcely help fancying it must have run there when it was a young house, playing at hide-and-seek with other houses, and forgotten the way out again.

His last attack was on his clerk, and he accuses his clerk of being a pickpocket,

"A poor excuse for picking a man's pocket every twenty-fifth of December"

Scrooge is furious that he has to give his clerk the day off on Christmas Day and pay him and he walked out with a 'growl 'once again suggesting his animalistic behaviour.

Dickens highlights for us how Scrooge's love for money had left him a very lonely man living in isolation. Remember the imagery of the pearl,

"solitary as an oyster"

Dickens gives us a visual picture of Scrooge's miserable, isolated lifestyle. He cleverly uses a repetition of the verb 'melancholy 'which highlights Scrooge's sad existence. The vivid description of Scrooge's house helps the reader visualise how this miser lived,

'gloomy suite of rooms'

Dickens uses a tone of mockery by personifying the house,

"It must have run there when it was a young house"

It was old enough now, and dreary enough, for nobody lived in it but Scrooge, the other rooms being all let out as offices. The yard was so dark that even Scrooge, who knew its every stone, was fain to grope with his hands. The fog and frost so hung about the black old gateway of the house, that it seemed as if the Genius of the Weather sat in mournful meditation on the threshold.

Now, it is a fact, that there was nothing at all particular about the knocker on the door, except that it was very large. It is also a fact, that Scrooge had seen it, night and morning, during his whole residence in that place; also that Scrooge had as little of what is called fancy about him as any man in the city of London, even including—which is a bold word—the corporation, aldermen, and livery. Let it also be borne in mind that Scrooge had not bestowed one thought on Marley, since his last mention of his seven years 'dead partner that afternoon. And then let any man explain to me, if he can, how it happened that Scrooge, having his key in the lock of the door, saw in the knocker, without its undergoing any intermediate process of change—not a knocker, but Marley's face.

Not a knocker, but Marley's face

Marley's face. It was not in impenetrable shadow as the other objects in the yard were, but had a dismal light about it, like a bad lobster in a dark cellar. It was not angry or ferocious but looked at Scrooge as Marley used to look: with ghostly spectacles turned up on its ghostly forehead.

Dickens goes on to describe its dreariness,

"dreary enough"

"yard was so dark"

and the

"black old gateway"

is representative of the dark imagery associated with Scrooge's house which so perfectly mirrors his character.

Surprisingly, Scrooge's door knocker changes into Marley's face with a strange light about it.

Marley's face was compared to having

"a dismal light about it, like a bad lobster in a dark cellar"

This imagery of the lobster is important because in Victorian times people did not have fridges and food was kept in a cold room for storage so when the lobster got rotten it gave of a green neon glow, the simile suggesting here that Marley now had a glow in him.

Dickens foreshadows Marley 'ghost when he appears later to Scrooge.

"with ghostly spectacles turned up upon its ghostly forehead"

Dickens creates a lot of suspense when Scrooge enters his dingy house, and the reader becomes curious upon Scrooge's entry as though expecting Marley to suddenly appear.

The hair was curiously stirred, as if by breath or hot air; and, though the eyes were wide open, they were perfectly motionless. That, and its livid colour, made it horrible; but its horror seemed to be in spite of the face and beyond its control, rather than a part of its own expression.

As Scrooge looked fixedly at this phenomenon, it was a knocker again.

To say that he was not startled, or that his blood was not conscious of a terrible sensation to which it had been a stranger from infancy, would be untrue. But he put his hand upon the key he had relinquished, turned it sturdily, walked in, and lighted his candle.

He did pause, with a moment's irresolution, before he shut the door; and he did look cautiously behind it first, as if he half expected to be terrified with the sight of Marley's pigtail sticking out into the hall. But there was nothing on the back of the door, except the screws and nuts that held the knocker on, so he said

"Pooh, pooh!" and closed it with a bang"

The sound resounded through the house like thunder. Every room above, and every cask in the wine-merchant's cellars below, appeared to have a separate peal of echoes of its own. Scrooge was not a man to be frightened by echoes. He fastened the door, and walked across the hall, and up the stairs; slowly too: trimming his candle as he went.

You may talk vaguely about driving a coach-and-six up a good old flight of stairs, or through a bad young Act of Parliament; but I mean to say you might have got a hearse up that staircase, and taken it broad-wise, with the splinter-bar towards the wall and the door towards the balustrades: and done it easy. There was plenty of width for that, and room to spare, which is perhaps the reason why Scrooge thought he saw a locomotive hearse going on before him in the gloom. Half-a-dozen gas-lamps out of the street wouldn't have lighted the entry too well, so you may suppose that it was pretty dark with Scrooge's dip.

Of course, this clearly foreshadows Marley's sudden visit,

"terrified at the sight of Marley's pigtail"

We see a change of tone here. Scrooge is suddenly transformed from a bold, brazen rude man to a frightened coward.

Dickens' tells us that Scrooge sensed something strange because he, 'paused' before he shut the door. He also looked carefully behind the door because he imagined seeing Marley.

Although there was nothing behind the door, Dickens prepares us for Marley's visit to Scrooge.
Scrooge said,

"Pooh, Pooh!" And closed it with a bang."

Dickens highlights Scrooge's fear by using auditory imagery and a simile,

"The sound resounded through the house like thunder"

The fact that the door made such a big noise tells us that Scrooge is so scared that he wants to shut something out of his life. The great sound of the door banging sounded like thunder.

The sound echoed all around even to the wine-merchant's cellars below.
So Scrooge,

"He fastened the door, and walked across the hall, and up the stairs"

He walked in the dark imagining a hearse on the stairs. Once again, the hearse can be symbolic of his death or when the Ghost shows him his tombstone later in the story.

Up Scrooge went, not caring a button for that. Darkness is cheap, and Scrooge liked it. But before he shut his heavy door, he walked through his rooms to see that all was right.

Scrooge walked through the rooms

He had just enough recollection of the face to desire to do that.

Sitting-room, bedroom, lumber-room. All as they should be. Nobody under the table, nobody under the sofa; a small fire in the grate; spoon and basin ready; and the little saucepan of gruel (Scrooge had a cold in his head) upon the hob. Nobody under the bed; nobody in the closet; nobody in his dressing- gown, which was hanging up in a suspicious attitude against the wall. Lumber-room as usual. Old fire-guard, old shoes, two fish-baskets, washing-stand on three legs, and a poker.

Quite satisfied, he closed his door, and locked himself in; double-locked himself in, which was not his custom. Thus secured against surprise, he took off his cravat; put on his dressing-gown and slippers, and his nightcap; and sat down before the fire to take his gruel.

It was a very low fire indeed; nothing on such a bitter night. He was obliged to sit close to it, and brood over it, before he could extract the least sensation of warmth from such a handful of fuel. The fireplace was an old one, built by some Dutch merchant long ago, and paved all round with quaint Dutch tiles, designed to illustrate the Scriptures.

Scrooge's fears were once again intensified when he walks through his rooms to make sure that everything was alright – he looked under the table, under the sofa and ensured that nobody was there because Marley's face haunted him,

"He had just enough recollection of the face to desire to do that."

Dicken's foreshadows and prepares us for Scrooge's fear when the ghost arrives later.

He even looks under the bed, in the closet, and even inside his dressing gown. That's how afraid he was. He made double sure that everything was in its place – lumber room as usual, old shoes, poker etc.

"Quite satisfied, he closed his door, and locked himself in; double-locked himself in, which was not his custom."

Now he felt secured and safe, dressed in his night clothes

"Thus secured against surprise."

and in a miserly way, sat comfortably by a barely lit fire.

"It was a very low fire indeed"

Dickens invites us into Scrooge's house and shows us his mean lifestyle. It was a bitterly cold night, but he used very little coal. He had to sit very close to the fire to feel the heat, so he wasn't only mean towards his clerk for coal he deprived himself too just to save money.

The Dutch tiles in Scrooge's house represented a biblical imagery of characters and events from the bible. The audience or even Dickens may have hoped that this would have tugged at his conscience and reminded him of his religious obligation to the poor and needy in society.

There were Cains and Abels, Pharaoh's daughters; Queens of Sheba, Angelic messengers descending through the air on clouds like feather-beds, Abrahams, Belshazzars, Apostles putting off to sea in butter-boats, hundreds of figures to attract his thoughts; and yet that face of Marley, seven years dead, came like the ancient Prophet's rod, and swallowed up the whole.

If each smooth tile had been a blank at first, with power to shape some picture on its surface from the disjointed fragments of his thoughts, there would have been a copy of old Marley's head on every one. "Humbug!" said Scrooge; and walked across the room.

After several turns, he sat down again. As he threw his head back in the chair, his glance happened to rest upon a bell, a disused bell, that hung in the room, and communicated for some purpose now forgotten with a chamber in the highest story of the building. It was with great astonishment, and with a strange, inexplicable dread, that as he looked, he saw this bell begin to swing. It swung so softly in the outset that it scarcely made a sound; but soon it rang out loudly, and so did every bell in the house.

This might have lasted half a minute, or a minute, but it seemed an hour. The bells ceased as they had begun, together. They were succeeded by a clanking noise, deep down below; as if some person were dragging a heavy chain over the casks in the wine-merchant's cellar. Scrooge then remembered to have heard that ghosts in haunted houses were described as dragging chains.

The cellar-door flew open with a booming sound, and then he heard the noise much louder, on the floors below; then coming up the stairs; then coming straight towards his door.

"It's humbug still!" said Scrooge. "I won't believe it."

His colour changed though, when, without a pause, it came on through the heavy door, and passed into the room before his eyes. Upon its coming in, the dying flame leaped up, as though it cried, "I know him; Marley's Ghost!" and fell again.

The use of auditory imagery is imperative here, and it's mysterious and sudden ringing petrified Scrooge,

'Inexplicable dread'

There's a mounting tension at this point in the story and the mood is somewhat altered. The suspense is riveting and the audience becomes curious as to what's going to happen next and lo and behold,

'The cellar door flew open with a booming sound, and then he heard the noise much louder, on the floors below; then coming up the stairs; then coming straight towards his door'

Marley's ghost enters through the door

The tension is palpable here and Scrooge's alarmed reaction shocks the reader.

Dickens gives us a splendid imagery of the,

'dying flame leaped up'

and one can associate that to Dickens message where socialism was dying in society and he hopes by introducing the supernatural to Scrooge that that flame would leap up, which of course it did at the end, and social responsibility was revived in Scrooge.

Dickens creates visual imagery by Marley dragging heavy chains to heighten tension and fear in Scrooge

The same face: the very same. Marley in his pigtail, usual waistcoat, tights and boots; the tassels on the latter bristling, like his pigtail, and his coat-skirts, and the hair upon his head. The chain he drew was clasped about his middle.

It was long, and wound about him like a tail; and it was made (for Scrooge observed it closely) of cash-boxes, keys, padlocks, ledgers, deeds, and heavy purses wrought in steel. His body was transparent; so that Scrooge, observing him, and looking through his waistcoat, could see the two buttons on his coat behind.

Scrooge had often heard it said that Marley had no bowels, but he had never believed it until now.

No, nor did he believe it even now. Though he looked the phantom through and through, and saw it standing before him; though he felt the chilling influence of its death-cold eyes; and marked the very texture of the folded kerchief bound about its head and chin, which wrapper he had not observed before; he was still incredulous, and fought against his senses.

"How now!" said Scrooge, caustic and cold as ever. "What do you want with me?"
"Much!"—Marley's voice, no doubt about it. "Who are you?"
"Ask me who I was."

"Who were you then?" said Scrooge, raising his voice. "You're particular, for a shade." He was going to say "to a shade," but substituted this, as more appropriate. "In life I was your partner, Jacob Marley."
"Can you—can you sit down?" asked Scrooge, looking doubtfully at him. "I can."
"Do it, then."

Scrooge asked the question, because he didn't know whether a ghost so transparent might find himself in a condition to take a chair; and felt that in the event of its being impossible, it might involve the necessity of an embarrassing explanation. But the ghost sat down on the opposite side of the fireplace, as if he were quite used to it.

"You don't believe in me," observed the Ghost.
"I don't," said Scrooge.

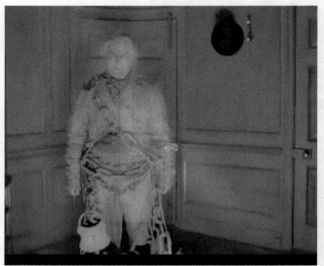

Chain made of cash-boxes, keys, padlocks

To alleviate his apprehension, Scrooge demands with trepidation,

"What do you want with me?"

Scrooge asks: "can you - can you sit down?"

"What evidence would you have of my reality beyond that of your senses?"

"I don't know," said Scrooge.

"Why do you doubt your senses?"

"Because," said Scrooge, "a little thing affects them. A slight disorder of the stomach makes them cheats. You may be an undigested bit of beef, a blot of mustard, a crumb of cheese, a fragment of an underdone potato. There's more of gravy than of grave about you, whatever you are!"

Scrooge was not much in the habit of cracking jokes, nor did he feel, in his heart, by any means waggish then. The truth is, that he tried to be smart, as a means of distracting his own attention, and keeping down his terror; for the spectre's voice disturbed the very marrow in his bones.

To sit, staring at those fixed glazed eyes, in silence for a moment, would play, Scrooge felt, the very deuce with him. There was something very awful, too, in the spectre's being provided with an infernal atmosphere of its own.

Scrooge could not feel it himself, but this was clearly the case; for though the Ghost sat perfectly motionless, its hair, and skirts, and tassels, were still agitated as by the hot vapour from an oven.

You see this toothpick?" said Scrooge, returning quickly to the charge, for the reason just assigned; and wishing, though it were only for a second, to divert the vision's stony gaze from himself.

"I do," replied the Ghost.

"You are not looking at it," said Scrooge.

"But I see it," said the Ghost, "notwithstanding."

"Well!" returned Scrooge, "I have but to swallow this, and be for the rest of my days persecuted by a legion of goblins, all of my own creation. Humbug, I tell you! humbug!"

At this the spirit raised a frightful cry, and shook its chain with such a dismal and appalling noise, that Scrooge held on tight to his chair, to save himself from falling in a swoon. But how much greater was his horror, when the phantom taking off the bandage round its head, as if it were too warm to wear indoors, its lower jaw dropped down upon its breast!

Dickens very carefully crafted Marley's ghost. He enchained him and the chains can symbolically represent imprisonment Marley became imprisoned by his own uncharitable mean actions like Scrooge when he was on Earth. He also carried cash boxes, ledgers and deeds.

Marley: "Why do you doubt your senses?"

These items were linked to a materialistic world of money and power. Scrooge is trying to put on a facade and act brave challenging the ghost, but in reality the spectra's voice had disturbed,
the 'very marrow in his bones'

When Scrooge's response to the ghost was,
"Humbug, I tell you - Humbug!"

The Spirit reacted ferociously and 'raised a frightful cry'

Spirit raised a frightful cry

Out of fear, Scrooge
'held on tight to his chair'

Scrooge fell upon his knees, and clasped his hands before his face.

"Mercy!" he said. "Dreadful apparition, why do you trouble me?"

"Man of the worldly mind!" replied the Ghost, "do you believe in me or not?"

"I do," said Scrooge. "I must. But why do spirits walk the earth, and why do they come to me?"

"It is required of every man," the Ghost returned, "that the spirit within him should walk abroad among his fellowmen, and travel far and wide; and if that spirit goes not forth in life, it is condemned to do so after death. It is doomed to wander through the world—oh, woe is me! — and witness what it cannot share, but might have shared on earth, and turned to happiness!"

Again the spectre raised a cry, and shook its chain and wrung its shadowy hands.

"You are fettered," said Scrooge, trembling. "Tell me why?"

"I wear the chain I forged in life," replied the Ghost. "I made it link by link, and yard by yard; I girded it on of my own free will, and of my own free will I wore it. Is its pattern strange to you?"

Scrooge trembled more and more.

"Or would you know," pursued the Ghost, "the weight and length of the strong coil you bear yourself? It was full as heavy and as long as this, seven Christmas Eves ago. You have laboured on it, since. It is a ponderous chain!"

Scrooge glanced about him on the floor, in the expectation of finding himself surrounded by some fifty or sixty fathoms of iron cable: but he could see nothing.

"Jacob," he said, imploringly. "Old Jacob Marley, tell me more. Speak comfort to me, Jacob!"

"I have none to give," the Ghost replied. "It comes from other regions, Ebenezer Scrooge, and is conveyed by other ministers, to other kinds of men. Nor can I tell you what I would. A very little more is all permitted to me. I cannot rest, I cannot stay, I cannot linger anywhere. My spirit never walked beyond our counting-house— mark me! — in life my spirit never roved beyond the narrow limits of our money-changing hole; and weary journeys lie before me!"

Dickens 'mortification of Scrooge seems to be deliberate as though belittling him seemed be his ultimate goal. We see a terrified Scrooge and the tension and suspense rapidly rises when the Spirit strips the bandage off it's head and it's lower jaw dropped down upon its breast! Dickens presents us with an image of a fallen Scrooge on his knees begging for mercy.

The Ghost addresses Scrooge as,

"Man of the worldly mind!"

He explains to Scrooge that,

Ghost - I wear the chain I forged in life

He too, he says was like Scrooge on earth, selfish, mean and unkind and he urges Scrooge to repent and share with the poor and bring happiness to them otherwise,

"the weight and length of the strong coil you bear yourself?"

We are surprised to see an awakening in Scrooge and he urges the Ghost to

"Speak comfort to me, Jacob"

The Ghost replies

"I have none to give"

It was a habit with Scrooge, whenever he became thoughtful, to put his hands in his breeches pockets. Pondering on what the Ghost had said, he did so now, but without lifting up his eyes, or getting off his knees.

"You must have been very slow about it, Jacob," Scrooge observed, in a business-like manner, though with humility and deference.
"Slow!" the Ghost repeated.
"Seven years dead," mused Scrooge. "And travelling all the time!"
"The whole time," said the Ghost. "No rest, no peace. Incessant torture of remorse."
"You travel fast?" said Scrooge.
"On the wings of the wind," replied the Ghost.
"You might have got over a great quantity of ground in seven years," said Scrooge.

The Ghost, on hearing this, set up another cry, and clanked its chain so hideously in the dead silence of the night, that the Ward would have been justified in indicting it for a nuisance.

Oh! Captive, bound, and double-ironed," cried the phantom, "not to know, that ages of incessant labour by immortal creatures, for this earth must pass into eternity before the good of which it is susceptible is all developed. Not to know that any Christian spirit working kindly in its little sphere, whatever it may be, will find its mortal life too short for its vast means of usefulness. Not to know that no space of regret can make amends for one life's opportunity misused! Yet such was I! Oh! such was I!"

"But you were always a good man of business, Jacob," faltered Scrooge, who now began to apply this to himself.
"Business!" cried the Ghost, wringing its hands again. "Mankind was my business. The common welfare was my business; charity, mercy, forbearance, and benevolence, were, all, my business. The dealings of my trade were but a drop of water in the comprehensive ocean of my business!"

It held up its chain at arm's length, as if that were the cause of all its unavailing grief, and flung it heavily upon the ground again.

"At this time of the rolling year," the spectre said, "I suffer most. Why did I walk through crowds of fellow-beings with my eyes turned down, and never raise them to that blessed Star which led the Wise Men to a poor abode! Were there no poor homes to which its light would have conducted me!"

But yet again the Ghost became furious at Scrooge's questioning and,

'clanked its chain'

and yelled at Scrooge calling him a prisoner of his fate,

"Oh! Captive, bound, and doubled-ironed"

Warning Scrooge with this prison imagery that if he didn't mend the error of his ways, he will be held captive and imprisoned just the way he, Marley is roaming the earth because of the error of his ways, when he was alive.

The Ghost becomes furious as we see by Dickens use of the exclamation marks. When Scrooge mentions that Marley was a good man of business,

"Business!"

the Ghost yells out.

He makes it clear to Scrooge

"Mankind was my business"

"charity, mercy, forbearance, and benevolence were all my business

The Ghost is imparting Dickens serious message of Social Responsibility not only to Scrooge but to all of us.

Marley says "Mankind was my business"

The Ghost is imparting Dickens serious message of Social Responsibility not only to Scrooge but to all of us.

Scrooge was very much dismayed to hear the spectre going on at this rate, and began to quake exceedingly.

"Hear me!" cried the Ghost. "My time is nearly gone."
"I will," said Scrooge. "But don't be hard upon me! Don't be flowery, Jacob! Pray!"
"How it is that I appear before you in a shape that you can see, I may not tell. I have sat invisible beside you many and many a day."

It was not an agreeable idea. Scrooge shivered, and wiped the perspiration from his brow.
"That is no light part of my penance," pursued the Ghost. "I am here to- night to warn you, that you have yet a chance and hope of escaping my fate. A chance and hope of my procuring, Ebenezer."
"You were always a good friend to me," said Scrooge. "Thank'ee!"
"You will be haunted," resumed the Ghost, "by Three Spirits."

Scrooge's countenance fell almost as low as the Ghost's had done.
"Is that the chance and hope you mentioned, Jacob?" he demanded, in a faltering voice.
"It is."
"I—I think I'd rather not," said Scrooge.
"Without their visits," said the Ghost, "you cannot hope to shun the path I tread. Expect the first to-morrow, when the bell tolls One."
"Couldn't I take 'em all at once, and have it over, Jacob?" hinted Scrooge.
"Expect the second on the next night at the same hour. The third upon the next night when the last stroke of Twelve has ceased to vibrate. Look to see me no more; and look that, for your own sake, you remember what has passed between us!"

When it had said these words, the spectre took its wrapper from the table, and bound it round its head, as before. Scrooge knew this, by the smart sound its teeth made, when the jaws were brought together by the bandage. He ventured to raise his eyes again, and found his supernatural visitor confronting him in an erect attitude, with its chain wound over and about its arm.

Marley tells Scrooge why he has come

"to warn you, that you have yet a chance and hope of escaping my fate"

Marley warns Scrooge about his fate

The Ghost tells Scrooge that he will be visited by

"Three Spirits"

The apparition walked backward from him; and at every step it took, the window raised itself a little, so that when the spectre reached it, it was wide open.

It beckoned Scrooge to approach, which he did. When they were within two paces of each other, Marley's Ghost held up its hand, warning him to come no nearer. Scrooge stopped.

Not so much in obedience, as in surprise and fear: for on the raising of the hand, he became sensible of confused noises in the air; incoherent sounds of lamentation and regret; wailings inexpressibly sorrowful and self-accusatory. The spectre, after listening for a moment, joined in the mournful dirge; and floated out upon the bleak, dark night.

Scrooge followed to the window: desperate in his curiosity. He looked out.

The air was filled with phantoms, wandering hither and thither in restless haste, and moaning as they went. Every one of them wore chains like Marley's Ghost; some few (they might be guilty governments) were linked together; none were free. Many had been personally known to Scrooge in their lives.

The Ghost went out through the window and Scrooge saw the air filled with phantoms in chains and they were roaming and moaning, and none were free.

Scrooge recognised some of them and they were paying for their greed and lack of empathy towards the poor when they were on earth

Marley's ghost exits through window

The Air was filled with phantoms, wandering hither and thither in restless haste

He had been quite familiar with one old ghost, in a white waistcoat, with a monstrous iron safe attached to its ankle, who cried piteously at being unable to assist a wretched woman with an infant, whom it saw below, upon a door- step. The misery with them all was, clearly, that they sought to interfere, for good, in human matters, and had lost the power for ever.

Whether these creatures faded into mist, or mist enshrouded them, he could not tell. But they and their spirit voices faded together; and the night became as it had been when he walked home.

Scrooge closed the window, and examined the door by which the Ghost had entered. It was double-locked, as he had locked it with his own hands, and the bolts were undisturbed. He tried to say "Humbug!" but stopped at the first syllable. And being, from the emotion he had undergone, or the fatigues of the day, or his glimpse of the Invisible World, or the dull conversation of the Ghost, or the lateness of the hour, much in need of repose; went straight to bed, without undressing, and fell asleep upon the instant.

End of STAVE one

Phantom unable to assist a wretched woman with an infant

Dickens informs the reader that it is their contribution that can alleviate the misery of those less fortunate than ourselves, not the spirits because

"The misery with them all was, clearly, that they sought to interfere, for good, in human matters, and had lost the power for ever"

Scrooge is skeptical, bolts the door to shut out any further interruptions, but is too fatigued to ponder further his bizarre encounter with his former deceased business partner Jacob Marley, and so ends Stave one of Charles Dickens' A Christmas Carol'.

This scene is set in Scrooge's bedroom and he is visited by the Spirit of Christmas Past. It has a bright light on its head. The Ghost takes him to his School when he was a boy. He was neglected and left alone, and Scrooge cried when he saw this. Then the Ghost shows him his kind sister Fan who tells him that their father wants him to come home. Fan died very young leaving his nephew Fred behind. Next the Ghost shows him a Christmas when he worked for Mr Fezziwig who overflowed with kindness and good nature.

Mr Fezziwig made everyone happy by throwing a wonderful Christmas party for them. Now Scrooge thinks about his shoddy, ugly treatment of his clerk, Bob Cratchit.

Then the Ghost shows him his fiancée Belle. She tells him that he is obsessed with money and that he doesn't love her. She then breaks off her engagement to him. Scrooge then sees Belle's life as a happily married woman with children and her husband tells her that he saw Scrooge and that he is rather lonely. By this time Scrooge becomes irate because he cannot bear to see anymore, and he insists that the Ghost takes him home. He tries to extinguish the Spirit's light but is unsuccessful.

End of SUMMARY on STAVE two

When Scrooge awoke, it was so dark, that looking out of bed, he could scarcely distinguish the transparent window from the opaque walls of his chamber. He was endeavouring to pierce the darkness with his ferret eyes, when the chimes of a neighbouring church struck the four quarters. So he listened for the hour.

To his great astonishment the heavy bell went on from six to seven, and from seven to eight, and regularly up to twelve; then stopped. Twelve! It was past two when he went to bed. The clock was wrong. An icicle must have got into the works. Twelve!

He touched the spring of his repeater, to correct this most preposterous clock. Its rapid little pulse beat twelve: and stopped.

"Why, it isn't possible," said Scrooge, "that I can have slept through a whole day and far into another night. It isn't possible that anything has happened to the sun, and this is twelve at noon!"

The idea being an alarming one, he scrambled out of bed, and groped his way to the window. He was obliged to rub the frost off with the sleeve of his dressing-gown before he could see anything; and could see very little then. All he could make out was, that it was still very foggy and extremely cold, and that there was no noise of people running to and fro, and making a great stir, as there unquestionably would have been if night had beaten off bright day, and taken possession of the world.

This was a great relief, because "three days after sight of this First of Exchange pay to Mr. Ebenezer Scrooge or his order," and so forth, would have become a mere United States 'security if there were no days to count by.

Scrooge went to bed again, and thought, and thought, and thought it over and over and over, and could make nothing of it. The more he thought, the more perplexed he was; and the more he endeavoured not to think, the more he thought.

Scrooge is confused by the time when he awoke.

"Why, it isn't possible," said Scrooge, "that I can have slept through a whole day and far into another night.

Scrooge is confused by the time of day

Scrooge now alarmed, scrambled our of bed, to the window, where he made out,

that it was still very foggy and extremely cold, and that there was no noise of people running to and fro

still very foggy and extremely cold

To Scrooge, the night was

'a great relief'

He went back to bed feeling very confused.

Marley's Ghost bothered him exceedingly. Every time he resolved within himself, after mature inquiry, that it was all a dream, his mind flew back again, like a strong spring released, to its first position, and presented the same problem to be worked all through, "Was it a dream or not?"

Scrooge lay in this state until the chime had gone three quarters more, when he remembered, on a sudden, that the Ghost had warned him of a visitation when the bell tolled one. He resolved to lie awake until the hour was passed; and, considering that he could no more go to sleep than go to Heaven, this was perhaps the wisest resolution in his power.

The quarter was so long, that he was more than once convinced he must have sunk into a doze unconsciously, and missed the clock. At length it broke upon his listening ear.

"Ding, dong!"
"A quarter past," said Scrooge, counting.
"Ding, dong!"
"Half-past!" said Scrooge.
"Ding, dong!"
"A quarter to it," said Scrooge.
"Ding, dong!"
"The hour itself," said Scrooge, triumphantly, "and nothing else!"

He spoke before the hour bell sounded, which it now did with a deep, dull, hollow, melancholy One. Light flashed up in the room upon the instant, and the curtains of his bed were drawn.

The curtains of his bed were drawn aside, I tell you, by a hand. Not the curtains at his feet, nor the curtains at his back, but those to which his face was addressed. The curtains of his bed were drawn aside; and Scrooge, starting up into a half-recumbent attitude, found himself face to face with the unearthly visitor who drew them: as close to it as I am now to you, and I am standing in the spirit at your elbow.

Scrooge scans his First of Exchange pay

Perplexed, Scrooge could not decide whether Marley's ghost was real or a figment of his imagination.

"Was it a dream or not?"

So because the Ghost had warned him of a visitation when the bell tolled at ONE, Scrooge

resolved to lie awake until the hour was passed

The symbolism of the bell surfaces again as though warning Scrooge about the imminent arrival of the Ghost of Christmas Past and the ordeal he is about to face.

'the hour bell sounded, which it now did with a deep, dull, hollow, melancholy ONE'

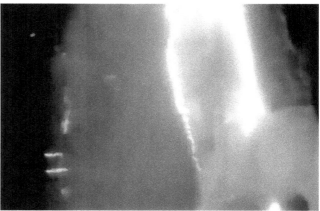

Light flashed up – the curtains of his bed were drawn

It was a strange figure—like a child: yet not so like a child as like an old man, viewed through some supernatural medium, which gave him the appearance of having receded from the view, and being diminished to a child's proportions. Its hair, which hung about its neck and down its back, was white as if with age; and yet the face had not a wrinkle in it, and the tenderest bloom was on the skin. The arms were very long and muscular; the hands the same, as if its hold were of uncommon strength. Its legs and feet, most delicately formed, were, like those upper members, bare. It wore a tunic of the purest white; and round its waist was bound a lustrous belt, the sheen of which was beautiful. It held a branch of fresh green holly in its hand; and, in singular contradiction of that wintry emblem, had its dress trimmed with summer flowers. But the strangest thing about it was, that from the crown of its head there sprung a bright clear jet of light, by which all this was visible; and which was doubtless the occasion of its using, in its duller moments, a great extinguisher for a cap, which it now held under its arm.

Even this, though, when Scrooge looked at it with increasing steadiness, was not its strangest quality. For as its belt sparkled and glittered now in one part and now in another, and what was light one instant, at another time was dark, so the figure itself fluctuated in its distinctness: being now a thing with one arm, now with one leg, now with twenty legs, now a pair of legs without a head, now a head without a body: of which dissolving parts, no outline would be visible in the dense gloom wherein they melted away. And in the very wonder of this, it would be itself again; distinct and clear as ever.

"Are you the Spirit, sir, whose coming was foretold to me?" asked Scrooge.
"I am!"
The voice was soft and gentle. Singularly low, as if instead of being so close beside him, it were at a distance.
"Who, and what are you?" Scrooge demanded.
"I am the Ghost of Christmas Past."
"Long Past?" inquired Scrooge: observant of its dwarfish stature. "No. Your past."

At ONE a strange figure appeared, and Dickens presents us with a vivid description of the Ghost, and he uses many oxymorons to create a visual picture for us.

'yet not so like a child as like an old man'

yet not so like a child as like an old man

'It wore a tunic of purest white'

suggesting the Ghost's angel-like purity because it came to help Scrooge to redeem himself from the error of his ways. The 'fresh green holly' which the Ghost carried can symbolise the spirit of Christmas and we can connote that it can represent the thorns on Christ's crown when he was crucified. Hence Dickens message - that we must be like Christ and make sacrifices for the poor and accept our social responsibilities.

Scrooge asks – "Are you the Spirit foretold"

The Ghost also carried a bright light on its head.

Perhaps, Scrooge could not have told anybody why, if anybody could have asked him; but he had a special desire to see the Spirit in his cap; and begged him to be covered.

What!" exclaimed the Ghost, "would you so soon put out, with worldly hands, the light I give? Is it not enough that you are one of those whose passions made this cap, and force me through whole trains of years to wear it low upon my brow!"

Scrooge reverently disclaimed all intention to offend or any knowledge of having wilfully "bonneted" the Spirit at any period of his life. He then made bold to inquire what business brought him there.
"Your welfare!" said the Ghost.

Scrooge expressed himself much obliged, but could not help thinking that a night of unbroken rest would have been more conducive to that end. The Spirit must have heard him thinking, for it said immediately:
"Your reclamation, then. Take heed!"

It put out its strong hand as it spoke, and clasped him gently by the arm. "Rise! and walk with me!"

It would have been in vain for Scrooge to plead that the weather and the hour were not adapted to pedestrian purposes; that bed was warm, and the thermometer a long way below freezing; that he was clad but lightly in his slippers, dressing-gown, and nightcap; and that he had a cold upon him at that time. The grasp, though gentle as a woman's hand, was not to be resisted. He rose: but finding that the Spirit made towards the window, clasped his robe in supplication.

"I am a mortal," Scrooge remonstrated, "and liable to fall."

"Bear but a touch of my hand there," said the Spirit, laying it upon his heart, "and you shall be upheld in more than this!"

As the words were spoken, they passed through the wall, and stood upon an open country road, with fields on either hand.

This light imagery symbolises awakening which the Ghost hopes Scrooge will achieve, so the Ghost is trying to bring light into Scrooge's dark life. Ironically, Scrooge asks the Ghost to extinguish his light, to the fury of the Ghost it retorts, Then

"would you so soon put out, with worldly hands, the light I give you?"

The Ghost informs Scrooge that his business was his welfare.
"Your welfare!"

and warns Scrooge to take heed and be aware.

It put out its strong hand as it spoke

Scrooge remonstrate that he is mortal and "liable to fall"
but the Spirit reassures Scrooge

Spirit - "Bear but a touch of my hand there"

The ghost takes him on a journey to the countryside.

The city had entirely vanished. Not a vestige of it was to be seen. The darkness and the mist had vanished with it, for it was a clear, cold, winter day, with snow upon the ground.

"Good Heaven!" said Scrooge, clasping his hands together, as he looked about him. "I was bred in this place. I was a boy here!"

The Spirit gazed upon him mildly. Its gentle touch, though it had been light and instantaneous, appeared still present to the old man's sense of feeling. He was conscious of a thousand odours floating in the air, each one connected with a thousand thoughts, and hopes, and joys, and cares long, long, forgotten!

"Your lip is trembling," said the Ghost. "And what is that upon your cheek?"

Scrooge muttered, with an unusual catching in his voice, that it was a pimple; and begged the Ghost to lead him where he would.

"You recollect the way?" inquired the Spirit.
"Remember it!" cried Scrooge with fervour; "I could walk it blindfold."

"Strange to have forgotten it for so many years!" observed the Ghost. "Let us go on."

They walked along the road, Scrooge recognising every gate, and post, and tree; until a little market-town appeared in the distance, with its bridge, its church, and winding river. Some shaggy ponies now were seen trotting towards them with boys upon their backs, who called to other boys in country gigs and carts, driven by farmers. All these boys were in great spirits, and shouted to each other, until the broad fields were so full of merry music, that the crisp air laughed to hear it!

"These are but shadows of the things that have been," said the Ghost. "They have no consciousness of us."

The jocund travellers came on; and as they came, Scrooge knew and named them every one. Why was he rejoiced beyond all bounds to see them! Why did his cold eye glisten, and his heart leap up as they went past!

Scrooge is astounded by the sudden transformation from city to countryside which he recognised instantly,

"Good Heaven!"
"I was bred in this place. I was a boy here!"

Scrooge – "I was a boy here!"

Dickens sets the scene for reminiscence. Scrooge was

conscious of a thousand odours floating in the air, each one connected with a thousand thoughts, and hopes, and joys, and cares long, long, forgotten!

Dickens further reinforces the past events, by describing how Scrooge immediately recollects the

'Boys in country gigs and carts'
'until the broad fields were so full of merry music, that the crisp air laughed to hear it'

'boys in country gigs and carts'

Why was he filled with gladness when he heard them give each other Merry Christmas, as they parted at cross-roads and bye-ways, for their several homes! What was merry Christmas to Scrooge? Out upon merry Christmas! What good had it ever done to him?

"The school is not quite deserted," said the Ghost. "A solitary child, neglected by his friends, is left there still." Scrooge said he knew it. And he sobbed.

They left the high-road, by a well-remembered lane, and soon approached a mansion of dull red brick, with a little weathercock-surmounted cupola, on the roof, and a bell hanging in it. It was a large house, but one of broken fortunes; for the spacious offices were little used, their walls were damp and mossy, their windows broken, and their gates decayed. Fowls clucked and strutted in the stables; and the coach-houses and sheds were over-run with grass. Nor was it more retentive of its ancient state, within; for entering the dreary hall, and glancing through the open doors of many rooms, they found them poorly furnished, cold, and vast. There was an earthy savour in the air, a chilly bareness in the place, which associated itself somehow with too much getting up by candle-light, and not too much to eat.

They went, the Ghost and Scrooge, across the hall, to a door at the back of the house. It opened before them, and disclosed a long, bare, melancholy room, made barer still by lines of plain deal forms and desks. At one of these a lonely boy was reading near a feeble fire; and Scrooge sat down upon a form, and wept to see his poor forgotten self as he used to be.

Not a latent echo in the house, not a squeak and scuffle from the mice behind the panelling, not a drip from the half-thawed water-spout in the dull yard behind, not a sigh among the leafless boughs of one despondent poplar, not the idle swinging of an empty store-house door, no, not a clicking in the fire, but fell upon the heart of Scrooge with a softening influence, and gave a freer passage to his tears.

The boys were in great spirits, there was an exciting atmosphere of music and enjoyment.

Dickens uses a personification to describe this jovial, happy scenario.

Even the air laughed in merriment to hear the music. By using the personification Dickens made the ambience of the countryside which Scrooge is witnessing come alive. He gave it animate qualities to express the excitement.

The Ghost then orders Scrooge to take a journey with him and he shows Scrooge his School,

"A solitary child, neglected by his friends, is left there still"

"A solitary child, neglected by his friends"

Note Dickens earlier description of Scrooge,

"Solitary as an oyster"

pointing out that Scrooge was no stranger to loneliness. The repetition of the adjective 'solitary' suggests this. Scrooge saw himself all alone reading by the fire and he began to sob and wept to see his poor forgotten self as he used to be.

Then the spirit showed him a little boy, Scrooge's younger self reading.

The Spirit touched him on the arm, and pointed to his younger self, intent upon his reading. Suddenly a man, in foreign garments: wonderfully real and distinct to look at: stood outside the window, with an axe stuck in his belt, and leading by the bridle an ass laden with wood.

"Why, it's Ali Baba!" Scrooge exclaimed in ecstasy. "It's dear old honest Ali Baba! Yes, yes, I know! One Christmas time, when yonder solitary child was left here all alone, he did come, for the first time, just like that. Poor boy! And Valentine," said Scrooge, "and his wild brother, Orson; there they go! And what's his name, who was put down in his drawers, asleep, at the Gate of Damascus; don't you see him! And the Sultan's Groom turned upside down by the Genii; there he is upon his head! Serve him right. I'm glad of it. What business had he to be married to the Princess!"

To hear Scrooge expending all the earnestness of his nature on such subjects, in a most extraordinary voice between laughing and crying; and to see his heightened and excited face; would have been a surprise to his business friends in the city, indeed.

"There's the Parrot!" cried Scrooge. "Green body and yellow tail, with a thing like a lettuce growing out of the top of his head; there he is! Poor Robin Crusoe, he called him, when he came home again after sailing round the island. 'Poor Robin Crusoe, where have you been, Robin Crusoe?' The man thought he was dreaming, but he wasn't. It was the Parrot, you know. There goes Friday, running for his life to the little creek! Halloa! Hoop! Halloo!"

Then, with a rapidity of transition very foreign to his usual character, he said, in pity for his former self, "Poor boy!" and cried again.

"I wish," Scrooge muttered, putting his hand in his pocket, and looking about him, after drying his eyes with his cuff: "but it's too late now."
"What is the matter?" asked the Spirit.

Dickens spices up the narrative by introducing the local woodsman as,
'a man, in foreign garments'

a man in foreign garments, Ali Baba

Scrooge's exclaimed,
"It's dear old honest Ali Baba!"

Dickens gets Scrooge to recall events that made him think about his sad past,
"There's the Parrot!" cried Scrooge

"Green body and yellow tail, with a lettuce growing on his head"

Here Scrooge seemed happy to identify with the characters in his book as though they were his real friends,
"Halloa! Hoop! Halloo!"

Notice he repeats these same words of excitement in the end when he redeems himself.

Nothing," said Scrooge. "Nothing. There was a boy singing a Christmas Carol at my door last night. I should like to have given him something: that's all."

The Ghost smiled thoughtfully, and waved its hand: saying as it did so, "Let us see another Christmas!"

Scrooge's former self grew larger at the words, and the room became a little darker and more dirty. The panels shrunk, the windows cracked; fragments of plaster fell out of the ceiling, and the naked laths were shown instead; but how all this was brought about, Scrooge knew no more than you do. He only knew that it was quite correct; that everything had happened so; that there he was, alone again, when all the other boys had gone home for the jolly holidays.

He was not reading now, but walking up and down despairingly. Scrooge looked at the Ghost, and with a mournful shaking of his head, glanced anxiously towards the door.

It opened; and a little girl, much younger than the boy, came darting in, and putting her arms about his neck, and often kissing him, addressed him as her "Dear, dear brother."

"I have come to bring you home, dear brother!" said the child, clapping her tiny hands, and bending down to laugh. "To bring you home, home, home!"
"Home, little Fan?" returned the boy.
"Yes!" said the child, brimful of glee. "Home, for good and all.

Home, for ever and ever. Father is so much kinder than he used to be, that home's like Heaven! He spoke so gently to me one dear night when I was going to bed, that I was not afraid to ask him once more if you might come home; and he said Yes, you should; and sent me in a coach to bring you. And you're to be a man!" said the child, opening her eyes, "and are never to come back here; but first, we're to be together all the Christmas long, and have the merriest time in all the world."

This sad vision of himself immediately reverts his attention to the little boy wh o attempted to sing a Christmas Carol at his door.

Now Scrooge regrets his action of terrifying the boy with a ruler and now wishes that he

"should like to have given him something"

Scrooge then sees his sister Fan who came to take him home. Scrooge was ecstatic.

"I have come to bring you home, dear brother!"

Fan assures Scrooge that

'Father is so much kinder than he used to be'

and that

"home's like Heaven!"

and he will;

"have the merriest time in all the world"

"You are quite a woman, little Fan!" exclaimed the boy. exclaimed the boy.

She clapped her hands and laughed, and tried to touch his head; but being too little, laughed again, and stood on tiptoe to embrace him. Then she began to drag him, in her childish eagerness, towards the door; and he, nothing loth to go, accompanied her.

A terrible voice in the hall cried, "Bring down Master Scrooge's box, there!" and in the hall appeared the schoolmaster himself, who glared on Master Scrooge with a ferocious condescension, and threw him into a dreadful state of mind by shaking hands with him. He then conveyed him and his sister into the veriest old well of a shivering best-parlour that ever was seen, where the maps upon the wall, and the celestial and terrestrial globes in the windows, were waxy with cold. Here he produced a decanter of curiously light wine, and a block of curiously heavy cake, and administered instalments of those dainties to the young people: at the same time, sending out a meagre servant to offer a glass of "something" to the postboy, who answered that he thanked the gentleman, but if it was the same tap as he had tasted before, he had rather not. Master Scrooge's trunk being by this time tied on to the top of the chaise, the children bade the schoolmaster good-bye right willingly; and getting into it, drove gaily down the garden-sweep: the quick wheels dashing the hoar frost and snow from off the dark leaves of the evergreens like spray.

Always a delicate creature, whom a breath might have withered," said the Ghost. "But she had a large heart!"

"So she had," cried Scrooge. "You're right. I will not gainsay it, Spirit. God forbid!"

"She died a woman," said the Ghost, "and had, as I think, children." "One child," Scrooge returned.

"True," said the Ghost. "Your nephew!"

Scrooge seemed uneasy in his mind; and answered briefly, "Yes."

Dickens gives young Scrooge a glimmer of hope and reunion with his family and estranged Father. Young Scrooge remarks

"You are quite a woman, little Fan!"

Dickens set the scene for the departure of young Scrooge and his sister Fan from the School. Master Scrooge is thrown into

"a dreadful state of mind"

by the schoolmaster but expecting the worst, young Scrooge is pleasantly surprised by being conveyed into the

'best-parlour that ever was seen'

where he and his sister are treated to

'light wine and heavy cake'

Dickens then goes on to describe the post-coach departure in vivid detail, it

drove gaily down the garden-sweep: the quick wheels dashing the hoar frost and snow from off the dark leaves of the evergreens like spray.

One can connote that the coach which Dickens personifies was happy for Scrooge's good fortune and danced its way to its destination, taking Scrooge home to be loved and cared for.

Scrooge and the Ghost discuss his sister,

"But she had a large heart!"

but she died leaving her child behind.

Although they had but that moment left the school behind them, they were now in the busy thoroughfares of a city, where shadowy passengers passed and repassed; where shadowy carts and coaches battled for the way, and all the strife and tumult of a real city were. It was made plain enough, by the dressing of the shops, that here too it was Christmas time again; but it was evening, and the streets were lighted up.

The Ghost stopped at a certain warehouse door, and asked Scrooge if he knew it.

"Know it!" said Scrooge. "Was I apprenticed here!"

They went in. At sight of an old gentleman in a Welsh wig, sitting behind such a high desk, that if he had been two inches taller he must have knocked his head against the ceiling, Scrooge cried in great excitement:

"Why, it's old Fezziwig! Bless his heart; it's Fezziwig alive again!"

Old Fezziwig laid down his pen, and looked up at the clock, which pointed to the hour of seven. He rubbed his hands; adjusted his capacious waistcoat; laughed all over himself, from his shoes to his organ of benevolence; and called out in a comfortable, oily, rich, fat, jovial voice:

"Yo ho, there! Ebenezer! Dick!"

Scrooge's former self, now grown a young man, came briskly in, accompanied by his fellow-'prentice.

"Dick Wilkins, to be sure!" said Scrooge to the Ghost. "Bless me, yes. There he is. He was very much attached to me, was Dick. Poor Dick! Dear, dear!"

"Yo ho, my boys!" said Fezziwig. "No more work to-night. Christmas Eve, Dick. Christmas, Ebenezer! Let's have the shutters up," cried old Fezziwig, with a sharp clap of his hands, "before a man can say Jack Robinson!"

You wouldn't believe how those two fellows went at it!

the quick wheels dashing the hoar frost

Scrooge felt uneasy because maybe he thought about his mistreatment of his nephew and his sheer rudeness towards him when he invited him for Christmas.
Scrooge is stopped at a certain warehouse door, where the Ghost asked him if he knew it.
"Know it! – Was I apprenticed here!

The Ghost stopped at a certain warehouse

On entry, Scrooge immediately recognises his former employer
"Why, it's old Fezziwig! Bless his heart"
The young adult Scrooge together with fellow-'prentice Dick Wilkins are summoned by Old Fezziwig. Notice how Dickens describes in detail Old Fezziwig's appearance and mannerisms
He rubbed his hands; adjusted his capacious waistcoat; laughed all over himself, from his shoes to his organ of benevolence; and called out in a comfortable, oily, rich, fat, jovial voice

They charged into the street with the shutters—one, two, three—had 'em up in their places— four, five, six—barred 'em and pinned 'em—seven, eight, nine—and came back before you could have got to twelve, panting like race-horses.

"Hilli-ho!" cried old Fezziwig, skipping down from the high desk, with wonderful agility. "Clear away, my lads, and let's have lots of room here! Hilli-ho, Dick! Chirrup, Ebenezer!"

Clear away! There was nothing they wouldn't have cleared away, or couldn't have cleared away, with old Fezziwig looking on. It was done in a minute. Every movable was packed off, as if it were dismissed from public life for evermore; the floor was swept and watered, the lamps were trimmed, fuel was heaped upon the fire; and the warehouse was as snug, and warm, and dry, and bright a ball-room, as you would desire to see upon a winter's night.

In came a fiddler with a music-book, and went up to the lofty desk, and made an orchestra of it, and tuned like fifty stomach-aches. In came Mrs. Fezziwig, one vast substantial smile

In came the three Miss Fezziwigs, beaming and lovable. In came the six young followers whose hearts they broke. In came all the young men and women employed in the business.

In came the housemaid, with her cousin, the baker. In came the cook, with her brother's particular friend, the milkman.

In came the boy from over the way, who was suspected of not having board enough from his master; trying to hide himself behind the girl from next door but one, who was proved to have had her ears pulled by her mistress.

In they all came, one after another; some shyly, some boldly, some gracefully, some awkwardly, some pushing, some pulling; in they all came, anyhow and everyhow. Away they all went, twenty couple at once; hands half round and back again the other way; down the middle and up again; round and round in various stages of affectionate grouping; old top couple always turning up in the wrong place; new top couple starting off again, as soon as they got there; all top couples at last, and not a bottom one to help them!

Old Fezziwig at his desk

Dick Wilkins with Scrooge as a young man

Dickens juxtaposes the merriment, joy and fun experienced at Fezziwigs party to that of the dismal hardship and solitude experienced at School.

At Fezziwig's, in came the

'fiddler'
'wife, Mrs Fezziwig'
'three Miss Fezziwigs'
'six young followers whose hearts they broke'
'young men and women employed'
'housemaid, with her cousin, the baker'
'cook, with her brother's friend, the milkman'
'boy from over the way'

'In they all came, one after the other'

When this result was brought about, old Fezziwig, clapping his hands to stop the dance, cried out, "Well done!" and the fiddler plunged his hot face into a pot of porter, especially provided for that purpose.

But scorning rest, upon his reappearance, he instantly began again, though there were no dancers yet, as if the other fiddler had been carried home, exhausted, on a shutter, and he were a bran-new man resolved to beat him out of sight, or perish.

There were more dances, and there were forfeits, and more dances, and there was cake, and there was negus, and there was a great piece of Cold Roast, and there was a great piece of Cold Boiled, and there were mince-pies, and plenty of beer. But the great effect of the evening came after the Roast and Boiled, when the fiddler (an artful dog, mind! The sort of man who knew his business better than you or I could have told it him!) struck up "Sir Roger de Coverley." Then old Fezziwig stood out to dance with Mrs. Fezziwig. Top couple, too; with a good stiff piece of work cut out for them; three or four and twenty pair of partners; people who were not to be trifled with; people who would dance, and had no notion of walking.

But if they had been twice as many—ah, four times—old Fezziwig would have been a match for them, and so would Mrs. Fezziwig. As to her, she was worthy to be his partner in every sense of the term. If that's not high praise, tell me higher, and I'll use it. A positive light appeared to issue from Fezziwig's calves. They shone in every part of the dance like moons. You couldn't have predicted, at any given time, what would have become of them next.

And when old Fezziwig and Mrs. Fezziwig had gone all through the dance; advance and retire, both hands to your partner, bow and curtsey, corkscrew, thread-the-needle, and back again to your place; Fezziwig "cut"— cut so deftly, that he appeared to wink with his legs, and came upon his feet again without a stagger.

Dickens is emphasising the many friends encountered by Scrooge in his new life as an apprentice compared to the solitude at School.

Dick and Scrooge as a young man, dancing

Dickens continues to promote the gaiety of the event by the inexhaustible actions of the fiddler

'scorning rest, he instantly began again'

'scorning rest, he instantly began to play'

Again, Dickens continues the theme of inexhaustible dances
'There were more dances'
'there were forfeits'
'and more dances'
and inexhaustible banqueting
'there was cake'
'there was negus'
'there were mince-pies'
'plenty of beer'

When the clock struck eleven, this domestic ball broke up. Mr. and Mrs. Fezziwig took their stations, one on either side of the door, and shaking hands with every person individually as he or she went out, wished him or her a Merry Christmas.

When everybody had retired but the two 'prentices, they did the same to them; and thus the cheerful voices died away, and the lads were left to their beds; which were under a counter in the back-shop.

During the whole of this time, Scrooge had acted like a man out of his wits. His heart and soul were in the scene, and with his former self. He corroborated everything, remembered everything, enjoyed everything, and underwent the strangest agitation. It was not until now, when the bright faces of his former self and Dick were turned from them, that he remembered the Ghost, and became conscious that it was looking full upon him, while the light upon its head burnt very clear.

"A small matter," said the Ghost, "to make these silly folks so full of gratitude."
"Small!" echoed Scrooge.

The Spirit signed to him to listen to the two apprentices, who were pouring out their hearts in praise of Fezziwig: and when he had done so, said,

"Why! Is it not? He has spent but a few pounds of your mortal money: three or four perhaps. Is that so much that he deserves this praise?"
"It isn't that," said Scrooge, heated by the remark, and speaking unconsciously like his former, not his latter, self. "It isn't that, Spirit. He has the power to render us happy or unhappy; to make our service light or burdensome; a pleasure or a toil. Say that his power lies in words and looks; in things so slight and insignificant that it is impossible to add and count 'em up: what then? The happiness he gives, is quite as great as if it cost a fortune."

He felt the Spirit's glance, and stopped.
"What is the matter?" asked the Ghost.

"Nothing particular," said Scrooge.

Fezziwig stood out to dance with Mrs. Fezziwig

Scrooge becomes conscious of the Ghost 'looking full upon him'

The Ghost looking full upon Scrooge

The Ghost asks Scrooge "What is the matter?"

"Nothing particular," said Scrooge

"Something, I think?" the Ghost insisted.
"No," said Scrooge, "No. I should like to be able to say a word or two to my clerk just now. That's all."

His former self turned down the lamps as he gave utterance to the wish; and Scrooge and the Ghost again stood side by side in the open air.

"My time grows short," observed the Spirit. "Quick!"

This was not addressed to Scrooge, or to any one whom he could see, but it produced an immediate effect. For again Scrooge saw himself. He was older now; a man in the prime of life. His face had not the harsh and rigid lines of later years; but it had begun to wear the signs of care and avarice. There was an eager, greedy, restless motion in the eye, which showed the passion that had taken root, and where the shadow of the growing tree would fall.

He was not alone, but sat by the side of a fair young girl in a mourning- dress: in whose eyes there were tears, which sparkled in the light that shone out of the Ghost of Christmas Past.

"It matters little," she said, softly. "To you, very little. Another idol has displaced me; and if it can cheer and comfort you in time to come, as I would have tried to do, I have no just cause to grieve."
"What Idol has displaced you?" he rejoined.
"A golden one."

"This is the even-handed dealing of the world!" he said. "There is nothing on which it is so hard as poverty; and there is nothing it professes to condemn with such severity as the pursuit of wealth!"

The ghost notices that Scrooge is uncomfortable, and he ask Scrooge why he feels this way. Something is bothering Scrooge.

The Ghost directs Scrooge to the place where he was apprenticed and he was delighted to see Fezziwig, all jovial and benevolent. He threw a sumptuous Christmas party for his staff. This can be juxtaposed with Scrooge's treatment of his clerk Bob Cratchit who he accused of picking his pocket because he had to pay him for not working on Christmas Day.

"I should like to be able to say a word or two to my clerk just now."

Scrooge is feeling guilty for his uncharitable behaviour towards Bob.

Dickens creates a sense of urgency as Scrooge and the Ghost again stood side by side in the open air. The Spirit observed

"My time grows short

"My time grows short," observed the Spirit

Scrooge sees himself as an older man now and Dickens describe him as wearing the,

'signs of care and avarice'

He was sitting next to a girl wearing a mourning dress and she tells Scrooge that

"Another idol has displaced me"

The 'idol 'that his girlfriend is referring to is Scrooge's greed for money.

"You fear the world too much," she answered, gently. "All your other hopes have merged into the hope of being beyond the chance of its sordid reproach. I have seen your nobler aspirations fall off one by one, until the master-passion, Gain, engrosses you. Have I not?"
"What then?" he retorted. "Even if I have grown so much wiser, what then? I am not changed towards you."

She shook her head.

"Am I?"
"Our contract is an old one. It was made when we were both poor and content to be so, until, in good season, we could improve our worldly fortune by our patient industry. You are changed. When it was made, you were another man."
"I was a boy," he said impatiently.

"Your own feeling tells you that you were not what you are," she returned. "I am. That which promised happiness when we were one in heart, is fraught with misery now that we are two. How often and how keenly I have thought of this, I will not say. It is enough that I have thought of it, and can release you."
"Have I ever sought release?"
"In words. No. Never."
"In what, then?"

"In a changed nature; in an altered spirit; in another atmosphere of life; another Hope as its great end. In everything that made my love of any worth or value in your sight. If this had never been between us," said the girl, looking mildly, but with steadiness, upon him; "tell me, would you seek me out and try to win me now? Ah, no!"

He seemed to yield to the justice of this supposition, in spite of himself. But he said with a struggle, "You think not."

Scrooge as a young man sat by his girlfriend

The 'idol 'that his girlfriend is referring to is Scrooge's greed for money.
She is mourning losing him because of his 'avarice ' and he condemns poverty and says he prefers to pursue wealth instead. She says that she has also seen that his,
"nobler aspirations fall off one by one, until the master-passion, gain, engrossed you"

Referring to the sense of greed that had overtaken and dominated his life, so she left him, and they parted.
Dickens uses a very effective tactic here to actually present us with the actual conversation between Scrooge and Belle.

This conversation is very emotional, and the reader tends to sympathise with both Scrooge and Belle because Scrooge seems to be remorseful when he impatiently says,
"I was a boy."

Scrooge listens to the young couple

"I would gladly think otherwise if I could," she answered, "Heaven knows! When I have learned a Truth like this, I know how strong and irresistible it must be. But if you were free to-day, to-morrow, yesterday, can even I believe that you would choose a dowerless girl—you who, in your very confidence with her, weigh everything by Gain: or, choosing her, if for a moment you were false enough to your one guiding principle to do so, do I not know that your repentance and regret would surely follow? I do; and I release you. With a full heart, for the love of him you once were."
He was about to speak; but with her head turned from him, she resumed.

"You may—the memory of what is past half makes me hope you will— have pain in this. A very, very brief time, and you will dismiss the recollection of it, gladly, as an unprofitable dream, from which it happened well that you awoke. May you be happy in the life you have chosen!"

She left him, and they parted.

"Spirit!" said Scrooge, "show me no more! Conduct me home. Why do you delight to torture me?"
"One shadow more!" exclaimed the Ghost.
"No more!" cried Scrooge. "No more. I don't wish to see it. Show me no more!"

But the relentless Ghost pinioned him in both his arms, and forced him to observe what happened next.

They were in another scene and place: a room, not very large or handsome, but full of comfort. Near to the winter fire sat a beautiful young girl, so like that last that Scrooge believed it was the same, until he saw her, now a comely matron, sitting opposite her daughter.

The noise in this room was perfectly tumultuous, for there were more children there, than Scrooge in his agitated state of mind could count; and, unlike the celebrated herd in the poem, they were not forty children conducting themselves like one, but every child was conducting itself like forty.

Dickens makes Scrooge regret his youthful words and actions to his former girlfriend, by expressing his feelings in sorrowful expressions of guilt.

Dickens create the irreconcilable farewell as Elle explains why Gain, not her, is her rival in love.

"you who
 weigh everything by Gain"

She was angry that Scrooge chose her over money, and she wished him luck in his new chosen way of life – married to money.
Then she leaves.

Scrooge insisted on going home and he accused the ghost of torturing him.

But the Ghost was strong and it insisted that Scrooge observe what happened next.

She left him, and they part

At this point Scrooge did not want to see anymore, and cried

"No more!" - "Show me no more!"

The consequences were uproarious beyond belief; but no one seemed to care; on the contrary, the mother and daughter laughed heartily, and enjoyed it very much; and the latter, soon beginning to mingle in the sports, got pillaged by the young brigands most ruthlessly.

What would I not have given to be one of them! Though I never could have been so rude, no, no! I wouldn't for the wealth of all the world have crushed that braided hair, and torn it down; and for the precious little shoe, I wouldn't have plucked it off, God bless my soul! to save my life. As to measuring her waist in sport, as they did, bold young brood, I couldn't have done it; I should have expected my arm to have grown round it for a punishment, and never come straight again. And yet I should have dearly liked, I own, to have touched her lips; to have questioned her, that she might have opened them; to have looked upon the lashes of her downcast eyes, and never raised a blush; to have let loose waves of hair, an inch of which would be a keepsake beyond price: in short, I should have liked, I do confess, to have had the lightest licence of a child, and yet to have been man enough to know its value.

But now a knocking at the door was heard, and such a rush immediately ensued that she with laughing face and plundered dress was borne towards it the centre of a flushed and boisterous group, just in time to greet the father, who came home attended by a man laden with Christmas toys and presents. Then the shouting and the struggling, and the onslaught that was made on the defenceless porter!

The scaling him with chairs for ladders to dive into his pockets, despoil him of brown-paper parcels, hold on tight by his cravat, hug him round his neck, pommel his back, and kick his legs in irrepressible affection! The shouts of wonder and delight with which the development of every package was received!

"No more!" – "Show me no more!"

The use of the exclamation marks shows that he is adamant and refused to see any more, but the Ghost compelled him to observe another scene.

Dickens present the alternative events had Scrooge decided not to forsake a family life with Belle for monetary gain.

Dickens describes the carefree nature of a happy family. It's full of action, and excitement as opposed to Scrooge's forlorn, lonely, unhappy existence .
Scrooge remarks,

'What would I not have given to be one of them!'

Scrooge regrets not being a family man with children

I should have liked, I do confess, to have had the lightest licence of a child

Dickens continues the theme of family life at Christmas, by describing the boisterousness and joy of children waiting to receive their presents when a father returns home. In this case, a father who came home attended by a defenseless porter laden with Christmas toys and presents.

scaling him with chairs for ladders to dive into his pockets, despoil him of brown-paper parcels

The terrible announcement that the baby had been taken in the act of putting a doll's frying-pan into his mouth, and was more than suspected of having swallowed a fictitious turkey, glued on a wooden platter! The immense relief of finding this a false alarm! The joy, and gratitude, and ecstasy! They are all indescribable alike. It is enough that by degrees the children and their emotions got out of the parlour, and by one stair at a time, up to the top of the house; where they went to bed, and so subsided.

And now Scrooge looked on more attentively than ever, when the master of the house, having his daughter leaning fondly on him, sat down with her and her mother at his own fireside; and when he thought that such another creature, quite as graceful and as full of promise, might have called him father, and been a spring-time in the haggard winter of his life, his sight grew very dim indeed.

"Belle," said the husband, turning to his wife with a smile, "I saw an old friend of yours this afternoon."
"Who was it?"
"Guess!"
"How can I? Tut, don't I know?" she added in the same breath, laughing as he laughed. "Mr. Scrooge."

"Mr. Scrooge it was. I passed his office window; and as it was not shut up, and he had a candle inside, I could scarcely help seeing him. His partner lies upon the point of death, I hear; and there he sat alone. Quite alone in the world, I do believe."
"Spirit!" said Scrooge in a broken voice, "remove me from this place."
"I told you these were shadows of the things that have been," said the Ghost. "That they are what they are, do not blame me!"
"Remove me!" Scrooge exclaimed, "I cannot bear it!"

Dickens temper this joy with the mishaps that can happen when so much is going on at such festive time like Christmas.

The terrible announcement that the baby was

more than suspected of having swallowed a fictitious turkey

followed by the

immense relief of finding this a false alarm!

Dickens emphasises the point

They are all indescribable alike

Joy and immense relief wrapped up in conflicting emotions but subdued when

'they went to bed, and so subsided'

Scrooge discovers with sadness and regret that the husband's wife is his former fiancé, Belle.

Belle's husband tells her that he saw Scrooge sitting in his office,

"Quite alone in the world"

Scrooge tormented by the lost opportunity of experiencing a family life demanded that the Ghost takes him home. Scrooge exclaimed

"Remove me!" - "I cannot bear it!"

He turned upon the Ghost, and seeing that it looked upon him with a face, in which in some strange way there were fragments of all the faces it had shown him, wrestled with it.

"Leave me!
 Take me back.
 Haunt me no longer!"

In the struggle, if that can be called a struggle in which the Ghost with no visible resistance on its own part was undisturbed by any effort of its adversary, Scrooge observed that its light was burning high and bright; and dimly connecting that with its influence over him, he seized the extinguisher- cap, and by a sudden action pressed it down upon its head.

The Spirit dropped beneath it, so that the extinguisher covered its whole form; but though Scrooge pressed it down with all his force, he could not hide the light: which streamed from under it, in an unbroken flood upon the ground.

He was conscious of being exhausted, and overcome by an irresistible drowsiness; and, further, of being in his own bedroom. He gave the cap a parting squeeze, in which his hand relaxed; and had barely time to reel to bed, before he sank into a heavy sleep.

End of STAVE two

On arriving home, in his fury, Scrooge demands,

"Leave me!
 Take me back.
 Haunt me no longer!"

Scrooge is emotionally drained and cannot bear to harassed by this Spirit no longer.

Scrooge then attempted to extinguish the bright light emanating from the Spirit by forcing an extinguisher-cap over its head, but unsuccessfully.

Dickens introduces imagery to reinforce the fact that truth represent by light cannot be extinguished

The Spirit dropped beneath it, so that the extinguisher covered its whole form; but though Scrooge pressed it down with all his force, he could not hide the light: which streamed from under it, in an unbroken flood upon the ground.

Scrooge pressed it down with all his force

Scrooge exhausted and overcome by drowsiness, sank into a heavy sleep.

The clock strikes ONE and Scrooge sees a light in the next room. Scrooge goes in and sees the Ghost of Christmas Present. The Ghost is different in physical appearance to the previous ghost. It resembled a giant wearing a green robe trimmed with fur and it carried a torch shaped like 'plenty's horn'. The room has been transformed into a festive sumptuous Christmas scene with holly, ivy and mistletoe and lots of scrumptious food and wines. The Spirit represents 'plenty 'considering that Scrooge thinks that Christmas is a waste,

"Out upon Merry Christmas"

and he regards those who celebrate Christmas as "fools". Holding the Ghost's robe, Scrooge is taken on a journey through the city, shown Christmas festivities and the air of excitement associated with Christmas. The Ghost sprinkled incense on the food and the mood of the people. Hence the food became tasty and the people's mood suddenly became very jovial. Scrooge was taken to Bob Cratchit's house and the Ghost showed him their Christmas celebrations. Despite their poverty there is a beautiful camaraderie and love flowing in the family. Bob arrives carrying Tiny Tim who is sick, and we see a certain change in Scrooge's attitude. He displays a keen sense of sympathy when he enquires about whether Tiny Tim will live. The Spirit tells him that unless there are changes in the future, meaning social change, Tiny Tim will die. Scrooge is reminded of his unfeeling, unsympathetic attitude towards the Charity Collectors.

"If they would rather die, they had better do it and decrease the surplus population"

The Ghost takes Scrooge across the country and showed him a family of miners, sailors, and lighthouse keepers celebrating Christmas with cheer and contentment. Scrooge is then taken to his nephew Fed's house. They were having a Christmas party with a jovial atmosphere - singing and playing games. Scrooge eagerly watches them.

Towards the end of the stave the Ghost ages in appearance. Two miserable, dirty looking children appeared from under the Ghost's cloak. The Ghost tells Scrooge that the boy is 'Ignorance 'and the girl is 'Want 'and that they are children of man who symbolise Ignorance and Want. When Scrooge asks if anything can be done for them, the Ghost reminds him of his curt reply to the two Charity workers

"are there no workhouses"

The Ghost disappears, the clock strikes TWELVE and another Spirit appears.

Awaking in the middle of a prodigiously tough snore, and sitting up in bed to get his thoughts together, Scrooge had no occasion to be told that the bell was again upon the stroke of ONE. He felt that he was restored to consciousness in the right nick of time, for the especial purpose of holding a conference with the second messenger despatched to him through Jacob Marley's intervention. But finding that he turned uncomfortably cold when he began to wonder which of his curtains this new spectre would draw back, he put them every one aside with his own hands; and lying down again, established a sharp look-out all round the bed. For he wished to challenge the Spirit on the moment of its appearance, and did not wish to be taken by surprise, and made nervous.

Gentlemen of the free-and-easy sort, who plume themselves on being acquainted with a move or two, and being usually equal to the time-of-day, express the wide range of their capacity for adventure by observing that they are good for anything from pitch-and-toss to manslaughter; between which opposite extremes, no doubt, there lies a tolerably wide and comprehensive range of subjects. Without venturing for Scrooge quite as hardily as this, I don't mind calling on you to believe that he was ready for a good broad field of strange appearances, and that nothing between a baby and rhinoceros would have astonished him very much.

Now, being prepared for almost anything, he was not by any means prepared for nothing; and, consequently, when the Bell struck One, and no shape appeared, he was taken with a violent fit of trembling. Five minutes, ten minutes, a quarter of an hour went by, yet nothing came.

All this time, he lay upon his bed, the very core and centre of a blaze of ruddy light, which streamed upon it when the clock proclaimed the hour; and which, being only light, was more alarming than a dozen ghosts, as he was powerless to make out what it meant, or would be at; and was sometimes apprehensive that he might be at that very moment an interesting case of spontaneous combustion, without having the consolation of knowing it.

The Bell seems to come alive, heralding the arrival of the Ghost. Scrooge saw,

'a blaze of ruddy light'

Shining from the adjoining room and a strange voice called him by his name and asked him to enter. He was surprised to see the transformation in his room.

Blaze of ruddy light streaming upon it

The room was ablaze with Christmas festivities. There was an array of scrumptious food and drinks ever imaginable and in such plentiful amounts. The room overflowed with the Christmas Spirit.

A Christmas Carol was published in 1843 which coincided with fun, feasting, exchanging of gifts and singing of Christmas Carols.

Dickens used this opportune time to pass on his message of Social Responsibility and for people to reflect upon their actions. Hence the introduction of the Ghost of Christmas Present.

During Victorian times Ghost stories were very popular especially on Christmas Eve. Dickens believed that the Victorian Middle-Class people did not practice what they preached. They were not charitable and viewed the workhouses as sufficient means to house the poor as Scrooge said previously,

"Are there no workhouses?"

They firmly held on to the beliefs of Malthus who believed that if the poor died it will be for the good of the remaining population as Scrooge said previously,

At last, however, he began to think—as you or I would have thought at first; for it is always the person not in the predicament who knows what ought to have been done in it, and would unquestionably have done it too—at last, I say, he began to think that the source and secret of this ghostly light might be in the adjoining room, from whence, on further tracing it, it seemed to shine. This idea taking full possession of his mind, he got up softly and shuffled in his slippers to the door.

The moment Scrooge's hand was on the lock, a strange voice called him by his name, and bade him enter. He obeyed.

It was his own room. There was no doubt about that. But it had undergone a surprising transformation. The walls and ceiling were so hung with living green, that it looked a perfect grove; from every part of which, bright gleaming berries glistened. The crisp leaves of holly, mistletoe, and ivy reflected back the light, as if so many little mirrors had been scattered there; and such a mighty blaze went roaring up the chimney, as that dull petrification of a hearth had never known in Scrooge's time, or Marley's, or for many and many a winter season gone. Heaped up on the floor, to form a kind of throne, were turkeys, geese, game, poultry, brawn, great joints of meat, sucking-pigs, long wreaths of sausages, mince-pies, plum-puddings, barrels of oysters, red- hot chestnuts, cherry-cheeked apples, juicy oranges, luscious pears, immense twelfth-cakes, and seething bowls of punch, that made the chamber dim with their delicious steam. In easy state upon this couch, there sat a jolly Giant, glorious to see; who bore a glowing torch, in shape not unlike Plenty's horn, and held it up, high up, to shed its light on Scrooge, as he came peeping round the door.

"Come in!" exclaimed the Ghost. "Come in! and know me better, man!"

Scrooge entered timidly, and hung his head before this Spirit. He was not the dogged Scrooge he had been; and though the Spirit's eyes were clear and kind, he did not like to meet them.

"I am the Ghost of Christmas Present," said the Spirit. "Look upon me!"

"if the poor had to die so let them"

It was this view that incensed Dickens and he challenged it by creating this special genre 'A Christmas Carol', to teach these Middle-Class selfish Victorians a moral lesson.

Hence, he very meticulously and very carefully crafted the character of each of the three Spirits with their overwhelming presence, to carry this moral message whilst using the character of Scrooge to represent the Capitalist class.

Dickens gives a vivid detailed description of the festive room so that we can visualise it. It was plentiful - something Scrooge would have viewed as a total waste.

Sitting on the couch was a jolly Giant, carrying a torch which it held up to illuminate Scrooge.

there sat a jolly Giant

The Ghost bade him enter and he obediently did so.

'Scrooge entered timidly'

Note Dickens use of the adverb 'timidly 'suggesting a change in Scrooge as juxtaposed to that of Marley's ghost where Scrooge challenged Marley.

"He was not the dogged Scrooge he had been"

The Ghost of Christmas Present commanded Scrooge to

"Look upon me!"

Scrooge reverently did so. It was clothed in one simple green robe, or mantle, bordered with white fur. This garment hung so loosely on the figure, that its capacious breast was bare, as if disdaining to be warded or concealed by any artifice. Its feet, observable beneath the ample folds of the garment, were also bare; and on its head it wore no other covering than a holly wreath, set here and there with shining icicles. Its dark brown curls were long and free; free as its genial face, its sparkling eye, its open hand, its cheery voice, its unconstrained demeanour, and its joyful air. Girded round its middle was an antique scabbard; but no sword was in it, and the ancient sheath was eaten up with rust.

"You have never seen the like of me before!" exclaimed the Spirit.
"Never," Scrooge made answer to it.
"Have never walked forth with the younger members of my family; meaning (for I am very young) my elder brothers born in these later years?" pursued the Phantom.
"I don't think I have," said Scrooge. "I am afraid I have not. Have you had many brothers, Spirit?"

"More than eighteen hundred," said the Ghost.
"A tremendous family to provide for!" muttered Scrooge. The Ghost of Christmas Present rose.
"Spirit," said Scrooge submissively, "conduct me where you will. I went forth last night on compulsion, and I learnt a lesson which is working now. To-night, if you have aught to teach me, let me, let me profit by it."

"Touch my robe!"
Scrooge did as he was told, and held it fast.

Holly, mistletoe, red berries, ivy, turkeys, geese, game, poultry, brawn, meat, pigs, sausages, oysters, pies, puddings, fruit, and punch, all vanished instantly. So did the room, the fire, the ruddy glow, the hour of night, and they stood in the city streets on Christmas morning, where (for the weather was severe) the people made a rough, but brisk and not unpleasant kind of music, in scraping the snow from the pavement in front of their dwellings, and from the tops of their houses, whence it was mad delight to the boys to see it come plumping down into the road below, and splitting into artificial little snow-storms.

We see a very changed meek and humbled Scrooge, ready to learn his lesson,

"To-night, if you have aught to teach me, let me profit by it"

Scrooge touched the Spirit's robe as requested. Off on a journey did Scrooge go with the phantom, through the city streets on Christmas morning.

"Touch my robe!"

Scrooge is transported to the Christmas market where all manner of fruits, meats and drinks are displayed.

Fruits, meats and drink displayed

The house fronts looked black enough, and the windows blacker, contrasting with the smooth white sheet of snow upon the roofs, and with the dirtier snow upon the ground; which last deposit had been ploughed up in deep furrows by the heavy wheels of carts and waggons; furrows that crossed and re-crossed each other hundreds of times where the great streets branched off; and made intricate channels, hard to trace in the thick yellow mud and icy water. The sky was gloomy, and the shortest streets were choked up with a dingy mist, half thawed, half frozen, whose heavier particles descended in a shower of sooty atoms, as if all the chimneys in Great Britain had, by one consent, caught fire, and were blazing away to their dear hearts 'content. There was nothing very cheerful in the climate or the town, and yet was there an air of cheerfulness abroad that the clearest summer air and brightest summer sun might have endeavoured to diffuse in vain.

For, the people who were shovelling away on the housetops were jovial and full of glee; calling out to one another from the parapets, and now and then exchanging a facetious snowball—better-natured missile far than many a wordy jest—laughing heartily if it went right and not less heartily if it went wrong. The poulterers 'shops were still half open, and the fruiterers 'were radiant in their glory. There were great, round, pot-bellied baskets of chestnuts, shaped like the waistcoats of jolly old gentlemen, lolling at the doors, and tumbling out into the street in their apoplectic opulence.

There were ruddy, brown-faced, broad-girthed Spanish Onions, shining in the fatness of their growth like Spanish Friars, and winking from their shelves in wanton slyness at the girls as they went by, and glanced demurely at the hung-up mistletoe. There were pears and apples, clustered high in blooming pyramids; there were bunches of grapes, made, in the shopkeepers' benevolence to dangle from conspicuous hooks, that people's mouths might water gratis as they passed;

there were bunches of grapes, made, in the shopkeepers' benevolence to dangle from conspicuous hooks, that people's mouths might water gratis as they passed;

Dickens gives us a lengthy description of the weather using pathetic fallacy, the setting was dull and gloomy.

'There was nothing very cheerful in the climate or the town and yet there was an air of cheerfulness abroad'

Scrooge saw that despite their poverty, the people were

'jovial and full of glee'

Dickens describes in detail the daily activities of the ordinary people, particularly, the tradesmen and shopkeepers. What they did. Their appearance. The produce that they sold.

There were great, round, pot-bellied baskets of chestnuts, shaped like the waistcoats of jolly old gentlemen, lolling at the doors, and tumbling out into the street in their apoplectic opulence.

The Spirit and Scrooge at the Market

Dickens continues his vivid description of the scenery to make the reader feel as though that they are there within the scene.
Remember, the novel was first published in December 1843 just prior to Christmas.

Dicken's creates the lull before the storm – everything is quiet on this early Christmas morning and waiting before the burst of the Christmas festivities when people began to pour into the streets.

There were pears and apples, clustered high in blooming pyramids there were piles of filberts, mossy and brown, recalling, in their fragrance, ancient walks among the woods, and pleasant shufflings ankle deep through withered leaves; there were Norfolk Biffins, squat and swarthy, setting off the yellow of the oranges and lemons, and, in the great compactness of their juicy persons, urgently entreating and beseeching to be carried home in paper bags and eaten after dinner. The very gold and silver fish, set forth among these choice fruits in a bowl, though members of a dull and stagnant- blooded race, appeared to know that there was something going on; and, to a fish, went gasping round and round their little world in slow and passionless excitement.

The Grocers'! oh, the Grocers'! nearly closed, with perhaps two shutters down, or one; but through those gaps such glimpses! It was not alone that the scales descending on the counter made a merry sound, or that the twine and roller parted company so briskly, or that the canisters were rattled up and down like juggling tricks, or even that the blended scents of tea and coffee were so grateful to the nose, or even that the raisins were so plentiful and rare, the almonds so extremely white, the sticks of cinnamon so long and straight, the other spices so delicious, the candied fruits so caked and spotted with molten sugar as to make the coldest lookers-on feel faint and subsequently bilious. Nor was it that the figs were moist and pulpy, or that the French plums blushed in modest tartness from their highly-decorated boxes, or that everything was good to eat and in its Christmas dress: but they customers were all so hurried and so eager in the hopeful promise of the day, that they tumbled up against each other at the door, crashing their wicker baskets wildly, and left their purchases upon the counter, and came running back to fetch them, and committed hundreds of the like mistakes, in the best humour possible; while the Grocer and his people were so frank and fresh that the polished hearts with which they fastened their aprons behind might have been their own, worn outside for general inspection, and for Christmas daws to peck at if they chose.

But soon the steeples called good people all, to church and chapel, and away they came, flocking through the streets in their best clothes, and with their gayest faces.

there were piles of filberts, mossy and brown

Everything is available to buy.

raisins were so plentiful and rare

Yet, again, everything was plentiful.

everything was good to eat

Again, everything was good to eat. Scrooge saw the start of the Christmas spirit when people poured into the streets, participating in various activities. Yet he refused to become part of this exciting and fulfilling Christmas experience.

And at the same time there emerged from scores of bye- streets, lanes, and nameless turnings, innumerable people, carrying their dinners to the bakers 'shops. The sight of these poor revellers appeared to interest the Spirit very much, for he stood with Scrooge beside him in a baker's doorway, and taking off the covers as their bearers passed, sprinkled incense on their dinners from his torch. And it was a very uncommon kind of torch, for once or twice when there were angry words between some dinner- carriers who had jostled each other, he shed a few drops of water on them from it, and their good humour was restored directly. For they said, it was a shame to quarrel upon Christmas Day. And so it was! God love it, so it was!

In time the bells ceased, and the bakers were shut up; and yet there was a genial shadowing forth of all these dinners and the progress of their cooking, in the thawed blotch of wet above each baker's oven; where the pavement smoked as if its stones were cooking too.

"Is there a peculiar flavour in what you sprinkle from your torch?" asked Scrooge.
"There is. My own."
"Would it apply to any kind of dinner on this day?" asked Scrooge. "To any kindly given. To a poor one most."
"Why to a poor one most?" asked Scrooge.
"Because it needs it most."

"Spirit," said Scrooge, after a moment's thought, "I wonder you, of all the beings in the many worlds about us, should desire to cramp these people's opportunities of innocent enjoyment."

"I!" cried the Spirit.
"You would deprive them of their means of dining every seventh day, often the only day on which they can be said to dine at all," said Scrooge. "Wouldn't you?"
"I!" cried the Spirit.
"You seek to close these places on the Seventh Day?" said Scrooge. "And it comes to the same thing."
"I seek!" exclaimed the Spirit.

"Forgive me if I am wrong. It has been done in your name, or at least in that of your family," said Scrooge.

'Humbug' he referred to it as.

The Spirit displayed a very noble gesture. He sprinkled incense from his torch onto people's dinners. He also added cheer to the angry shoppers by shedding,

"a few drops of water on them"

and restoring their good humour.

"a few drops of water on them"

This conforms with the traditional Christian blessing administered to everyday items in Victorian times.

"a few drops of water on them"

Scrooge accuses the Ghost of closing the shops on the Sabbath day - the Seventh Day - and depriving the poor people of enjoying a dinner on a Sunday.

The Spirit became furious,

"I seek!"

and he set upon a verbal attack on Scrooge and his avaricious and selfish nature.

"There are some upon this earth of yours," returned the Spirit, "who lay claim to know us, and who do their deeds of passion, pride, ill-will, hatred, envy, bigotry, and selfishness in our name, who are as strange to us and all our kith and kin, as if they had never lived. Remember that, and charge their doings on themselves, not us."

Scrooge promised that he would; and they went on, invisible, as they had been before, into the suburbs of the town. It was a remarkable quality of the Ghost (which Scrooge had observed at the baker's), that notwithstanding his gigantic size, he could accommodate himself to any place with ease; and that he stood beneath a low roof quite as gracefully and like a supernatural creature, as it was possible he could have done in any lofty hall.

And perhaps it was the pleasure the good Spirit had in showing off this power of his, or else it was his own kind, generous, hearty nature, and his sympathy with all poor men, that led him straight to Scrooge's clerk's; for there he went, and took Scrooge with him, holding to his robe; and on the threshold of the door the Spirit smiled, and stopped to bless Bob Cratchit's dwelling with the sprinkling of his torch. Think of that! Bob had but fifteen "Bob" a-week himself; he pocketed on Saturdays but fifteen copies of his Christian name; and yet the Ghost of Christmas Present blessed his four-roomed house!

Then up rose Mrs. Cratchit, Cratchit's wife, dressed out but poorly in a twice-turned gown, but brave in ribbons, which are cheap and make a goodly show for sixpence; and she laid the cloth, assisted by Belinda Cratchit, second of her daughters, also brave in ribbons; while Master Peter Cratchit plunged a fork into the saucepan of potatoes, and getting the corners of his monstrous shirt collar (Bob's private property, conferred upon his son and heir in honour of the day) into his mouth, rejoiced to find himself so gallantly attired, and yearned to show his linen in the fashionable Parks.

The Spirit reminds Scrooge that the Capitalist class like him only pretend to know God but are totally uncharitable and have a total disregard for the sufferings of the poor.

He further accuses Scrooge of
"passion, pride, ill-will, hatred, envy, bigotry, and selfishness"
against the poor socialist class.

They then moved into the suburbs of the town. Being very sympathetic with,
"all poor men"
the Ghost takes Scrooge to Bob Cratchit's house. Scrooge witnesses the Cratchit's Christmas filled with warmth and love flowing through the very veins of the house.

Bob Cratchit's dwelling with the sprinkling

Mrs Cratchit, appeared in a,
'twice-turned gown, brave in ribbons, which are cheap'

Mrs Cratchit and children preparing dinner

And now two smaller Cratchits, boy and girl, came tearing in, screaming that outside the baker's they had smelt the goose, and known it for their own; and basking in luxurious thoughts of sage and onion, these young Cratchits danced about the table, and exalted Master Peter Cratchit to the skies, while he (not proud, although his collars nearly choked him) blew the fire, until the slow potatoes bubbling up, knocked loudly at the saucepan-lid to be let out and peeled.

"What has ever got your precious father then?" said Mrs. Cratchit. "And your brother, Tiny Tim! And Martha warn't as late last Christmas Day by half-an-hour?"
"Here's Martha, mother!" said a girl, appearing as she spoke.
"Here's Martha, mother!" cried the two young Cratchits. "Hurrah! There's such a goose, Martha!"
"Why, bless your heart alive, my dear, how late you are!" said Mrs. Cratchit kissing her a dozen times, and taking off her shawl and bonnet for her with officious zeal.

"We'd a deal of work to finish up last night," replied the girl, "and had to clear away this morning, mother!"
"Well! Never mind so long as you are come," said Mrs. Cratchit. "Sit ye down before the fire, my dear, and have a warm, Lord bless ye!"

"No, no! There's father coming," cried the two young Cratchits, who were everywhere at once. "Hide, Martha, hide!"

So Martha hid herself, and in came little Bob, the father, with at least three feet of comforter exclusive of the fringe, hanging down before him; and his threadbare clothes darned up and brushed, to look seasonable; and Tiny Tim upon his shoulder. Alas for Tiny Tim, he bore a little crutch, and had his limbs supported by an iron frame!

"Why, where's our Martha?" cried Bob Cratchit, looking round.
"Not coming," said Mrs. Cratchit.
"Not coming!" said Bob, with a sudden declension in his high spirits; for he had been Tim's blood horse all the way from church, and had come home rampant. "Not coming upon Christmas Day!"

We see that Martha, the daughter, worked on Christmas Day. When Dickens was a child, most people worked on Christmas Day. The situation changed when Christmas became more prominent and the Victorian middle-class employers gave their employees a paid holiday. For example, previously in the office Scrooge accused Bob of

'picking his pocket'

because he would have to pay Bob for not work on Christmas Day.

So in comes Bob Cratchit in his,

'thread-bare clothes darned up and brushed'

and the cripple

'Tiny Tim upon his shoulder'

Tiny Tim upon his shoulder

There is such an admirable camaraderie among the Cratchit family with Martha hiding to surprise her loving father.

Tiny Tim was sick and he bore a little crutch. Dickens portrays Bob as a very warm and affectionate father which we can denote from his disappointment on learning that Martha will not be coming for Christmas dinner.

"Not coming!"

said Bob,

'with a sudden declension in his high spirits'

Martha didn't like to see him disappointed, if it were only in joke; so she came out prematurely from behind the closet door, and ran into his arms, while the two young Cratchits hustled Tiny Tim, and bore him off into the wash-house, that he might hear the pudding singing in the copper.

"And how did little Tim behave?" asked Mrs. Cratchit, when she had rallied Bob on his credulity, and Bob had hugged his daughter to his heart's content.
"As good as gold," said Bob, "and better. Somehow he gets thoughtful, sitting by himself so much, and thinks the strangest things you ever heard. He told me, coming home, that he hoped the people saw him in the church, because he was a cripple, and it might be pleasant to them to remember upon Christmas Day, who made lame beggars walk, and blind men see."

Bob's voice was tremulous when he told them this, and trembled more when he said that Tiny Tim was growing strong and hearty.

His active little crutch was heard upon the floor, and back came Tiny Tim before another word was spoken, escorted by his brother and sister to his stool before the fire; and while Bob, turning up his cuffs—as if, poor fellow, they were capable of being made more shabby—compounded some hot mixture in a jug with gin and lemons, and stirred it round and round and put it on the hob to simmer; Master Peter, and the two ubiquitous young Cratchits went to fetch the goose, with which they soon returned in high procession.

Such a bustle ensued that you might have thought a goose the rarest of all birds; a feathered phenomenon, to which a black swan was a matter of course —and in truth it was something very like it in that house. Mrs. Cratchit made the gravy (ready beforehand in a little saucepan) hissing hot; Master Peter mashed the potatoes with incredible vigour; Miss Belinda sweetened up the apple-sauce; Martha dusted the hot plates; Bob took Tiny Tim beside him in a tiny corner at the table; the two young Cratchits set chairs for everybody, not forgetting themselves, and mounting guard upon their posts, crammed spoons into their mouths, lest they should shriek for goose before their turn came to be helped.

Martha didn't want to see him disappointed, so she quickly ran into his arms from her hiding place.

Martha didn't like to see him disappointed

Bob's emotions are exhibited when he tells his family about Tiny Tim and what Tim told him coming home from church that day. Tim hoped that,

'the people saw him in the church, because he was a cripple, and it might be pleasant to them to remember upon Christmas Day, who made lame beggars walk and blind men see'

By using the innocence of crippled Tiny Tim, Dickens portrays for us the terrible plight of the disabled people in Victorian Britain.

Dickens describes in vivid detail the frantic hustle and bustle of preparing and delivering the Christmas dinner. Every member of the Cratchit family making a contribution in expectation of experiencing an outstanding dinner.

Master Peter

'mashed the potatoes with incredible vigour'

Miss Belinda

'sweetened up the apple-sauce'

And Martha

'dusted the hot plates'

At last the dishes were set on, and grace was said. It was succeeded by a breathless pause, as Mrs. Cratchit, looking slowly all along the carving- knife, prepared to plunge it in the breast; but when she did, and when the long expected gush of stuffing issued forth, one murmur of delight arose all round the board, and even Tiny Tim, excited by the two young Cratchits, beat on the table with the handle of his knife, and feebly cried Hurrah!

There never was such a goose. Bob said he didn't believe there ever was such a goose cooked. Its tenderness and flavour, size and cheapness, were the themes of universal admiration. Eked out by apple-sauce and mashed potatoes, it was a sufficient dinner for the whole family; indeed, as Mrs. Cratchit said with great delight (surveying one small atom of a bone upon the dish), they hadn't ate it all at last! Yet every one had had enough, and the youngest Cratchits in particular, were steeped in sage and onion to the eyebrows! But now, the plates being changed by Miss Belinda, Mrs. Cratchit left the room alone—too nervous to bear witnesses—to take the pudding up and bring it in.

Suppose it should not be done enough! Suppose it should break in turning out! Suppose somebody should have got over the wall of the back-yard, and stolen it, while they were merry with the goose—a supposition at which the two young Cratchits became livid! All sorts of horrors were supposed.

Hallo! A great deal of steam! The pudding was out of the copper. A smell like a washing-day! That was the cloth. A smell like an eating-house and a pastrycook's next door to each other, with a laundress's next door to that! That was the pudding!

In half a minute Mrs. Cratchit entered—flushed, but smiling proudly—with the pudding, like a speckled cannon-ball, so hard and firm, blazing in half of half-a-quartern of ignited brandy, and bedight with Christmas holly stuck into the top.

Oh, a wonderful pudding! Bob Cratchit said, and calmly too, that he regarded it as the greatest success achieved by Mrs. Cratchit since their marriage.

Mrs Cratchit – prepared to plunge it in

Finally, with grace said, and the knife plunged into the goose,
'the two young Cratchits, beat on the table with the handle of his knife'

Bob declared and all agreed
'he didn't believe there ever was such a goose cooked'

Dickens creates suspense by making Mrs Cratchit
'too nervous to bear witnesses'

as to her cooking of the pudding.
'All sorts of horrors were supposed'

Mrs. Cratchit entered—flushed, but smiling

Bob's sense of appreciation of his wife's cooking is priceless. Note the use of the exclamation mark denoting excitement.
"Oh, a wonderful pudding!"

Mrs. Cratchit said that now the weight was off her mind, she would confess she had had her doubts about the quantity of flour. Everybody had something to say about it, but nobody said or thought it was at all a small pudding for a large family. It would have been flat heresy to do so. Any Cratchit would have blushed to hint at such a thing.	The use of the superlative, 'greatest success 'further enhances his appreciation of his wife. Being very poor, the pudding was very small, but none of the Cratchits mentioned it.
At last the dinner was all done, the cloth was cleared, the hearth swept, and the fire made up. The compound in the jug being tasted, and considered perfect, apples and oranges were put upon the table, and a shovel-full of chestnuts on the fire. Then all the Cratchit family drew round the hearth, in what Bob Cratchit called a circle, meaning half a one; and at Bob Cratchit's elbow stood the family display of glass. Two tumblers, and a custard-cup without a handle.	We notice that the custard cup had no handle and again Dickens reveals the Cratchit's contentment because they believed that the two tumblers, and custard-cup,
	'held the hot stuff from the jug, as well as golden goblets would have done'
These held the hot stuff from the jug, however, as well as golden goblets would have done; and Bob served it out with beaming looks, while the chestnuts on the fire sputtered and cracked noisily. Then Bob proposed:	One can connote that even the chestnuts joined in the Cratchit's merriment.
	'the chestnuts on the fire sputtered and cracked noisily'
"A Merry Christmas to us all, my dears. God bless us!" Which all the family re-echoed. "God bless us every one!" said Tiny Tim, the last of all.	The use of the onomatopoeia 'sputtered 'and 'cracked ' can suggest that even the chestnuts danced on the fire to become part of the 'Cratchit's fun and excitement.
He sat very close to his father's side upon his little stool. Bob held his withered little hand in his, as if he loved the child, and wished to keep him by his side, and dreaded that he might be taken from him	Dickens paints a very emotive picture of the relationship between Bob Cratchit and Tiny Tim and hence the reader gets emotionally involved.
	'Bob held his withered little hand in his'
	'dreaded that he might be taken from him'
"Spirit," said Scrooge, with an interest he had never felt before, "tell me if Tiny Tim will live." "I see a vacant seat," replied the Ghost, "in the poor chimney-corner, and a crutch without an owner, carefully preserved. If these shadows remain unaltered by the Future, the child will die."	To describe a little child's hand as 'withered 'is very sad because it may perhaps be looking like an old person's hand.
	Scrooge asks the Ghost if Tiny Tim will live and the Ghost told Scrooge that he will live if the Social problems and lack of empathy towards the poor improves.
"No, no," said Scrooge. "Oh, no, kind Spirit! say he will be spared."	Furthermore, through the Ghost, Dickens relays the simple truth that Tiny Tim was going to die,
	"If these shadows remain unaltered by the Future, the child will die"
	The reader is pleasantly surprised at Scrooge's reaction,
	"No, no", said Scrooge
	"Oh, no, kind Spirit! say he will be spared."

TEXT Stave 3	EXPLANATION
"If these shadows remain unaltered by the Future, none other of my race," returned the Ghost, "will find him here. What then? If he be like to die, he had better do it, and decrease the surplus population."	The Ghost repeated what Scrooge said to the charity collectors,
	"and decrease the surplus population"
Scrooge hung his head to hear his own words quoted by the Spirit, and was overcome with penitence and grief.	Scrooge felt embarrassed when the Ghost echoed his words and Scrooge was,
	'overcome with penitence and grief'
"Man," said the Ghost, "if man you be in heart, not adamant, forbear that wicked cant until you have discovered What the surplus is, and Where it is. Will you decide what men shall live, what men shall die? It may be, that in the sight of Heaven, you are more worthless and less fit to live than millions like this poor man's child. Oh God! to hear the Insect on the leaf pronouncing on the too much life among his hungry brothers in the dust!"	We can now juxtapose Scrooge's changed, admirable behaviour to that of the display of his earlier cold, ruthless behaviour towards the poor.
	He shows genuine concern for Tiny Tim's sad situation, and we witness a certain awakening in Scrooge.
	The Ghost uses a biblical imagery,
	"in the sight of Heaven"
Scrooge bent before the Ghost's rebuke, and trembling cast his eyes upon the ground. But he raised them speedily, on hearing his own name.	Scrooge felt humiliated at the Ghost's rebuke and he trembled with disgust and fear for his actions.
"Mr. Scrooge!" said Bob; "I'll give you Mr. Scrooge, the Founder of the Feast!"	The Ghost makes it clear to Scrooge that God does not approve of his uncharitable, avaricious attitude,
"The Founder of the Feast indeed!" cried Mrs. Cratchit, reddening. "I wish I had him here. I'd give him a piece of my mind to feast upon, and I hope he'd have a good appetite for it."	"you are more worthless and less fit to live than millions like this poor man's child"
"My dear," said Bob, "the children! Christmas Day."	because he said that the poor must die.
"It should be Christmas Day, I am sure," said she, "on which one drinks the health of such an odious, stingy, hard, unfeeling man as Mr. Scrooge. You know he is, Robert! Nobody knows it better than you do, poor fellow!"	Dickens had so carefully crafted Bob's character to be so virtuous and loving. His toast to Scrooge,
"My dear," was Bob's mild answer, "Christmas Day."	"I'll give you Mr Scrooge, the Founder of the Feast"
"I'll drink his health for your sake and the Day's," said Mrs. Cratchit, "not for his. Long life to him! A merry Christmas and a happy new year! He'll be very merry and very happy, I have no doubt!"	to the annoyance of his wife who labels Scrooge as
	"an odious, stingy, hard, unfeeling man"
The children drank the toast after her. It was the first of their proceedings which had no heartiness. Tiny Tim drank it last of all, but he didn't care twopence for it.	Bob did not welcome his wife's criticism of Scrooge and was forced to wish
	"Long life to him"

Scrooge was the Ogre of the family. The mention of his name cast a dark shadow on the party, which was not dispelled for full five minutes.

After it had passed away, they were ten times merrier than before, from the mere relief of Scrooge the Baleful being done with. Bob Cratchit told them how he had a situation in his eye for Master Peter, which would bring in, if obtained, full five-and-sixpence weekly. The two young Cratchits laughed tremendously at the idea of Peter's being a man of business; and Peter himself looked thoughtfully at the fire from between his collars, as if he were deliberating what particular investments he should favour when he came into the receipt of that bewildering income. Martha, who was a poor apprentice at a milliner's, then told them what kind of work she had to do, and how many hours she worked at a stretch, and how she meant to lie abed to-morrow morning for a good long rest; to-morrow being a holiday she passed at home.

Also how she had seen a countess and a lord some days before, and how the lord "was much about as tall as Peter;" at which Peter pulled up his collars so high that you couldn't have seen his head if you had been there. All this time the chestnuts and the jug went round and round; and by-and-bye they had a song, about a lost child travelling in the snow, from Tiny Tim, who had a plaintive little voice, and sang it very well indeed.

There was nothing of high mark in this. They were not a handsome family; they were not well dressed; their shoes were far from being water-proof; their clothes were scanty; and Peter might have known, and very likely did, the inside of a pawnbroker's. But, they were happy, grateful, pleased with one another, and contented with the time; and when they faded, and looked happier yet in the bright sprinklings of the Spirit's torch at parting, Scrooge had his eye upon them, and especially on Tiny Tim, until the last.

By this time it was getting dark, and snowing pretty heavily; and as Scrooge and the Spirit went along the streets, the brightness of the roaring fires in kitchens, parlours, and all sorts of rooms, was wonderful.

Bob toasts Scrooge – Founder of the feast

Dickens juxtaposes the loathing of Scrooge by Bob's family

'The mention of his name cast a dark shadow'

to Bob's embracement of the Christmas Spirit.

Dickens highlights the concerns of parents like Bob about employment opportunities for their children.

Both Peter and Martha were not convinced and

laughed tremendously at the idea of Peter's being a man of business'

Dickens introduces the theme of fantasy as Martha tells the family about

'how she had seen a countess and a lord some days before, and how the lord "was much about as tall as Peter"

Fantasy helped alleviate the true reality of struggle ever prevalent in society for the needy who depended on others for their meagre income.

The merriment continues with food and drink,

'they had a song' … 'from Tiny Tim'

The Cratchits were not a wealthy family and Peter probably knew

'the inside of a pawnbroker's' But

'they were happy, grateful, pleased with one another'

Here, the flickering of the blaze showed preparations for a cosy dinner, with hot plates baking through and through before the fire, and deep red curtains, ready to be drawn to shut out cold and darkness. There all the children of the house were running out into the snow to meet their married sisters, brothers, cousins, uncles, aunts, and be the first to greet them. Here, again, were shadows on the window-blind of guests assembling; and there a group of handsome girls, all hooded and fur-booted, and all chattering at once, tripped lightly off to some near neighbour's house; where, woe upon the single man who saw them enter —artful witches, well they knew it—in a glow!

But, if you had judged from the numbers of people on their way to friendly gatherings, you might have thought that no one was at home to give them welcome when they got there, instead of every house expecting company, and piling up its fires half-chimney high. Blessings on it, how the Ghost exulted! How it bared its breadth of breast, and opened its capacious palm, and floated on, outpouring, with a generous hand, its bright and harmless mirth on everything within its reach! The very lamplighter, who ran on before, dotting the dusky street with specks of light, and who was dressed to spend the evening somewhere, laughed out loudly as the Spirit passed, though little kenned the lamplighter that he had any company but Christmas!

And now, without a word of warning from the Ghost, they stood upon a bleak and desert moor, where monstrous masses of rude stone were cast about, as though it were the burial-place of giants; and water spread itself wheresoever it listed, or would have done so, but for the frost that held it prisoner; and nothing grew but moss and furze, and coarse rank grass. Down in the west the setting sun had left a streak of fiery red, which glared upon the desolation for an instant, like a sullen eye, and frowning lower, lower, lower yet, was lost in the thick gloom of darkest night.

they had a song - from Tiny Tim

Dickens paints a vivid picture of social excitement at Christmas within the community, introducing new social groups and their different ways of celebrating the joys of Christmas.

There all the children of the house were running out into the snow to meet their married sisters, brothers, cousins, uncles, aunts, and be the first to greet them

Dickens muses about the lamplighter and empty houses
'you might have thought that no one was at home'

Dickens emphasises that even the lamplighter is 'dressed to spend the evening somewhere'

his companion is Christmas itself.

Dickens suddenly switches the location to open a new page on events.

they stood upon a bleak and desert moor

"What place is this?" asked Scrooge.

"A place where Miners live, who labour in the bowels of the earth," returned the Spirit. "But they know me. See!"

A light shone from the window of a hut, and swiftly they advanced towards it. Passing through the wall of mud and stone, they found a cheerful company assembled round a glowing fire. An old, old man and woman, with their children and their children's children, and another generation beyond that, all decked out gaily in their holiday attire. The old man, in a voice that seldom rose above the howling of the wind upon the barren waste, was singing them a Christmas song—it had been a very old song when he was a boy—and from time to time they all joined in the chorus. So surely as they raised their voices, the old man got quite blithe and loud; and so surely as they stopped, his vigour sank again.

The Spirit did not tarry here, but bade Scrooge hold his robe, and passing on above the moor, sped—whither?

Not to sea? To sea.

To Scrooge's horror, looking back, he saw the last of the land, a frightful range of rocks, behind them; and his ears were deafened by the thundering of water, as it rolled and roared, and raged among the dreadful caverns it had worn, and fiercely tried to undermine the earth.

Built upon a dismal reef of sunken rocks, some league or so from shore, on which the waters chafed and dashed, the wild year through, there stood a solitary lighthouse. Great heaps of sea-weed clung to its base, and storm-birds —born of the wind one might suppose, as sea-weed of the water—rose and fell about it, like the waves they skimmed.

But even here, two men who watched the light had made a fire, that through the loophole in the thick stone wall shed out a ray of brightness on the awful sea. Joining their horny hands over the rough table at which they sat, they wished each other Merry Christmas in their can of grog; and one of them: the elder, too, with his face all damaged and scarred with hard weather, as the figure-head of an old ship might be: struck up a sturdy song that was like a Gale in itself.

Dickens gives us a vivid description of the empty bleak setting of the miners,

"who labour in the bowels of the earth."

This bleak setting can be associated with the bleak, sad, empty lives of the poor, struggling miners.

Scrooge and the Ghost went along the streets, passing through the wall of mud and stone, observing how everybody so joyously enjoyed the Christmas Spirit, with children playing and singing.

But the Spirit did not tarry. Next, they wizzed out to sea to a lighthouse to see how two men who were all alone managed to give Christmas a cheerful meaning by singing and drinking. Their loneliness did not deter them from enjoying the Christmas spirit and they were so content.

'there stood a solitary lighthouse'

Again,
'they wished each other Merry Christmas'

Again the Ghost sped on, above the black and heaving sea—on, on—until, being far away, as he told Scrooge, from any shore, they lighted on a ship. They stood beside the helmsman at the wheel, the look-out in the bow, the officers who had the watch; dark, ghostly figures in their several stations; but every man among them hummed a Christmas tune, or had a Christmas thought, or spoke below his breath to his companion of some bygone Christmas Day, with homeward hopes belonging to it. And every man on board, waking or sleeping, good or bad, had had a kinder word for another on that day than on any day in the year; and had shared to some extent in its festivities; and had remembered those he cared for at a distance, and had known that they delighted to remember him.

It was a great surprise to Scrooge, while listening to the moaning of the wind, and thinking what a solemn thing it was to move on through the lonely darkness over an unknown abyss, whose depths were secrets as profound as Death: it was a great surprise to Scrooge, while thus engaged, to hear a hearty laugh. It was a much greater surprise to Scrooge to recognise it as his own nephew's and to find himself in a bright, dry, gleaming room, with the Spirit standing smiling by his side, and looking at that same nephew with approving affability!

"Ha, ha!" laughed Scrooge's nephew. "Ha, ha, ha!"

If you should happen, by any unlikely chance, to know a man more blest in a laugh than Scrooge's nephew, all I can say is, I should like to know him too. Introduce him to me, and I'll cultivate his acquaintance.

It is a fair, even-handed, noble adjustment of things, that while there is infection in disease and sorrow, there is nothing in the world so irresistibly contagious as laughter and good-humour. When Scrooge's nephew laughed in this way: holding his sides, rolling his head, and twisting his face into the most extravagant contortions: Scrooge's niece, by marriage, laughed as heartily as he. And their assembled friends being not a bit behindhand, roared out lustily.

Scrooge observes the spirit of Christmas in action against the harshness of sea or storm,

The Ghost then sped on to a ship. Although they were out at sea, without their families, they all hummed a Christmas tune, and were kind to each other.

they lighted on a ship

Dickens portrays the joys experienced by families and their children, miners, lighthouse keepers, mariners, and others at Christmas, but not Scrooge who is indifferent and see no value in such sentiments. But like ice that eventually melts when exposed to heat, Scrooge is gradually exposed to the values of generosity and love.

Dickens, again, switches location to provide a closer exposure to the values of the Christmas spirit.

Suddenly, Scrooge heard a familiar laugh, and was surprised that it was his nephew's hearty laugh.

He found himself in a bright, dry, gleaming room. It was Fred's house and he and his wife were howling with laughter, and so were their friends.

Dickens muses on the therapy of laughter

'while there is infection in disease and sorrow, there is nothing in the world so irresistibly contagious as laughter and good-humour'

"Ha, ha! Ha, ha, ha, ha!"

"He said that Christmas was a humbug, as I live!" cried Scrooge's nephew. "He believed it too!"

"More shame for him, Fred!" said Scrooge's niece, indignantly.

Bless those women; they never do anything by halves. They are always in earnest.

She was very pretty: exceedingly pretty. With a dimpled, surprised- looking, capital face; a ripe little mouth, that seemed made to be kissed—as no doubt it was; all kinds of good little dots about her chin, that melted into one another when she laughed; and the sunniest pair of eyes you ever saw in any little creature's head.

Altogether she was what you would have called provoking, you know; but satisfactory, too. Oh, perfectly satisfactory!

"He's a comical old fellow," said Scrooge's nephew, "that's the truth: and not so pleasant as he might be. However, his offences carry their own punishment, and I have nothing to say against him."

"I'm sure he is very rich, Fred," hinted Scrooge's niece. "At least you always tell me so."

"What of that, my dear!" said Scrooge's nephew. "His wealth is of no use to him. He don't do any good with it. He don't make himself comfortable with it. He hasn't the satisfaction of thinking—ha, ha, ha!—that he is ever going to benefit US with it."

"I have no patience with him," observed Scrooge's niece. Scrooge's niece's sisters, and all the other ladies, expressed the same opinion.

"Oh, I have!" said Scrooge's nephew. "I am sorry for him; I couldn't be angry with him if I tried. Who suffers by his ill whims! Himself, always. Here, he takes it into his head to dislike us, and he won't come and dine with us. What's the consequence? He don't lose much of a dinner."

Scrooge inside his nephew's house

Fred, Scrooge's nephew, is convinced that Scrooge is lacking in this therapy, as he remarks

"He said that Christmas was a humbug, as I live! "He believed it too!"

Fred's wife, Fred's niece, Fred

The atmosphere was joyfully electric. They were discussing Scrooge and Fred says that,

"His wealth is of no use to him. He don't do any good with it"

Fred very skillfully defends his uncle amid the criticisms levelled against him by the ladies. He defends him by saying,

"I am sorry for him; I couldn't be angry with him if I tried"

"Indeed, I think he loses a very good dinner," interrupted Scrooge's niece. Everybody else said the same, and they must be allowed to have been competent judges, because they had just had dinner; and, with the dessert upon the table, were clustered round the fire, by lamplight.

"Well! I'm very glad to hear it," said Scrooge's nephew, "because I haven't great faith in these young housekeepers. What do you say, Topper?"

Topper had clearly got his eye upon one of Scrooge's niece's sisters, for he answered that a bachelor was a wretched outcast, who had no right to express an opinion on the subject.

Whereat Scrooge's niece's sister—the plump one with the lace tucker: not the one with the roses—blushed.

"Do go on, Fred," said Scrooge's niece, clapping her hands. "He never finishes what he begins to say! He is such a ridiculous fellow!"

Scrooge's nephew revelled in another laugh, and as it was impossible to keep the infection off; though the plump sister tried hard to do it with aromatic vinegar; his example was unanimously followed.

"I was only going to say," said Scrooge's nephew, "that the consequence of his taking a dislike to us, and not making merry with us, is, as I think, that he loses some pleasant moments, which could do him no harm. I am sure he loses pleasanter companions than he can find in his own thoughts, either in his mouldy old office, or his dusty chambers. I mean to give him the same chance every year, whether he likes it or not, for I pity him. He may rail at Christmas till he dies, but he can't help thinking better of it—I defy him—if he finds me going there, in good temper, year after year, and saying Uncle Scrooge, how are you? If it only puts him in the vein to leave his poor clerk fifty pounds, that's something; and I think I shook him yesterday."

Fred: "I couldn't be angry with him if I tried"

Topper is more interested in love and had clearly

'got his eye upon one of Scrooge's niece's sisters'

Dickens creates the natural events of self-interest as Topper defers judgement by saying of himself that

"a bachelor was a wretched outcast, who had no right to express an opinion on the subject"

Topper: eye on Scrooge's niece's sisters

Fred is sad that Scrooge is missing out on
"not making merry with us"

And that Scrooge,
"loses some pleasant moments which could do him no harm"

It was their turn to laugh now at the notion of his shaking Scrooge. But being thoroughly good-natured, and not much caring what they laughed at, so that they laughed at any rate, he encouraged them in their merriment, and passed the bottle joyously.

After tea, they had some music. For they were a musical family, and knew what they were about, when they sung a Glee or Catch, I can assure you: especially Topper, who could growl away in the bass like a good one, and never swell the large veins in his forehead, or get red in the face over it.

Scrooge's niece played well upon the harp; and played among other tunes a simple little air (a mere nothing: you might learn to whistle it in two minutes), which had been familiar to the child who fetched Scrooge from the boarding-school, as he had been reminded by the Ghost of Christmas Past.

When this strain of music sounded, all the things that Ghost had shown him, came upon his mind; he softened more and more; and thought that if he could have listened to it often, years ago, he might have cultivated the kindnesses of life for his own happiness with his own hands, without resorting to the sexton's spade that buried Jacob Marley.

But they didn't devote the whole evening to music. After a while they played at forfeits; for it is good to be children sometimes, and never better than at Christmas, when its mighty Founder was a child himself.

Stop! There was first a game at blind-man's buff. Of course there was. And I no more believe Topper was really blind than I believe he had eyes in his boots. My opinion is, that it was a done thing between him and Scrooge's nephew; and that the Ghost of Christmas Present knew it.

Dickens makes the theme of laughter infectious by the guests displaying empathy with Fred in his efforts to change Scrooge's mind about Christmas

'It was their turn to laugh now at the notion of his shaking Scrooge'

Events move to enjoyment of music and song

'For they were a musical family'

'For they were a musical family'

As Scrooge is observing this excitement and merriment, he began to reminiscence about the Ghost's lessons, and
'he softened more and more'

He regrets not having listened to it because if he did, he might have crafted out a life of kindness,
'for his own happiness'

no more believe Topper was really blind

The way he went after that plump sister in the lace tucker, was an outrage on the credulity of human nature. Knocking down the fire-irons, tumbling over the chairs, bumping against the piano, smothering himself among the curtains, wherever she went, there went he!

He always knew where the plump sister was. He wouldn't catch anybody else. If you had fallen up against him (as some of them did).

On purpose, he would have made a feint of endeavouring to seize you, which would have been an affront to your understanding, and would instantly have sidled off in the direction of the plump sister. She often cried out that it wasn't fair; and it really was not. But when at last, he caught her; when, in spite of all her silken rustlings, and her rapid flutterings past him, he got her into a corner whence there was no escape; then his conduct was the most execrable. For his pretending not to know her; his pretending that it was necessary to touch her head-dress, and further to assure himself of her identity by pressing a certain ring upon her finger, and a certain chain about her neck; was vile, monstrous! No doubt she told him her opinion of it, when, another blind-man being in office, they were so very confidential together, behind the curtains.

Scrooge's niece was not one of the blind-man's buff party, but was made comfortable with a large chair and a footstool, in a snug corner, where the Ghost and Scrooge were close behind her. But she joined in the forfeits, and loved her love to admiration with all the letters of the alphabet.

Likewise at the game of How, When, and Where, she was very great, and to the secret joy of Scrooge's nephew, beat her sisters hollow: though they were sharp girls too, as Topper could have told you. There might have been twenty people there, young and old, but they all played, and so did Scrooge; for wholly forgetting in the interest he had in what was going on, that his voice made no sound in their ears, he sometimes came out with his guess quite loud, and very often guessed quite right, too; for the sharpest needle, best Whitechapel, warranted not to cut in the eye, was not sharper than Scrooge; blunt as he took it in his head to be.

Dickens builds excitement in Scrooge as he watches the fun of Topper

'Knocking down the fire-irons, tumbling over the chairs, bumping against the piano, smothering himself among the curtains'

Topper – 'tumbling over the chairs'

Dickens managed to get us involved in the excitement of the Christmas spirit.

Our opinions of Scrooge now takes a drastic turn. We are both happy and emotional at Scrooge's gradual change.

Dickens takes us on an emotional journey with Scrooge.

Dickens introduces the theme of joy through party games where fun and laughter is prevalent among both young and old

'There might have been twenty people there, young and old, but they all played, and so did Scrooge'

The Ghost was greatly pleased to find him in this mood, and looked upon him with such favour, that he begged like a boy to be allowed to stay until the guests departed. But this the Spirit said could not be done.

"Here is a new game," said Scrooge.
"One half hour, Spirit, only one!"

It was a Game called Yes and No, where Scrooge's nephew had to think of something.

And the rest must find out what; he only answering to their questions yes or no, as the case was. The brisk fire of questioning to which he was exposed, elicited from him that he was thinking of an animal, a live animal, rather a disagreeable animal, a savage animal, an animal that growled and grunted sometimes, and talked sometimes, and lived in London, and walked about the streets, and wasn't made a show of, and wasn't led by anybody, and didn't live in a menagerie, and was never killed in a market, and was not a horse, or an ass, or a cow, or a bull, or a tiger, or a dog, or a pig, or a cat, or a bear. At every fresh question that was put to him, this nephew burst into a fresh roar of laughter; and was so inexpressibly tickled, that he was obliged to get up off the sofa and stamp. At last the plump sister, falling into a similar state, cried out:

"I have found it out! I know what it is, Fred!"
"I know what it is!"
"What is it?" cried Fred.
"It's your Uncle Scro-o-o-oge!"

Which it certainly was. Admiration was the universal sentiment, though some objected that the reply to "Is it a bear?" ought to have been "Yes;" inasmuch as an answer in the negative was sufficient to have diverted their thoughts from Mr. Scrooge, supposing they had ever had any tendency that way.

"He has given us plenty of merriment, I am sure," said Fred, "and it would be ungrateful not to drink his health.

Even the Ghost marvelled at Scrooge's change of attitude and was even pleased when Scrooge,

begged like a boy to be allowed to stay.

Dickens continues the theme of joy with new games to engage the mind.

Scrooge implores the Spirit

"Here is a new game,"
"One half hour, Spirit, only one!"

Dickens provides a detailed, informative description of the new game providing the reader with an activity that they might like to try once 'A Christmas Carol' is read.

Dickens was a keen observer of people and their actions. The games 'Blind-Man's Buff', 'How, When and Where' and 'Yes and No' are realistic descriptions of how people behaved and their actions, contemporary with the era in which the book was written.

Scrooge enjoying the party games

Fred never gives up hope and views Scrooge as a lost soul waiting for redemption, and says,

"it would be ungrateful not to drink his health"

Here is a glass of mulled wine ready to our hand at the moment; and I say,

"Uncle Scrooge!" '
"Well! Uncle Scrooge!" they cried.
"A Merry Christmas and a Happy New Year to the old man, whatever he is!" said Scrooge's nephew. "He wouldn't take it from me, but may he have it, nevertheless. Uncle Scrooge!"

Uncle Scrooge had imperceptibly become so gay and light of heart, that he would have pledged the unconscious company in return, and thanked them in an inaudible speech, if the Ghost had given him time. But the whole scene passed off in the breath of the last word spoken by his nephew; and he and the Spirit were again upon their travels.

Much they saw, and far they went, and many homes they visited, but always with a happy end. The Spirit stood beside sick beds, and they were cheerful; on foreign lands, and they were close at home; by struggling men, and they were patient in their greater hope; by poverty, and it was rich. In almshouse, hospital, and jail, in misery's every refuge, where vain man in his little brief authority had not made fast the door, and barred the Spirit out, he left his blessing, and taught Scrooge his precepts.

It was a long night, if it were only a night; but Scrooge had his doubts of this, because the Christmas Holidays appeared to be condensed into the space of time they passed together.

Fred – 'ungrateful not to drink his health'

Scrooge also observed how his nephew gave a toast in his honour. Scrooge became

'so gay and light of heart'
and he,
'thanked them in an inaudible speech'

Dickens switches the scene from Fred's house to various new venues where Scrooge's joy is tempered by the realities endured by the poor and underprivileged socialist class.

"The Spirit stood beside sick beds, and they were cheerful; on foreign lands, and they were close at home; by struggling men, and they were patient in their greater hope; by poverty, and it was rich. In almshouse, hospital, and jail, in misery's every refuge"

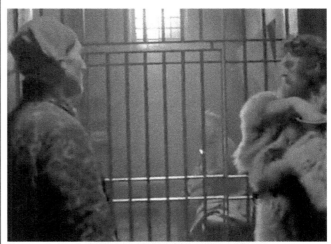

they visited: jail, in misery's every refuge

The Spirit
taught Scrooge his lessons.

It was strange, too, that while Scrooge remained unaltered in his outward form, the Ghost grew older, clearly older. Scrooge had observed this change, but never spoke of it, until they left a children's Twelfth Night party, when, looking at the Spirit as they stood together in an open place, he noticed that its hair was grey.

"Are spirits' lives so short?" asked Scrooge.
"My life upon this globe, is very brief," replied the Ghost. "It ends to- night."
"To-night!" cried Scrooge.
"To-night at midnight. Hark! The time is drawing near."

The chimes were ringing the three quarters past eleven at that moment.

"Forgive me if I am not justified in what I ask," said Scrooge, looking intently at the Spirit's robe, "but I see something strange, and not belonging to yourself, protruding from your skirts. Is it a foot or a claw?"
"It might be a claw, for the flesh there is upon it," was the Spirit's sorrowful reply. "Look here."

From the foldings of its robe, it brought two children; wretched, abject, frightful, hideous, miserable. They knelt down at its feet, and clung upon the outside of its garment.

"Oh, Man! look here. Look, look, down here!" exclaimed the Ghost.

They were a boy and girl. Yellow, meagre, ragged, scowling, wolfish; but prostrate, too, in their humility. Where graceful youth should have filled their features out, and touched them with its freshest tints, a stale and shrivelled hand, like that of age, had pinched, and twisted them, and pulled them into shreds. Where angels might have sat enthroned, devils lurked, and glared out menacing. No change, no degradation, no perversion of humanity, in any grade, through all the mysteries of wonderful creation, has monsters half so horrible and dread.

Scrooge started back, appalled. Having them shown to him in this way, he tried to say they were fine children, but the words choked themselves, rather than be parties to a lie of such enormous magnitude.

Scrooge noticed that

the Ghost grew older, clearly older

and he noticed that

its hair was grey.

'the Ghost grew older, clearly older'

Scrooge's curiosity got the better of him when he noticed something protruding from under the Ghost's robe.

Dickens creates a sense of suspense here, when the Ghost brings out two wretched and miserable looking children. Scrooge was shocked to see those ragged, scowling and wolffish looking children.

They were a boy and girl.

TEXT Stave 3	EXPLANATION
"Spirit! are they yours?" Scrooge could say no more.	The Spirit tells Scrooge that the children are not his,
"They are Man's," said the Spirit, looking down upon them. "And they cling to me, appealing from their fathers. This boy is Ignorance. This girl is Want. Beware them both, and all of their degree, but most of all beware this boy, for on his brow I see that written which is Doom, unless the writing be erased. Deny it!" cried the Spirit, stretching out its hand towards the city. "Slander those who tell it ye! Admit it for your factious purposes, and make it worse. And bide the end!"	"They are Man's" He introduces the wolfish children 'this boy is Ignorance' and 'this girl as 'Want' and tells Scrooge to beware of them and that on the boy's brow is written, 'Doom'
"Have they no refuge or resource?" cried Scrooge. "Are there no prisons?" said the Spirit, turning on him for the last time with his own words. "Are there no workhouses?"	Once again, the Spirit shamed Scrooge when he enquired about the children and made reference to Scrooge's earlier outburst, "Are there no prisons?" suggesting that these children are impoverished and are imprisoned by poverty and lastly the Ghost enquires of Scrooge,
The bell struck twelve.	
Scrooge looked about him for the Ghost, and saw it not. As the last stroke ceased to vibrate, he remembered the prediction of old Jacob Marley, and lifting up his eyes, beheld a solemn Phantom, draped and hooded, coming, like a mist along the ground, towards him.	"Are there no workhouses?" and he disappeared when the Bell struck TWELVE, leaving Scrooge guilty and ashamed because of his past behaviour but enough for Scrooge to reflect and make amends and show remorse for his callous behaviour.
END of STAVE three	

A scary, menacing looking figure, draped in a black garment and a hood visits Scrooge. This terrifying, faceless phantom is the Ghost of Christmas yet to come who shows Scrooge visions of his future.

First the Ghost takes Scrooge to the Centre of London where some businessmen are discussing someone's funeral. They don't want to attend his funeral because he is mean and unpopular. Scrooge does not understand who they are discussing but Dickens uses dramatic irony here because we clearly know that it is Scrooge that they are discussing but Scrooge promises to learn from this experience.

Next the Spirit takes Scrooge to a shop in the poor part of town where a charwoman, a laundress, and an undertaker's man had items to sell to a shopkeeper - from a dead person.

Dickens highlights the desperate plight of the poor in Victorian society by their need to acquire money by any means, however crooked, even the theft and disposal of the deceased's possessions, hence showing no respect for the dead.

Obviously, this dead man was detested by society and his death was a welcome relief to the poor. Scrooge is horrified to see the dead man all alone with no one mourning or caring for him.

Scrooge then asks the Spirit to show him someone who is emotionally involved in this man's death.

He is shown a young couple who is indebted to this man. This couple is glad that their creditor is dead, and the wife is,

"thankful in her soul"

that the man is dead which means that they don't have to pay a debt which they can't afford.

Scrooge wants to see some tenderness associated with death and the Spirit takes him to the Cratchit's home. Sadly, Tiny Tim has died, and the family is in mourning. Bob Cratchit is distraught, and he kisses the 'little face'. The grief-stricken family comfort each other and they reminisce and treasure the memory of Tiny Tim and the untold joy he brought to them. This emotive scenario about a child's death tugs at the heartstrings of the reader.

Dickens draws a juxtaposition between the emotional, endearing and warm attitude of the Cratchit's towards Tiny Tim's death to that of the cold, impassive, and unemotional response to the man's death.

Finally, the Ghost takes Scrooge to a graveyard, and he is shown his own gravestone on a very neglected grave

'overrun by grass and weeds'

He sees on the gravestone his name, EBENEZER SCROOGE, and now it begins to dawn on him that the dead man was him. He begs the Ghost to tell him if he can avoid his fate and emphasises that he has learnt lessons from the three Ghosts and that he can redeem himself and make amends if he is given the chance. The Ghost disappears.

End of SUMMARY on STAVE four

The Phantom slowly, gravely, silently, approached. When it came near him, Scrooge bent down upon his knee; for in the very air through which this Spirit moved it seemed to scatter gloom and mystery.

It was shrouded in a deep black garment, which concealed its head, its face, its form, and left nothing of it visible save one outstretched hand. But for this it would have been difficult to detach its figure from the night, and separate it from the darkness by which it was surrounded.

He felt that it was tall and stately when it came beside him, and that its mysterious presence filled him with a solemn dread. He knew no more, for the Spirit neither spoke nor moved.

"I am in the presence of the Ghost of Christmas Yet To Come?" said Scrooge.

The Spirit answered not, but pointed onward with its hand.

"You are about to show me shadows of the things that have not happened, but will happen in the time before us," Scrooge pursued. "Is that so, Spirit?"

The upper portion of the garment was contracted for an instant in its folds, as if the Spirit had inclined its head. That was the only answer he received.

Although well used to ghostly company by this time, Scrooge feared the silent shape so much that his legs trembled beneath him, and he found that he could hardly stand when he prepared to follow it. The Spirit paused a moment, as observing his condition, and giving him time to recover.

But Scrooge was all the worse for this. It thrilled him with a vague uncertain horror, to know that behind the dusky shroud, there were ghostly eyes intently fixed upon him, while he, though he stretched his own to the utmost, could see nothing but a spectral hand and one great heap of black.

'The Phantom slowly, gravely, silently approached'

Dickens use of the repeated adverbs suggests that something strange is going to happen. He also creates an eerie, mysterious atmosphere with the arrival of the Ghost of Christmas yet to come who

'scatter gloom and mystery'

The Phantom was,

'shrouded in a deep black garment'

This Phantom represents Death and Darkness. A 'shroud' is associated with Death, and 'black' with Darkness, as well as with mystery, as we see in this Stave.

The Phantom's head was concealled and it was surrounded by the very darkness which it represented.

'It was shrouded in a deep black garment'

Scrooge was terrified of the Ghost,

'his legs trembled beneath him'

Notice Dickens repetition of 'shroud' reminding us that this Ghost represent Death and Darkness.

"Ghost of the Future!" he exclaimed, "I fear you more than any spectre I have seen. But as I know your purpose is to do me good, and as I hope to live to be another man from what I was, I am prepared to bear you company, and do it with a thankful heart. Will you not speak to me?"

It gave him no reply. The hand was pointed straight before them.

"Lead on!" said Scrooge. "Lead on! The night is waning fast, and it is precious time to me, I know. Lead on, Spirit!"

The Phantom moved away as it had come towards him. Scrooge followed in the shadow of its dress, which bore him up, he thought, and carried him along.

They scarcely seemed to enter the city; for the city rather seemed to spring up about them, and encompass them of its own act. But there they were, in the heart of it; on 'Change, amongst the merchants; who hurried up and down, and chinked the money in their pockets, and conversed in groups, and looked at their watches, and trifled thoughtfully with their great gold seals; and so forth, as Scrooge had seen them often.

The Spirit stopped beside one little knot of business men. Observing that the hand was pointed to them, Scrooge advanced to listen to their talk.

"No," said a great fat man with a monstrous chin, "I don't know much about it, either way. I only know he's dead."
"When did he die?" inquired another.
"Last night, I believe."
"Why, what was the matter with him?" asked a third, taking a vast quantity of snuff out of a very large snuff-box. "I thought he'd never die."
"God knows," said the first, with a yawn.

Scrooge displays fear and submission
"I fear you more than any Spectre I have seen"

and he unashamedly tells the Ghost that he is prepared to learn lessons from him and that he

"hopes to live to be another man"
from what he was.

They went to the City
amongst the merchants

Phantom and Scrooge amongst the merchants

and stopped beside some business men. They were discussing the death of a man who was going to have a cheap funeral and that nobody was going to attend his funeral.

Business men discussing the death of a man

The self-interest and disrespect for the deceased is evident in their conversations

TEXT	EXPLANATION
"What has he done with his money?" asked a red-faced gentleman with a pendulous excrescence on the end of his nose, that shook like the gills of a turkey-cock.	A red-faced gentleman with a pendulous excrescence on the end of his nose asked
	What has he done with his money?"
"I haven't heard," said the man with the large chin, yawning again. "Left it to his company, perhaps. He hasn't left it to me. That's all I know."	to which, the man with the large chin, yawning retorts
	"He hasn't left it to me"
This pleasantry was received with a general laugh.	Mockingly, the same speaker comments
This pleasantry was received with a general laugh.	"It's likely to be a very cheap funeral"
"It's likely to be a very cheap funeral," said the same speaker; "for upon my life I don't know of anybody to go to it. Suppose we make up a party and volunteer?" "I don't mind going if a lunch is provided," observed the gentleman with the excrescence on his nose. "But I must be fed, if I make one."	and then the disrespectful remark
	I don't know of anybody to go to it
	The gentleman with the excrescences on his nose, has an ulterior motive
Another laugh.	"I don't mind going if a lunch is provided"
"Well, I am the most disinterested among you, after all," said the first speaker, "for I never wear black gloves, and I never eat lunch. But I'll offer to go, if anybody else will. When I come to think of it, I'm not at all sure that I wasn't his most particular friend; for we used to stop and speak whenever we met. Bye, bye!"	The first speaker
	"Well, I am the most disinterested among you, after all,"
	Unsure about his friendship with the deceased, he volunteers to go to the funeral if others will as well
Speakers and listeners strolled away, and mixed with other groups. Scrooge knew the men, and looked towards the Spirit for an explanation.	"But I'll offer to go, if anybody else will"
	The business men dispersed, and Scrooge looked towards the Spirit for an explanation as to who was the deceased man.
The Phantom glided on into a street. Its finger pointed to two persons meeting. Scrooge listened again, thinking that the explanation might lie here.	The Phantom points his finger to two other persons meeting. Scrooge listened again
He knew these men, also, perfectly. They were men of business: very wealthy, and of great importance. He had made a point always of standing well in their esteem: in a business point of view, that is; strictly in a business point of view.	'thinking that the explanation might lie here'
	as to the identity of the deceased man.

"How are you?" said one.	The first person remarks
"How are you?" returned the other.	
"Well!" said the first. "Old Scratch has got his own at last, hey?"	"Well!" - Old Scratch has got his own at last"
"So I am told," returned the second. "Cold, isn't it?"	Scrooge was still confused because he didn't know who the man was but Dickens uses dramatic irony because the reader knows that it is Scrooge.
"Seasonable for Christmas time. You're not a skater, I suppose?"	
"No. No. Something else to think of. Good morning!"	Scrooge feeling assured that the Spirit must have
Not another word. That was their meeting, their conversation, and their parting.	'some hidden purpose'
	and sets himself
Scrooge was at first inclined to be surprised that the Spirit should attach importance to conversations apparently so trivial; but feeling assured that they must have some hidden purpose, he set himself to consider what it was likely to be. They could scarcely be supposed to have any bearing on the death of Jacob, his old partner, for that was Past, and this Ghost's province was the Future. Nor could he think of any one immediately connected with himself, to whom he could apply them. But nothing doubting that to whomsoever they applied they had some latent moral for his own improvement, he resolved to treasure up every word he heard, and everything he saw; and especially to observe the shadow of himself when it appeared. For he had an expectation that the conduct of his future self would give him the clue he missed, and would render the solution of these riddles easy.	'to consider what it was likely to be'
	Scrooge scarcely supposes that it has
	'any bearing on the death of Jacob'
	because that was Past not the province of the Future
	Nor could he think of any one immediately connected with himself
	but that his conduct of his future self would
	'give him the clue he missed and would render the solution of these riddles easy'
	Scrooge scarcely supposes that it has
	'any bearing on the death of Jacob'
He looked about in that very place for his own image; but another man stood in his accustomed corner, and though the clock pointed to his usual time of day for being there, he saw no likeness of himself among the multitudes that poured in through the Porch.	because that was Past not the province of the Future
	Nor could he think of any one immediately connected with himself
	but that his conduct of his future self would
	'give him the clue he missed and would render the solution of these riddles easy'
	Scrooge looked about but saw
	'no likeness of himself'

It gave him little surprise, however; for he had been revolving in his mind a change of life, and thought and hoped he saw his new-born resolutions carried out in this.

Quiet and dark, beside him stood the Phantom, with its outstretched hand. When he roused himself from his thoughtful quest, he fancied from the turn of the hand, and its situation in reference to himself, that the Unseen Eyes were looking at him keenly. It made him shudder, and feel very cold.

They left the busy scene, and went into an obscure part of the town, where Scrooge had never penetrated before, although he recognised its situation, and its bad repute.

The ways were foul and narrow; the shops and houses wretched; the people half-naked, drunken, slipshod, ugly. Alleys and archways, like so many cesspools, disgorged their offences of smell, and dirt, and life, upon the straggling streets; and the whole quarter reeked with crime, with filth, and misery.

Far in this den of infamous resort, there was a low-browed, beetling shop, below a pent-house roof, where iron, old rags, bottles, bones, and greasy offal, were bought. Upon the floor within, were piled up heaps of rusty keys, nails, chains, hinges, files, scales, weights, and refuse iron of all kinds.

Much relieved, Scrooge

'thought and hoped'

that his

'new-born resolutions'

had been carried out. Consequently, he could not be the deceased man.

Next they went to

'an obscure part of town'

where Scrooge had never been but recognised its bad repute.

'The ways were foul and narrow'
'the shops and houses wretched'

the people were

'half-naked, drunken, slipshod, ugly'

and the whole quarter

'reeked with crime, with filth, and misery'

'An obscure part of the town'

Dickens provides a detailed description of the business practices in this

'den of infamous resort'

Dickens cites a beetling shop and the trading within it, to expose the social depravities necessary for the poor to survive economically.

Secrets that few would like to scrutinise were bred and hidden in mountains of unseemly rags, masses of corrupted fat, and sepulchres of bones. Sitting in among the wares he dealt in, by a charcoal stove, made of old bricks, was a grey-haired rascal, nearly seventy years of age; who had screened himself from the cold air without, by a frousy curtaining of miscellaneous tatters, hung upon a line; and smoked his pipe in all the luxury of calm retirement.

Scrooge and the Phantom came into the presence of this man, just as a woman with a heavy bundle slunk into the shop. But she had scarcely entered, when another woman, similarly laden, came in too; and she was closely followed by a man in faded black, who was no less startled by the sight of them, than they had been upon the recognition of each other. After a short period of blank astonishment, in which the old man with the pipe had joined them, they all three burst into a laugh.

"Let the charwoman alone to be the first!" cried she who had entered first. "Let the laundress alone to be the second; and let the undertaker's man alone to be the third. Look here, old Joe, here's a chance! If we haven't all three met here without meaning it!"

"You couldn't have met in a better place," said old Joe, removing his pipe from his mouth.

"Come into the parlour. You were made free of it long ago, you know; and the other two an't strangers. Stop till I shut the door of the shop. Ah! How it skreeks! There an't such a rusty bit of metal in the place as its own hinges, I believe; and I'm sure there's no such old bones here, as mine. Ha, ha! We're all suitable to our calling, we're well matched. Come into the parlour. Come into the parlour."

The parlour was the space behind the screen of rags. The old man raked the fire together with an old stair-rod, and having trimmed his smoky lamp (for it was night), with the stem of his pipe, put it in his mouth again.

'Secrets that few would like to scrutinise were bred and hidden in mountains of unseemly rags, masses of corrupted fat, and sepulchres of bones'

Dickens describes the shopkeeper as a

'grey-haired rascal, nearly seventy years'

and the attitude of his three clients as jovial

'they all three burst into a laugh'

The social interactions between the three clients the charwomen, the laundress, the undertaker's man, and the shopkeeper, old Joe, is one of business.

Old Joe retorts

"You couldn't have met in a better place"

and entices his clients to

"Come into the parlour"

Old Joe - "Come into the parlour"

While he did this, the woman who had already spoken threw her bundle on the floor, and sat down in a flaunting manner on a stool; crossing her elbows on her knees, and looking with a bold defiance at the other two.

"What odds then! What odds, Mrs. Dilber?" said the woman. "Every person has a right to take care of themselves. He always did."
"That's true, indeed!" said the laundress. "No man more so."
"Why then, don't stand staring as if you was afraid, woman; who's the wiser? We're not going to pick holes in each other's coats, I suppose?"
"No, indeed!" said Mrs. Dilber and the man together. "We should hope not."

"Very well, then!" cried the woman. "That's enough. Who's the worse for the loss of a few things like these? Not a dead man, I suppose."
"No, indeed," said Mrs. Dilber, laughing.
"If he wanted to keep 'em after he was dead, a wicked old screw," pursued the woman, "why wasn't he natural in his lifetime? If he had been, he'd have had somebody to look after him when he was struck with Death, instead of lying gasping out his last there, alone by himself."

"It's the truest word that ever was spoke," said Mrs. Dilber. "It's a judgment on him."

"I wish it was a little heavier judgment," replied the woman; "and it should have been, you may depend upon it, if I could have laid my hands on anything else. Open that bundle, old Joe, and let me know the value of it. Speak out plain. I'm not afraid to be the first, nor afraid for them to see it. We know pretty well that we were helping ourselves, before we met here, I believe. It's no sin. Open the bundle, Joe."

But the gallantry of her friends would not allow of this; and the man in faded black, mounting the breach first, produced his plunder. It was not extensive. A seal or two, a pencil-case, a pair of sleeve-buttons, and a brooch of no great value, were all. They were severally examined and appraised by old Joe, who chalked the sums he was disposed to give for each, upon the wall, and added them up into a total when he found there was nothing more to come.

While old Joe raked his fire, the Charwoman

'threw her bundle on the floor'

and remarks to the laundress, Mrs Dilber, in a light-hearted competitive manner

"What odds then! What odds, Mrs. Dilber?"

The charwoman justified the acquisition of the bundle by saying

"Who's the worse for the loss of a few things like these? Not a dead man, I suppose."

The laundress, Mrs Dilber, agreed laughing and said

"It's the truest word that ever was spoke,"
"It's a judgment on him"

Charwoman – "Open that bundle, old Joe"

But the undertaker's man first produced his plunder with acceptance by the women.

"That's your account," said Joe, "and I wouldn't give another sixpence, if I was to be boiled for not doing it. Who's next?"

Mrs. Dilber was next. Sheets and towels, a little wearing apparel, two old- fashioned silver teaspoons, a pair of sugar-tongs, and a few boots. Her account was stated on the wall in the same manner.
"I always give too much to ladies. It's a weakness of mine, and that's the way I ruin myself," said old Joe. "That's your account. If you asked me for another penny, and made it an open question, I'd repent of being so liberal and knock off half-a-crown."

"And now undo my bundle, Joe," said the first woman.

Joe went down on his knees for the greater convenience of opening it, and having unfastened a great many knots, dragged out a large and heavy roll of some dark stuff.

"What do you call this?" said Joe. "Bed-curtains!"
"Ah!" returned the woman, laughing and leaning forward on her crossed arms. "Bed-curtains!"

"You don't mean to say you took 'em down, rings and all, with him lying there?" said Joe.

"Yes I do," replied the woman. "Why not?"

"You were born to make your fortune," said Joe, "and you'll certainly do it."
"I certainly shan't hold my hand, when I can get anything in it by reaching it out, for the sake of such a man as He was, I promise you, Joe," returned the woman coolly. "Don't drop that oil upon the blankets, now."
"His blankets?" asked Joe.
"Whose else's do you think?" replied the woman. "He isn't likely to take cold without 'em, I dare say."

"I hope he didn't die of anything catching? Eh?" said old Joe, stopping in his work, and looking up.
"Don't you be afraid of that," returned the woman. "I an't so fond of his company that I'd loiter about him for such things, if he did.

Old Joe chalked the sums he was to give upon the wall, and said to the Undertaker's man
"That's your account,"
"and I wouldn't give another sixpence, if I was to be boiled for not doing it."

The Laundress, Mrs Dilber was next, and again Joe chalked her account on the wall stating
"I always give too much to ladies"

claiming that

"It's a weakness of mine, and that's the way I ruin myself"

Joe reveals is business acumen
"I'd repent of being so liberal and knock off half-a-crown"

Undertaker's man plunder inspected by Joe

Joe was indignant to find that the Charwoman's bundle contained

"Bed-curtains!"

but then remarked

"You were born to make your fortune"

The audacity of the charwoman is confirmed when Joe remarked
"His blankets?"

to which she replied
"He isn't likely to take cold without 'em, I dare say."

Ah! you may look through that shirt till your eyes ache; but you won't find a hole in it, nor a threadbare place. It's the best he had, and a fine one too. They'd have wasted it, if it hadn't been for me."
"What do you call wasting of it?" asked old Joe.
"Putting it on him to be buried in, to be sure," replied the woman with a laugh.
"Somebody was fool enough to do it, but I took it off again.

If calico an't good enough for such a purpose, it isn't good enough for anything. It's quite as becoming to the body. He can't look uglier than he did in that one."

Scrooge listened to this dialogue in horror. As they sat grouped about their spoil, in the scanty light afforded by the old man's lamp, he viewed them with a detestation and disgust, which could hardly have been greater, though they had been obscene demons, marketing the corpse itself.

"Ha, ha!" laughed the same woman, when old Joe, producing a flannel bag with money in it, told out their several gains upon the ground. "This is the end of it, you see! He frightened every one away from him when he was alive, to profit us when he was dead! Ha, ha, ha!"
"Spirit!" said Scrooge, shuddering from head to foot. "I see, I see. The case of this unhappy man might be my own. My life tends that way, now. Merciful Heaven, what is this!"

He recoiled in terror, for the scene had changed, and now he almost touched a bed: a bare, uncurtained bed: on which, beneath a ragged sheet, there lay a something covered up, which, though it was dumb, announced itself in awful language.

The room was very dark, too dark to be observed with any accuracy, though Scrooge glanced round it in obedience to a secret impulse, anxious to know what kind of room it was.

She even removed the deceased man's shirt and tells Joe

"you may look through that shirt till your eyes ache; but you won't find a hole in it, nor a threadbare place"

and justified her actions by saying

"They'd have wasted it, if it hadn't been for me."

She even took it of the dead man again

"Somebody was fool enough to do it, but I took it off again"

Dickens reinforces the message on social survival and attitudes of the poor by the actions of one of the woman who very blatantly tells the shopkeeper, old Joe, that she ripped off the bed-curtains and even took the blankets whilst the dead man lay in his bed.

They agreed that if the dead man had been kind and sympathetic towards others then he would not have died alone all by himself.

Dickens is making the point that those who could scavenge would do, without remorse or respect for the dead because it was a case of do or die.

Scrooge listened to this dialogue with horror, alarm and disgust.

At this point, Scrooge realised that they were talking about him,

"The case of this unhappy man might be my own"

He was so perplexed that he actually resorted to making a religious utterance,

"Merciful Heaven"

Without warning, Scrooge recoiled in terror as suddenly the scene changed to a very dark room where on an uncurtained bed was the body of the deceased man

A pale light, rising in the outer air, fell straight upon the bed; and on it, plundered and bereft, unwatched, unwept, uncared for, was the body of this man.

Scrooge glanced towards the Phantom. Its steady hand was pointed to the head. The cover was so carelessly adjusted that the slightest raising of it, the motion of a finger upon Scrooge's part, would have disclosed the face.

He thought of it, felt how easy it would be to do, and longed to do it; but had no more power to withdraw the veil than to dismiss the spectre at his side.

Oh cold, cold, rigid, dreadful Death, set up thine altar here, and dress it with such terrors as thou hast at thy command: for this is thy dominion! But of the loved, revered, and honoured head, thou canst not turn one hair to thy dread purposes, or make one feature odious. It is not that the hand is heavy and will fall down when released; it is not that the heart and pulse are still; but that the hand was open, generous, and true; the heart brave, warm, and tender; and the pulse a man's. Strike, Shadow, strike! And see his good deeds springing from the wound, to sow the world with life immortal!

No voice pronounced these words in Scrooge's ears, and yet he heard them when he looked upon the bed. He thought, if this man could be raised up now, what would be his foremost thoughts? Avarice, hard-dealing, griping cares? They have brought him to a rich end, truly!

He lay, in the dark empty house, with not a man, a woman, or a child, to say that he was kind to me in this or that, and for the memory of one kind word I will be kind to him.

A cat was tearing at the door, and there was a sound of gnawing rats beneath the hearth-stone. What they wanted in the room of death, and why they were so restless and disturbed, Scrooge did not dare to think.

"Spirit!" he said, "this is a fearful place. In leaving it, I shall not leave its lesson, trust me. Let us go!"

'plundered and bereft, unpatched, unswept, uncared for'

The Phantom directs Scrooge to remove the veil covering the deceased man's face, but Scrooge is hesitant because he,

'had no more power to withdraw the veil than to dismiss the spectre at his side'

Scrooge fails to remove the veil

Scrooge wondered if this man could come alive now, what would be his foremost thoughts?

'Avarice, hard dealing, griping cares?'

Having seen the dead man and his sad end, death has become a reality to Scrooge and at this moment he had an urge to change because he tells the Spirit,

"this is a fearful place. I'm leaving it, I shall not leave it's lesson."

Still the Ghost pointed with an unmoved finger to the head.

"I understand you," Scrooge returned, "and I would do it, if I could. But I have not the power, Spirit. I have not the power."

Again it seemed to look upon him.

"If there is any person in the town, who feels emotion caused by this man's death," said Scrooge quite agonised, "show that person to me, Spirit, I beseech you!"

The Phantom spread its dark robe before him for a moment, like a wing; and withdrawing it, revealed a room by daylight, where a mother and her children were.

She was expecting some one, and with anxious eagerness; for she walked up and down the room; started at every sound; looked out from the window; glanced at the clock; tried, but in vain, to work with her needle; and could hardly bear the voices of the children in their play.

At length the long-expected knock was heard. She hurried to the door, and met her husband; a man whose face was careworn and depressed, though he was young. There was a remarkable expression in it now; a kind of serious delight of which he felt ashamed, and which he struggled to repress.

He sat down to the dinner that had been hoarding for him by the fire; and when she asked him faintly what news (which was not until after a long silence), he appeared embarrassed how to answer.

"Is it good?" she said, "or bad?"—to help him. "Bad," he answered.
"We are quite ruined?"
"No. There is hope yet, Caroline."
"If he relents," she said, amazed, "there is! Nothing is past hope, if such a miracle has happened."
"He is past relenting," said her husband. "He is dead."

She was a mild and patient creature if her face spoke truth; but she was thankful in her soul to hear it, and she said so, with clasped hands.

The Ghost wanted Scrooge to see the dead man's face but Scrooge said that he did not have the power to do it.

Scrooge suspected that it was him but felt scared to confirm it wishing that it was not true, so he asked the Ghost to show him someone who felt emotion towards the dead man.

"If there is any person in the town, who feels emotion caused by this man's death,"

said Scrooge quite agonised

"show that person to me, Spirit, I beseech you"

The Phantom then spread its dark robe revealing

'a room by daylight, where a mother and her children were'

waiting anxiously for her husband to return with news about money they owed to a debt collector.

Phantom revealing mother and her children

On hearing the long-expected knock, she hurried to the door. The husband had

a kind of serious delight of which he felt ashamed, and which he struggled to repress

In a twist of fate, the husband tells her that the debt collector is dead and that their worries are over. Although, not wishing anyone's demise

'she was thankful in her soul to hear it'

She prayed forgiveness the next moment, and was sorry; but the first was the emotion of her heart.

"What the half-drunken woman whom I told you of last night, said to me, when I tried to see him and obtain a week's delay; and what I thought was a mere excuse to avoid me; turns out to have been quite true. He was not only very ill, but dying, then."

"To whom will our debt be transferred?"
"I don't know"

"But before that time we shall be ready with the money; and even though we were not, it would be a bad fortune indeed to find so merciless a creditor in his successor. We may sleep to-night with light hearts, Caroline!"

Yes. Soften it as they would, their hearts were lighter. The children's faces, hushed and clustered round to hear what they so little understood, were brighter; and it was a happier house for this man's death! The only emotion that the Ghost could show him, caused by the event, was one of pleasure.

"Let me see some tenderness connected with a death," said Scrooge; "or that dark chamber, Spirit, which we left just now, will be for ever present to me."

Scrooge – "Let me see some tenderness"

The husband relates how the half-drunken woman had told the truth about the debt collector being ill and dying.

In response, the wife, Caroline, asked

"To whom will our debt be transferred?"

The husband replied

"I don't know"

The husband is confident that should they have to repay to a successor then

"before that time we shall be ready with the money" and if not, it would be

"a bad fortune indeed to find so merciless a creditor in his successor"
Dickens builds tension in this story of debt where people find themselves in arrears unable to make payments who's only way out is to ask for more time to pay or have fate step-in, in this case, death to step-in and halt the debt. Remember Dickens father went to jail for not paying his debts.

Dickens makes it clear, that Caroline and her husband owed the deceased man money, and Scrooge now knows that should the future not be changed, the deceased man is himself.

Scrooge was very distraught to see this sad family scene which he had orchestrated, so he asked the Ghost to show him,

"Let me see some tenderness connected with a death"

The Ghost conducted him through several streets familiar to his feet; and as they went along, Scrooge looked here and there to find himself, but nowhere was he to be seen. They entered poor Bob Cratchit's house; the dwelling he had visited before; and found the mother and the children seated round the fire.

Quiet. Very quiet. The noisy little Cratchits were as still as statues in one corner, and sat looking up at Peter, who had a book before him. The mother and her daughters were engaged in sewing. But surely they were very quiet!

'And He took a child, and set him in the midst of them.'

Where had Scrooge heard those words? He had not dreamed them. The boy must have read them out, as he and the Spirit crossed the threshold. Why did he not go on?

The mother laid her work upon the table, and put her hand up to her face.

"The colour hurts my eyes," she said.

The colour? Ah, poor Tiny Tim!

"They're better now again," said Cratchit's wife. "It makes them weak by candle-light; and I wouldn't show weak eyes to your father when he comes home, for the world. It must be near his time."

"Past it rather," Peter answered, shutting up his book. "But I think he has walked a little slower than he used, these few last evenings, mother."

They were very quiet again. At last she said, and in a steady, cheerful voice, that only faltered once:

"I have known him walk with—I have known him walk with Tiny Tim upon his shoulder, very fast indeed."
"And so have I," cried Peter. "Often."
"And so have I," exclaimed another. So had all.
"But he was very light to carry," she resumed, intent upon her work, "and his father loved him so, that it was no trouble: no trouble. And there is your father at the door!"

The Spirit ushered him to the house of Bob Cratchit, the dwelling he had visited before. This time the Cratchit family was sad and sombre, the mother and the children seated around the fire.

'Quiet, Very quiet'
as opposed to Scrooge's previous visit which was full of merriment and laughter.

The Cratchit family mourn Tiny Tim's passing and awaited the return of Bob who had gone to attend church on Sunday, as was the custom, but sadly, this time without Tiny Tim.

Mrs Critchat tells the children that she does not want to show

"weak eyes to your father"

when he comes home.

Mrs Cratchit and the children recalled with affection how Bob would carry Tiny Tim on his shoulder, and how it was

'no trouble: no trouble'

Just then, Bob returned home, and Mrs Cratchit hurried out to meet him. His tea was ready for him.

Bob with tea and Cratchit family mourning

She hurried out to meet him; and little Bob in his comforter—he had need of it, poor fellow—came in. His tea was ready for him on the hob, and they all tried who should help him to it most.
Then the two young Cratchits got upon his knees and laid, each child a little cheek, against his face, as if they said, "Don't mind it, father. Don't be grieved!"

Bob was very cheerful with them, and spoke pleasantly to all the family. He looked at the work upon the table, and praised the industry and speed of Mrs. Cratchit and the girls. They would be done long before Sunday, he said.
"Sunday! You went to-day, then, Robert?" said his wife.
"Yes, my dear," returned Bob. "I wish you could have gone. It would have done you good to see how green a place it is. But you'll see it often. I promised him that I would walk there on a Sunday. My little, little child!" cried Bob. "My little child!"

He broke down all at once. He couldn't help it. If he could have helped it, he and his child would have been farther apart perhaps than they were.

He left the room, and went up-stairs into the room above, which was lighted cheerfully, and hung with Christmas.

There was a chair set close beside the child, and there were signs of some one having been there, lately. Poor Bob sat down in it, and when he had thought a little and composed himself, he kissed the little face. He was reconciled what had happened, and went down again quite happy.

They drew about the fire, and talked; the girls and mother working still. Bob told them of the extraordinary kindness of Mr. Scrooge's nephew, whom he had scarcely seen but once, and who, meeting him in the street that day, and seeing that he looked a little—"just a little down you know," said Bob, inquired what had happened to distress him.

'Bob was very cheerful with them, and spoke pleasantly to all the family'

Bob explained that he had attended church because he had

"promised him that I would walk there on a Sunday"

Such was his love for Tiny Tim.

Bob couldn't help his emotions and broke down crying.

'He left the room, and went up-stairs into the room above'

and sat down next to Tiny Tim to reconcile himself to what had happened.

Bob next to Tiny Tim to reconcile himself

Returning down-stairs, Bob told his family of the

'extraordinary kindness of Scrooge's nephew whom he had scarcely seen but once'

"On which," said Bob, "for he is the pleasantest-spoken gentleman you ever heard, I told him. 'I am heartily sorry for it, Mr. Cratchit, 'he said, 'and heartily sorry for your good wife. 'By the bye, how he ever knew that, I don't know."
"Knew what, my dear?"
"Why, that you were a good wife," replied Bob.

"Everybody knows that!" said Peter.

"Very well observed, my boy!" cried Bob. "I hope they do. 'Heartily sorry, 'he said, 'for your good wife. If I can be of service to you in any way, 'he said, giving me his card, 'that's where I live. Pray come to me. 'Now, it wasn't," cried Bob, "for the sake of anything he might be able to do for us, so much as for his kind way, that this was quite delightful. It really seemed as if he had known our Tiny Tim, and felt with us."

"I'm sure he's a good soul!" said Mrs. Cratchit.
"You would be surer of it, my dear," returned Bob, "if you saw and spoke to him. I shouldn't be at all surprised—mark what I say!—if he got Peter a better situation."
"Only hear that, Peter," said Mrs. Cratchit.
"And then," cried one of the girls, "Peter will be keeping company with some one, and setting up for himself."
"Get along with you!" retorted Peter, grinning.

"It's just as likely as not," said Bob, "one of these days; though there's plenty of time for that, my dear. But however and whenever we part from one another, I am sure we shall none of us forget poor Tiny Tim—shall we—or this first parting that there was among us?"

"Never, father!" cried they all.

"And I know," said Bob, "I know, my dears, that when we recollect how patient and how mild he was; although he was a little, little child; we shall not quarrel easily among ourselves, and forget poor Tiny Tim in doing it."

"No, never, father!" they all cried again.

"I am very happy," said little Bob, "I am very happy!"

Dickens juxtaposed the kindness without reservation of his nephew to the uncaring nature of his uncle.

Bob tells the family about Scrooge's nephew

Bob is still very emotional, and he talks about Tiny Tim's beautiful qualities,

"how patient and how mild he was"

and Bob goes on to say

"we shall not quarrel easily among ourselves, and forget poor Tiny Tim in doing it"

Such was the profound effect Tiny Tim had on the Cratchit family. They all cried again

"No, never, father!"

TEXT	EXPLANATION
Mrs. Cratchit kissed him, his daughters kissed him, the two young Cratchits kissed him, and Peter and himself shook hands. Spirit of Tiny Tim, thy childish essence was from God!	The scene is about to change again. Scrooge senses that
	"our parting moment is at hand"
"Spectre," said Scrooge, "something informs me that our parting moment is at hand. I know it, but I know not how. Tell me what man that was whom we saw lying dead?"	but is still unsure as to who the deceased man was, so he asked the Spectre to tell him
	"what man that was whom we saw lying dead?"
The Ghost of Christmas Yet To Come conveyed him, as before—though at a different time, he thought: indeed, there seemed no order in these latter visions, save that they were in the Future—into the resorts of business men, but showed him not himself.	No answer is given. Instead, the Spectre
	'conveyed him, as before—though at a different time'
	To Scrooge
	'there seemed no order in these latter visions'
Indeed, the Spirit did not stay for anything, but went straight on, as to the end just now desired, until besought by Scrooge to tarry for a moment.	except that
	'they were in the Future'
"This court," said Scrooge, "through which we hurry now, is where my place of occupation is, and has been for a length of time.	The Ghost of Christmas Yet To Come takes Scrooge
	'into the resorts of business men'
I see the house. Let me behold what I shall be, in days to come!"	but
	'showed him not himself'
The Spirit stopped; the hand was pointed elsewhere.	So, for now, Scrooge is still unsure if he is the deceased man.
"The house is yonder," Scrooge exclaimed. "Why do you point away?"	The Spirit pressed on with the journey.
The inexorable finger underwent no change.	As they journeyed, Scrooge recognises the locations through which they hurry but is still unsure of the final destination.
Scrooge hastened to the window of his office, and looked in. It was an office still, but not his. The furniture was not the same, and the figure in the chair was not himself. The Phantom pointed as before.	Scrooge is perplexed because instead of allowing him to see his house, the Spirit stopped
He joined it once again, and wondering why and whither he had gone, accompanied it until they reached an iron gate. He paused to look round before entering.	'the hand was pointed elsewhere'
	Scrooge exclaimed
	"Why do you point away?"
	Even at his office, he observed that
	'the figure in the chair was not himself'

A churchyard. Here, then; the wretched man whose name he had now to learn, lay underneath the ground. It was a worthy place. Walled in by houses; overrun by grass and weeds, the growth of vegetation's death, not life; choked up with too much burying; fat with repleted appetite. A worthy place!

The Spirit stood among the graves, and pointed down to One. He advanced towards it trembling. The Phantom was exactly as it had been, but he dreaded that he saw new meaning in its solemn shape.

"Before I draw nearer to that stone to which you point," said Scrooge, "answer me one question. Are these the shadows of the things that Will be, or are they shadows of things that May be, only?"

Still the Ghost pointed downward to the grave by which it stood.

"Men's courses will foreshadow certain ends, to which, if persevered in, they must lead," said Scrooge. "But if the courses be departed from, the ends will change. Say it is thus with what you show me!"

The Spirit was immovable as ever.

Scrooge crept towards it, trembling as he went; and following the finger, read upon the stone of the neglected grave his own name,

EBENEZER SCROOGE.

EBENEZER SCROOGE. - the grave stone

Joining the Spirit once again, still wondering where the journey will end, and who the deceased man was, they reached a churchyard.

Scrooge standing in the Churchyard

Here, then, the wretched man
'whose name he had now to learn'

lay underneath the ground
'overrun by grass and weeds'

Scrooge trembling, asked the Phantom to answer one question

"Are these the shadows of the things that Will be, or are they shadows of things that May be, only?"

No answer was forthcoming, except the pointed finger.

Scrooge debates out load how to change the future because he suspects that the wretched man was himself.

"But if the courses be departed from, the ends will change"

But the Spirit was

'immovable as ever'

Scrooge was left with one choice but to creep towards the stone to reveal the truth. Shocked, he read upon the neglected grave his own name

'EBENEZER SCROOGE'

"Am I that man who lay upon the bed?" he cried, upon his knees. The finger pointed from the grave to him, and back again.
"No, Spirit! Oh no, no!"

with the

'finger pointed from the grave to him, and back again'

The finger still was there.

"Spirit!" he cried, tight clutching at its robe, "hear me! I am not the man I was. I will not be the man I must have been but for this intercourse. Why show me this, if I am past all hope!"

For the first time the hand appeared to shake.

"Good Spirit," he pursued, as down upon the ground he fell before it: "Your nature intercedes for me, and pities me. Assure me that I yet may change these shadows you have shown me, by an altered life!"

The kind hand trembled.

"I will honour Christmas in my heart, and try to keep it all the year. I will live in the Past, the Present, and the Future. The Spirits of all Three shall strive within me. I will not shut out the lessons that they teach. Oh, tell me I may sponge away the writing on this stone!

In his agony, he caught the spectral hand. It sought to free itself, but he was strong in his entreaty, and detained it. The Spirit, stronger yet, repulsed him.

'The finger pointed from the grave to him and back again'

Scrooge pleaded

"No, Spirit! Oh no, no!"

and clutching the Spirit at it robe, pleaded

"Assure me that I yet may change these shadows you have shown me, by an altered life!"

and claiming

"I will honour Christmas in my heart"

and pledging

"I will not shut out the lessons that they teach"

Scrooge pledges to honour Christmas, and not shut out the lessons that they teach

Holding up his hands in a last prayer to have his fate reversed, he saw an alteration in the Phantom's hood and dress. It shrunk, collapsed, and dwindled down into a bedpost.

End of STAVE five

The Phantom hearing Scrooge's plea

Scrooge is uncertain about his future as the Phantom,

'shrunk, collapsed, and dwindled down into a bedpost'

Phantom: dwindled down into a bedpost

Dickens creates a storyline that in the real world exposed the hardships, struggles, and fears underprivileged people in his era endured but tempered with love and humanity which on occasion shone through.

Scrooge is relieved and excited to find himself back in the real world having been escorted through time Past, Present, and Future by Spirits intend on reforming his obnoxious ways towards his fellow man.

"The Spirits of all Three shall strive within me"

Scrooge is even grateful to Jacob Marley for starting him on the path to redemption.

"Oh Jacob Marley! Heaven, and the Christmas Time be praised for this!"

Laughing, crying, light as a feather, merry as a school-boy, giddy as a drunken man, not sure what day it is, Scrooge calls down to a boy from his open window who replies,

"Why, Christmas Day"

and offers the boy one shilling or half-a-crown if within five minutes, he returned with the man selling the big prize Turkey. Scrooge's generosity knew no bounds as he paid for a cab to take the boy with the Turkey to Bob Cratchit's house.

Next having shaved and dressed-up 'in all his best', Scrooge went into the streets and encountered what he had seen with the Ghost of Christmas Present, but this time adopted the path of redemption as shown by making amends to the portly gentleman who had walked into his shop the day before seeking a donation for the poor. Scrooge showed his new-found charitable spirit by offering him a substantial amount of money including back-payments. The man was astonished and overwhelmed by Scrooge's generosity and kindness.

Scrooge excited to explore, learn and practice his new-found generosity, went to church, walked about the streets, watched people hurrying to and fro, patted children on the head, questioned beggars, and looked down into kitchens, and up to the windows, finding that everything could yield him pleasure and happiness.

He felt more and more part of society and felt the need to make a contribution to it.

In the afternoon, apprehensive about his curt rejection of his nephew's invite to Christmas dinner, passed the door of his nephew's house a dozen times, before he dashed and knocked.

Scrooge need not had worried, Fred his nephew was ecstatic and shook his hand profusely,

"He was at home in five minutes"

stayed for dinner and participated in the wonderful party games.

Overjoyed with enthusiasm for his new found happiness and contribution to his fellow man, Scrooge had one last surprise to enact for Christmas.

Arriving early the next day, before Bob Cratchit, he admonished Bob for his lateness, but then admonished himself for underpaying Bob and offering to discuss Bob's affaires.

Better than his word, Scrooge did more. Tiny Tim did NOT die, and Scrooge became a second father to Tim.

Scrooge had 'no further intercourse with Spirits 'and that he 'knew how to keep Christmas well'.

End of SUMMARY on STAVE five

YES! and the bedpost was his own. The bed was his own, the room was his own. Best and happiest of all, the Time before him was his own, to make amends in!	This promising beginning warms the reader's heart towards Scrooge. We can juxtapose his avaricious harsh behaviour to his overwhelming sense of having the time,
"I will live in the Past, the Present, and the Future!" Scrooge repeated, as he scrambled out of bed. "The Spirits of all Three shall strive within me. Oh Jacob Marley! Heaven, and the Christmas Time be praised for this! I say it on my knees, old Jacob; on my knees!"	'to make amends in!' and determined to make sure, "The Spirits of all Three shall strive within me"
He was so fluttered and so glowing with his good intentions, that his broken voice would scarcely answer to his call. He had been sobbing violently in his conflict with the Spirit, and his face was wet with tear	Dickens uses biblical imagery to describe Scrooge's conversion. Scrooge proclaims, "Heaven, and the Christmas Time be praised for this!"
"They are not torn down," cried Scrooge, folding one of his bed-curtains in his arms, "they are not torn down, rings and all. They are here—I am here— the shadows of the things that would have been, may be dispelled. They will be. I know they will!"	Once again, we can juxtapose his earlier revulsion for Christmas and scorns idiots who celebrates Christmas and that any man, "should be boiled with his own pudding and buried with a stake of holly through his heart" Dickens tells us that Scrooge,
His hands were busy with his garments all this time; turning them inside out, putting them on upside down, tearing them, mislaying them, making them parties to every kind of extravagance.	'was so fluttered and so glowing with his good intentions'
"I don't know what to do!" cried Scrooge, laughing and crying in the same breath; and making a perfect Laocoön of himself with his stockings. "I am as light as a feather, I am as happy as an angel, I am as merry as a schoolboy. I am as giddy as a drunken man. A merry Christmas to everybody! A happy New Year to all the world. Hallo here! Whoop! Hallo!"	Dickens intention here is to develop a glow within the reader - to make the reader identify with Scrooge's new benevolent intent - that all of us, not only Scrooge, should become socially responsible. We see a redeemed Scrooge in tears,
He had frisked into the sitting-room, and was now standing there: perfectly winded.	'sobbing violently in his conflict with the Spirit'
"There's the saucepan that the gruel was in!" cried Scrooge, starting off again, and going round the fireplace. "There's the door, by which the Ghost of Jacob Marley entered!	He is very happy to find that the woman at the shop didn't tear his bed curtains down. "They are not torn down"
There's the corner where the Ghost of Christmas Present, sat!	This change in Scrooge is so refreshing to the reader and we share in his exuberance, as evidenced by Scrooge laughing and crying in the same breath as he said out loud,
	"I don't know what to do!" Dickens uses a series of similes which creates a visual picture of Scrooge's ecstasy, 'as light as a feather' – 'as happy as an angel' – 'as merry as a school boy'

There's the window where I saw the wandering Spirits! It's all right, it's all true, it all happened. Ha ha ha!"

Really, for a man who had been out of practice for so many years, it was a splendid laugh, a most illustrious laugh. The father of a long, long line of brilliant laughs!

"I don't know what day of the month it is!" said Scrooge. "I don't know how long I've been among the Spirits. I don't know anything. I'm quite a baby. Never mind. I don't care. I'd rather be a baby. Hallo! Whoop! Hallo here!"

He was checked in his transports by the churches ringing out the lustiest peals he had ever heard. Clash, clang, hammer; ding, dong, bell. Bell, dong, ding; hammer, clang, clash! Oh, glorious, glorious!

Running to the window, he opened it, and put out his head. No fog, no mist; clear, bright, jovial, stirring, cold; cold, piping for the blood to dance to; Golden sunlight; Heavenly sky; sweet fresh air; merry bells. Oh, glorious! Glorious!

"What's to-day!" cried Scrooge, calling downward to a boy in Sunday clothes, who perhaps had loitered in to look about him.
"Eh?" returned the boy, with all his might of wonder.
"What's to-day, my fine fellow?" said Scrooge. "To-day!" replied the boy. "Why, Christmas Day."

"What's to-day!" cried Scrooge, calling downward to a boy in Sunday clothes, who perhaps had loitered in to look about him.
"Eh?" returned the boy, with all his might of wonder.
"What's to-day, my fine fellow?" said Scrooge. "To-day!" replied the boy. "Why, Christmas Day."

"It's Christmas Day!" said Scrooge to himself. "I haven't missed it. The Spirits have done it all in one night. They can do anything they like. Of course they can. Of course they can.

"Hallo, my fine fellow!"
"Hallo!" returned the boy.
"Do you know the Poulterer's, in the next street but one, at the corner?" Scrooge inquired.
"I should hope I did," replied the lad.
"An intelligent boy!" said Scrooge.

Scrooge reminiscences about his encounter with the Spirits!

"It's all right, it's all true, it all happened. Ha ha ha!"

Dickens describes his laugh as,

'a splendid laugh, a most illustrious laugh.'
The father of a long, long line of brilliant laughs!'

Scrooge's euphoria causes him naturally to become confused as to time

"I don't know what day of the month it is!"

and his reversion to an energetic child,

"I'd rather be a baby. Hallo! Whoop! Hallo here!"

The use of several onomatopoeias with the ringing of the church bells,

'clash, clang, hammer, ding, dong'

suggest that Dickens wants us to hear through this auditory imagery, Scrooge's sense of euphoria.

Note the repetitive use of 'no' when Scrooge opens the window suggesting a mortal change from cold to warmth in Scrooge's character.

Dickens use of light imagery,

'Golden sunlight'

suggests that Scrooge has at last seen the light and has transform from darkness to light - selfishness to generosity.

Dickens use of biblical imagery,

'Heavenly sky'

implying that Scrooge is now closer to God.

"A remarkable boy! Do you know whether they've sold the prize Turkey that was hanging up there? - Not the little prize Turkey: the big one?"

"What, the one as big as me?" returned the boy.

"What a delightful boy!" said Scrooge. "It's a pleasure to talk to him. Yes, my buck!"

"It's hanging there now," replied the boy. "Is it?" said Scrooge. "Go and buy it."

"Walk-er!" exclaimed the boy.

"No, no," said Scrooge, "I am in earnest. Go and buy it, and tell 'em to bring it here, that I may give them the direction where to take it. Come back with the man, and I'll give you a shilling. Come back with him in less than five minutes and I'll give you half-a-crown!"

The boy was off like a shot. He must have had a steady hand at a trigger who could have got a shot off half so fast.

"I'll send it to Bob Cratchit's!" whispered Scrooge, rubbing his hands, and splitting with a laugh. "He sha'n't know who sends it. It's twice the size of Tiny Tim. Joe Miller never made such a joke as sending it to Bob's will be!"

The hand in which he wrote the address was not a steady one, but write it he did, somehow, and went down-stairs to open the street door, ready for the coming of the poulterer's man. As he stood there, waiting his arrival, the knocker caught his eye.

"I shall love it, as long as I live!" cried Scrooge, patting it with his hand. "I scarcely ever looked at it before. What an honest expression it has in its face! It's a wonderful knocker!—Here's the Turkey! Hallo! Whoop! How are you! Merry Christmas!"

It was a Turkey! He never could have stood upon his legs, that bird. He would have snapped 'em short off in a minute, like sticks of sealing-wax.

"Why, it's impossible to carry that to Camden Town," said Scrooge. "You must have a cab."

Scrooge calls out to a boy in the street and instructs him to buy the big prize Turkey hanging up in the next street and to bring the Poulterer as well. So pleased with the boy's response that Scrooge tells the boy

"Come back with him in less than five minutes and I'll give you half-a-crown!"

Scrooge instructs the boy to buy the Turkey

Scrooge rubbing his hands, and splitting with a laugh, whispered

"He shan't know who sends it. It's twice the size of Tiny Tim"

Down stairs, in front of the open door,

'ready for the coming of the poulterer's man'

the knocker caught his eye but this time there was no image of Jacob Marley. Scrooge cried

"What an honest expression it has in its face!"
"It's a wonderful knocker!"

Dickens now makes Scrooge perceive objects and his surroundings in a new light.

On arrival of the Turkey, Scrooge remarks

"He never could have stood upon his legs, that bird"

Scrooge remarks with delight

"Why, it's impossible to carry that to Camden Town" and said to the boy

"You must have a cab."

The chuckle with which he said this, and the chuckle with which he paid for the Turkey, and the chuckle with which he paid for the cab, and the chuckle with which he recompensed the boy, were only to be exceeded by the chuckle with which he sat down breathless in his chair again, and chuckled till he cried.

Shaving was not an easy task, for his hand continued to shake very much; and shaving requires attention, even when you don't dance while you are at it. But if he had cut the end of his nose off, he would have put a piece of sticking- plaister over it, and been quite satisfied.

He dressed himself "all in his best," and at last got out into the streets. The people were by this time pouring forth, as he had seen them with the Ghost of Christmas Present; and walking with his hands behind him, Scrooge regarded every one with a delighted smile. He looked so irresistibly pleasant, in a word, that three or four good-humoured fellows said, "Good morning, sir! A merry Christmas to you!" And Scrooge said often afterwards, that of all the blithe sounds he had ever heard, those were the blithest in his ears.

He had not gone far, when coming on towards him he beheld the portly gentleman, who had walked into his counting-house the day before, and said, "Scrooge and Marley's, I believe?" It sent a pang across his heart to think how this old gentleman would look upon him when they met; but he knew what path lay straight before him, and he took it.

"My dear sir," said Scrooge, quickening his pace, and taking the old gentleman by both his hands. "How do you do? I hope you succeeded yesterday. It was very kind of you. A merry Christmas to you, sir!"
"Mr. Scrooge?"
"Yes," said Scrooge. "That is my name, and I fear it may not be pleasant to you. Allow me to ask your pardon. And will you have the goodness"—here Scrooge whispered in his ear.

"Lord bless me!" cried the gentleman, as if his breath were taken away. "My dear Mr. Scrooge, are you serious?"

the Boy with the Poulterer with prize Turkey

We can denote Dickens overwhelming glee at his repetitive use of the verb,

'chuckle'

and of course Scrooge's remarkable sense of satisfaction in giving to others,

'and chuckled till he cried'

Scrooge greeted everyone on the street and,

'he looked so irresistibly pleasant'

He also made amends to the charity collector whom he rudely turned away the previous day.

Scrooge takes the charity collector by both his hands and said

"Allow me to ask your pardon"

before whispering in the collector's ear a sum

"My dear Mr. Scrooge, are you serious?"

"If you please," said Scrooge. "Not a farthing less. A great many back- payments are included in it, I assure you. Will you do me that favour?"

"My dear sir," said the other, shaking hands with him. "I don't know what to say to such munifi—"
"Don't say anything, please," retorted Scrooge. "Come and see me. Will you come and see me?"
"I will!" cried the old gentleman. And it was clear he meant to do it.
"Thank'ee," said Scrooge. "I am much obliged to you. I thank you fifty times. Bless you!"

He went to church, and walked about the streets, and watched the people hurrying to and fro, and patted children on the head, and questioned beggars, and looked down into the kitchens of houses, and up to the windows, and found that everything could yield him pleasure. He had never dreamed that any walk—that anything—could give him so much happiness. In the afternoon he turned his steps towards his nephew's house.

He passed the door a dozen times, before he had the courage to go up and knock. But he made a dash, and did it:
"Is your master at home, my dear?" said Scrooge to the girl. Nice girl! Very.
"Yes, sir."
"Where is he, my love?" said Scrooge.
"He's in the dining-room, sir, along with mistress. I'll show you up-stairs, if you please."
"Thank'ee. He knows me," said Scrooge, with his hand already on the dining-room lock. "I'll go in here, my dear."

He turned it gently, and sidled his face in, round the door. They were looking at the table (which was spread out in great array); for these young housekeepers are always nervous on such points, and like to see that everything is right.

"Fred!" said Scrooge.

Dear heart alive, how his niece by marriage started! Scrooge had forgotten, for the moment, about her sitting in the corner with the footstool, or he wouldn't have done it, on any account.

Scrooge replies

"Not a farthing less"

Dickens uses a series of verbs to get the reader involved in Scrooge's actions.

'He went to church'
'patted children on the head'
'found that everything could yield him pleasure'

Scrooge celebrating Christmas in Church

Scrooge is apprehensive,

'he passed the door a dozen times
before he had the courage to go up and knock'
at his nephew's house and his cordiality shocks us,

"Where is he, my love?"

when enquiring about his nephew.

Scrooge at His nephew's house

"Why bless my soul!" cried Fred, "who's that?"
"It's I. Your uncle Scrooge. I have come to dinner. Will you let me in, Fred?"

Let him in! It is a mercy he didn't shake his arm off. He was at home in five minutes. Nothing could be heartier. His niece looked just the same. So did Topper when he came. So did the plump sister when she came. So did every one when they came. Wonderful party, wonderful games, wonderful unanimity, won-der-ful happiness!

But he was early at the office next morning. Oh, he was early there. If he could only be there first, and catch Bob Cratchit coming late! That was the thing he had set his heart upon.

And he did it; yes, he did! The clock struck nine. No Bob. A quarter past. No Bob. He was full eighteen minutes and a half behind his time. Scrooge sat with his door wide open, that he might see him come into the Tank.

His hat was off, before he opened the door; his comforter too. He was on his stool in a jiffy; driving away with his pen, as if he were trying to overtake nine o'clock.

"Hallo!" growled Scrooge, in his accustomed voice, as near as he could feign it. "What do you mean by coming here at this time of day?"

" I am very sorry, sir," said Bob. "I am behind my time."
"You are?" repeated Scrooge. "Yes. I think you are. Step this way, sir, if you please."
"It's only once a year, sir," pleaded Bob, appearing from the Tank. "It shall not be repeated. I was making rather merry yesterday, sir."

"Now, I'll tell you what, my friend," said Scrooge, "I am not going to stand this sort of thing any longer. And therefore," he continued, leaping from his stool, and giving Bob such a dig in the waistcoat that he staggered back into the Tank again; "and therefore I am about to raise your salary!"

Bob trembled, and got a little nearer to the ruler.

He had a wonderful time at Fred's Christmas party,

"Nothing could be heartier"

and Dickens use of the adjective 'wonderful' further enhances this fact.

Scrooge dancing with Fred's wife

Next day, Bob arrives late, and is initially berated by Scrooge before Scrooge shocked Bob with his unusual, cheerful behaviour and a promise to raise his salary and he even buys more coal so that Bob can be kept warm.

Scrooge shocked Bob with his generosity

Scrooge became like a second father to Tiny Tim who did not die.

He had a momentary idea of knocking Scrooge down with it, holding him, and calling to the people in the court for help and a strait-waistcoat.

"A merry Christmas, Bob!" said Scrooge, with an earnestness that could not be mistaken, as he clapped him on the back. "A merrier Christmas, Bob, my good fellow, than I have given you, for many a year! I'll raise your salary, and endeavour to assist your struggling family, and we will discuss your affairs this very afternoon, over a Christmas bowl of smoking bishop, Bob! Make up the fires, and buy another coal-scuttle before you dot another i, Bob Cratchit!"

Scrooge was better than his word. He did it all, and infinitely more; and to Tiny Tim, who did not die, he was a second father. He became as good a friend, as good a master, and as good a man, as the good old city knew, or any other good old city, town, or borough, in the good old world. Some people laughed to see the alteration in him, but he let them laugh, and little heeded them; for he was wise enough to know that nothing ever happened on this globe, for good, at which some people did not have their fill of laughter in the outset; and knowing that such as these would be blind anyway, he thought it quite as well that they should wrinkle up their eyes in grins, as have the malady in less attractive forms. His own heart laughed: and that was quite enough for him.

He had no further intercourse with Spirits, but lived upon the Total Abstinence Principle, ever afterwards; and it was always said of him, that he knew how to keep Christmas well, if any man alive possessed the knowledge. May that be truly said of us, and all of us! And so, as Tiny Tim observed,

"God bless Us,
 Every One!"

End of STAVE five

The symbolism of the 'oyster' becomes apparent now because now Scrooge represents the Pearl full of beauty, kindness and love and not the lonely, isolated pearl as before.

'He became as a good a friend, as good a master, and as good a man'

in the

'good old world'

Dickens re-affirms the redemption of Scrooge by his continuous repetition of the adjective 'good'.

Scrooge is now a second father to Tiny Tim

Dickens shows the alteration in Scrooge by describing he new ability to laugh

'His own heart laughed: and that was quite enough for him'

Dickens turns 'A Christmas Carol' into an educational tool for social reform. Just as Scrooge is reformed, so can society be reformed making it a better place for all to live in.

Dickens concludes 'A Christmas Carol 'with a poignant message to the reader,

'And so, as Tiny Tim observed,

God bless Us,
Every One!'

EBENEZER SCROOGE

Dickens very carefully and meticulously crafted the character of Scrooge to represent a typical cold, avaricious capitalist class businessman who helps to move the plot along. Right at the outset, Dickens portrays him in a negative light - cold and unkind with a 'tight-fisted hand at the grindstone' implying that he is mean and uncharitable.

Dickens also uses pathetic fallacy to describe Scrooge's personality,

> 'Cold, snow, wintry' connoting that he is 'icy and frozen'

and doesn't have the ability to emit a glow of warmth to his fellow humans.

Dickens uses a metaphor for the weather to describe Scrooge's cold character. The imagery of the lonely pearl lodged inside the 'oyster' is a perfect analogy to describe Scrooge loneliness and isolation - he is devoid of any emotions and has no need for any sort of healthy communication. Scrooge's rejection of Christmas cheer and its significance - labelling it as "Humbug!" would cause the Victorian readers to surely raise eyebrows. Scrooge is miserly with coal for his clerk Bob Cratchit who desperately tries to warm himself with a candlelight. This implies that Scrooge is an imposing and dominant character especially when he accuses Bob of

> 'picking a man's pocket'

because he had to give him Christmas Day off. When his nephew visits him with a hearty 'Merry Christmas', his rudeness and ill-manners shocks the reader especially when he uses a graphic imagery to show his distaste of Christmas.

> "Every idiot who goes around with Merry Christmas should be
> boiled with his own pudding and buried with a stake of holly
> through his heart"

Scrooge is reluctant to give money to assist the wellbeing of the poor,

> "I can't afford to make idle people merry"

His reaction to those in prison "If they would rather die, they had better do it and decrease the surplus population" and yet again, his harsh reaction to the little carol singer,

> 'Scrooge seized the ruler with such energy of action,
> that the singer fled in terror'

display his deep self-centered attitude of distain and rejection of social issues. Dickens was intent on conveying to the reader his very important message of social responsibility and juxtaposes Scrooge's early behaviour from being money obsessed and obnoxious at the beginning to that of a joyous generosity and ecstasy of spirit at the end. Scrooge's purchase of the enormous turkey, raising Bob's salary, and his benevolent donation to the charity collectors is testament to his awakening and redemption brought about by his journey with Three Spirits. Each Spirit in turn takes Scrooge on a soulful, visionary journey, laying bare his cold uncharitable existence and awakening in him a desire for change and redemption towards his fellow man. The First Spirit, the Ghost of Christmas Past, transports Scrooge into the past, to come to terms with his unhappy childhood.

The Second Spirit, the Ghost of Christmas Present, takes Scrooge to see a wide variety of people in the city, and how they overcome inequality at Christmas time, finally arriving at the Cratchit's house to see adversity overcome by love. The Third Spirit, the Ghost of Christmas yet to come, transports Scrooge into the future, to shock Scrooge into redemption by showing him how terrible events might be if he doesn't redeem himself - people's joy at his death, his overgrown tombstone, and the early death of Tiny Tim.

Scrooge learnt many lessons from the Ghosts and acknowledges the error of his ways and was prepared to fully redeem himself and make amends for the wrongs he had done hence winning the respect, love, and forgiveness of the reader. Dickens echoed Tiny Tim's revered words,

> "God bless Us, Every One!"

and the use of a child's voice is poignant here because Tiny Tim was somewhat indirectly connected to Scrooge's redemption because Scrooge became like Tiny Tim's father in the end. We also see a sense of satisfaction in the narrator's voice.

Once again, Dickens has carefully crafted each member of the Cratchit family to represent the poor Socialist class in Victorian Britain. He uses the woes of the Cratchit family to convey his powerful Socialist belief to both the impartial reader and the avaricious Capitalist class of the Victorian era. The family too help to move the plot along and are responsible for much of the action in the novel.

Bob Cratchit is Scrooge's docile, mild mannered clerk who is the victim of Scrooge's caustic tongue-lashing. He is the epitome of love and affection which is transparent in his deep, loving bond with his family. Scrooge threatened to fire him when he involuntarily clapped when nephew Fred made his bold Christmas speech. One can draw a juxtaposition between Bob Cratchit and Scrooge's father who was cold and ruthless and almost left young Scrooge to spend Christmas alone at school until his sister Fan comes and merrily reports,

> "Father is so much kinder than he used to be"

Bob was also deeply concerned about Tiny Tim's health and he always carried him on his shoulders. His reaction of sadness when he learns that Martha his daughter won't be present at Christmas dinner was heart-warming.

> 'Bob hugged his daughter to his heart's content'

Bob is underpaid by Scrooge,

> 'fifteen shillings a week'

yet he is grateful for what he has and he is even noble enough to make a toast to him,

> "I'll give you Mr Scrooge, the Founder of the Feast!"

Although they were poor, with,

> 'a very small pudding and a custard cup without a handle'

they were very grateful for the little that they had.

Dickens uses the Cratchit's life as a platform to reflect at how the rich Capitalist class in Victorian society mistreated their staff and underpaid them. Bob as head of the family developed a healthy camaraderie and cordiality within his family structure, as seen on Christmas Day, allowing Dickens to point out to us the importance of the family structure in Victorian society which obviously Scrooge did not experience, hence one can connote that his wretched behaviour can partly stem from his neglected, lonely and unloved childhood.

Bob Cratchit therefore highlights for us how strong emotional family attachments can lead to strong adult development which Dickens was passionate about and which is reflected in his stable childhood upbringing where he enjoyed Christmas and in turn made Christmas a thoroughly enjoyable event for his own children, as he did for Bob Cratchit's family in this book. Mrs Cratchit was the epitome of virtue and Bob was very proud of her and praised her cooking. Bob regarded it, 'as the greatest success achieved by Mrs Cratchit'

She was,

'dressed out but poorly in a twice-turned gown'

and cheap ribbons but made sure that her family had a hearty Christmas dinner. She too just like Bob possessed a sense of overwhelming warmth and affection for her children despite her poverty,

'Mrs Cratchit, kissing Martha a dozen times'

upon her arrival.

Mrs Cratchit created such a zest and excitement among the young Cratchits around the table,

'basking in luxurious thoughts of sage and onion, these young Cratchits danced about the table'

She also addresses Bob in such an affectionate and heart-warming manner,

"what has ever got your precious father then"

fills the room with a beautiful glow emanating from her.

We should also admire her glee at seeing her family fully satisfied after their Christmas dinner which she so lovingly provided.

'It was a sufficient dinner for the whole family, indeed'

as Mrs Cratchit said with great delight.

She also smiled proudly when she brought the pudding, although it was a rather small pudding, none of the Cratchits made any comment about it's size. Dickens portrayal of Tiny Tim, handicapped and in need of medical assistance, highlights for us how sick people in the Victorian era in dire need of medical assistance, were coldly ignored by the rich Capitalist class like Scrooge.

Tiny Tim represents all things good and pure.   Tim told his father Bob that,

> 'he hoped the people saw him in the church, because
> he was a cripple, and it might be pleasant to them to
> remember upon Christmas Day, who made lame beggars
> walk and blind men see'

His biblical reference can be used to engineer social consciousness in the Capitalist Victorian society to those rich patrons who attended church but did not live according to the principles of Christian teachings of love and charity. Tiny Tim was indirectly responsible for the awakening of the social consciousness and charity within Scrooge. In the end, Scrooge becomes like a second father to Tiny Tim.

Dickens concludes the novel echoing Tiny Tim's prayer to all humanity,

> "God bless us everyone!"

Tiny Tim was a symbol of hope and Dickens vision for the future of socialism in Victorian Britain.

Dickens starts 'A Christmas Carol' with a short concise sentence,

> 'Marley was dead: to begin with'

to make it clear to the reader that when Marley arrives on the scene, he is not of this world but an apparition - phantom - Ghost! A Ghost who must forever drag the heavy chains of sin without reprieve and consequently no redemption because of his harsh business practices towards his clients when he was alive. Scrooge was Marley's business partner for many years, his sole friend, his sole executor, and Scrooge was in admiration of him. Marley was Scrooge's mentor, and Scrooge,

> 'never painted out Old Marley's name. There it
> stood year after year, above the warehouse door'

Scrooge's encounter with Marley's apparition began when he returned to where he lived in chambers which had once belonged to his deceased partner Jacob Marley. With the key in the lock, Scrooge saw

> 'not a knocker, but Marley's face'

Later, upstairs in his room, Scrooge is startled to hear the house bells ring by themselves, followed by the sounds of heavy chains being dragged over the casks in the cellar. The noise coming up the stairs, then

> 'it came through the heavy door, and passed into the room' Scrooge cried,
> "I know him! Marley's Ghost!"

Marley is described by Dickens just as Scrooge remembered him in life before his death, but now weighed down by chains made of

> 'cash-boxes, keys, padlocks, ledgers, deeds,
> and heavy purses wrought in steel'

clasped about his middle.

Marley's body was transparent, so that Scrooge

> 'looking through his waistcoat,
> could see the two buttons on his coat behind'

Dickens creates Marley as a very eerie, supernatural phantom anchored to the very tools that made him so despised by his clients and a curse to human generosity - Marley's obsession with making money without scruples from those that could least afford it - the poor in society. Dickens make use of the character of Jacob Marley as a voice piece to paint a vivid picture of the retribution that awaits those who trample on the less fortunate in his Victorian society.

'I wear the chain I forged in life, I made it link by link'

Dickens uses the character of Marley as an instrument to convert Scrooge from his destructive path, by the use of visual imagery of Marley together with Marley's utterances depicting the rewards of greed and avarice,

"Oh! captive, bound, and double-ironed,
not to know, that ages of incessant labour"

and as a herald of 'chance and hope' as to what awaits Scrooge later on,

"I am here to-night to warn you, that you have
yet a chance and hope of escaping my fate"

Again, acting as a messenger and as a circus ring-master, Marley tells Scrooge,

"You will be haunted by Three Spirits"

over the next three nights, and to expect the first when the bell tolls one.

Marley frightened Scrooge so much with his harrowing appearance and stark utterances that Scrooge asked,

"Couldn't I take 'em all at once, and have it over, Jacob?"

Marley ignores this plea, and continues to tell Scrooge the times to expect the final two Spirits, before departing through the window,

'the air filled with phantoms, wandering hither and thither
in restless haste, and moaning as they went. Every one
of them wore chains like Marley's Ghost'

Dickens has made Jacob Marley the pathfinder that will set Ebenezer Scrooge free from the restless moaning, torment, and eternal roaming for all time, in the spirit world, by the simple actions of rejecting greed, avarice, selfishness, hate exploitation, and accepting that we are all humans and where possible we should always act constructively to assist others less fortunate than ourselves.

Dickens uses a metaphor to represent Scrooge's life when presenting the Ghosts. The Ghost of Christmas Past takes Scrooge on an arduous journey back to his past. This Ghost is juxtaposed in its appearance as part child and part old man.

> 'It was s strange figure - like a child:
> yet not so like a child as like an old man'

It has white hair but a young face, this Ghost represents the different stages in Scrooge's life. It is clad in a white tunic, perhaps to represent Scrooge's childhood innocence and purity.

The Ghost holds a branch of holly representing the Christmas cheer and the thorns can symbolise the thorns on Christ's crown when he died on the cross or it can represent the Ghost pricking of Scrooge's guilty conscience or it can also symbolise Scrooge's sharp, pricking tongue. There was a bright beam of light emanating from the Ghost's head. With this light imagery one can connote that the Ghost is trying to bring some light into Scrooge's life or show understanding and wisdom and help him to acknowledge the error of his ways and redeem himself.

The Ghost reveals to us what Scrooge's childhood was like when it wizzes Scrooge off to his old school and shows a lonely schoolboy and his ill-treatment by his father.

The Ghost takes Scrooge to a warehouse where he did his apprenticeship and enjoyed such a wonderful Christmas party. The Ghost pricks at Scrooge's conscience. Whereas, Fezziwig shows generosity towards others, this is in complete contrast to Scrooge's past treatment of his clerk Bob Cratchit. The Ghost then exposes Scrooge's avaricious nature when he swapped love for money. Belle, his former fiancée, breaks her engagement to him because money is more important than her love. Now, Scrooge realises his loss, and is very sad to see that Belle is happily married with a loving family whilst he is left a very lonely man. The Ghost has made Scrooge realise his loss!

Scrooge was very distraught and wanted to leave the scene, so he attempted to wrench the light from the Ghost's head but was unsuccessful. The light here can represent Christ being the 'Light of the World' to help people redeem themselves like Scrooge, and this light cannot be extinguished. The Ghost's mission is done, its purpose to make Scrooge understand his past actions, completed, and now the baton of redemption can be passed to the next Spirit in chronological order, the Spirit of Christmas Present.

The sequence of the Ghost's arrival, the precision of the timing and the pealing of the bell are all symbols of Scrooge's stages of reflection leading to redemption, of his past atrocities and his journey towards the light of redemption. The Ghost's mission is done, its purpose to make Scrooge understand his past actions completed, and now the baton of redemption can be passed to the next Spirit. He awakes at ONE o'clock and recognises a light shining in the other room. The room is transformed into a plentiful lavish Christmas scene with every type of celebratory Christmas food.

Scrooge is confronted by a jolly giant of a Ghost draped in green robes and wearing a holly wreath, carrying a torch and sitting on a throne in the midst of all the sumptuous food. He represents each one on earth as suggested by his empty scabbard. He wizzes Scrooge off to the Cratchit's house to witness their meagre Christmas dinner filled with contentment and warm Christmas cheer. Bob even made a toast to Scrooge the founder of the feast despite Scrooge's harsh treatment of him. The Ghost then takes Scrooge on a journey to see the contentment in the miners, lighthouse men, and sailors despite their poverty. They are all celebrating the Christmas festivities with cheer and goodwill. Lastly, he takes him to Fred's house. Here too the air is filled with Christmas excitement, singing, playing games and Scrooge aught to reflect on his cruel rejection to the invite to Christmas dinner by his nephew Fred. The Ghost is pleasant and kind, and he brings about peace and makes people's dinners delicious by blessing it with a spray of incense. But despite this trait of kindness, the Ghost constantly reminds Scrooge of his unkindness especially when he said,

"if they would rather die, they had better do it,
    and decrease the surplus population"

to which Scrooge now hung his head in shame.

As the Ghost's appearance ages, he reveals the characters of 'Want' and 'Ignorance', saying that they were man's children implying that man created such monstrous - looking children because of his greed and selfishness. These two malnourished children had apt names 'Want' and 'Ignorance'. Dickens reaction to 'Want' is to alert the reader to the inadequate living suffered by the poor and outcasts, like those in prison, in society. When Scrooge enquires about resources for their well-being, the Ghost promptly reminds him of his earlier statements,

"Are there no prisons? Are there no workhouses?"
which made Scrooge feel rather ashamed.

Dickens reaction to 'Ignorance' is to hit out at the lack of schooling for the poor children in his Victorian era and he fought furiously to make changes hence creating the 'Ragged school', so that the poor children can have an education which Dickens was passionate about and believed that it was the passport to a successful life. The Ghost's mission is done, its purpose to make Scrooge understand his present actions, completed, and now the baton of redemption can be passed to the next Spirit in chronological order, the Spirit of Christmas yet to come.

The Bell strikes TWELVE and the ghost disappears.

This Ghost represented Scrooge's future and he is the personification of Death as represented by his long black cloak and hood. Shrouded in a deep black garment, the Ghost is like the 'Grim Reaper', a faceless phantom who doesn't speak. Scrooge admits that he fears him the most and this Spectral image makes Scrooge tremble with fear. It creates an eerie sense of mystery and suspense.

The Ghost zooms off with Scrooge into the financial district of the city where some businessmen are discussing the death of a mean, unpopular man who has just died. They say that he will have a cheap funeral and they are not very willing to attend his funeral. Dickens uses dramatic irony because we know that they are referring to Scrooge, but he does not have a clue that the dead man was him. Dickens creates a very poignant emotive scene to show us the destructive effects of abject poverty and how it can reduce desperate people to animalistic behaviour. This clearly shows us how Dickens 'spits out venom' writing in a bitter tone and displaying his disgust and revulsion at the decadent, selfish lifestyles of the rich capitalist classes, like Scrooge in Victorian Britain, who practiced no social responsibility.

Dickens shows us the shop where a cleaning woman, a laundress and an undertaker meet to sell their goods. These goods were ripped off a dead man and even his bed curtains were stolen from him and sold. Scrooge is shocked at this behaviour and he reminiscences about his fate realising that he could end up like this unfortunate man, unbeknown to him that he represented the 'the dead man'. He is then taken to the dead man's bed but he is too afraid to learn who the man is. Scrooge asks the Ghost to show him,
> "anyone who feels emotion caused by this man's death"
and he is shown a couple who owes him money and are facing ruin. The wife is delighted that the man is dead so that they will have time to pay the money back. Scrooge is very saddened by this scenario.

He then asks the Ghost to take him to a scene where there is
> "some tenderness connected with Death"
He is then taken to the Cratchits where the distraught family is mourning Tiny Tim's death. They speak fondly of Tiny Tim and the precious gift that he was to them. They are all visibly shaken by his death especially Bob.

Finally, the Ghost leads Scrooge to a graveyard where he sees his own gravestone with his name engraved on it. He is mortified and he promises to redeem himself immediately. He says that he has learnt a lot of lessons from all three Ghosts and he will make amends for his past follies. We are delighted to see a changed Scrooge who is exuberant and excited, and he makes things right by giving Bob Cratchit a raise, gives money for charity to the charity-collector which he previously turned away, and bought the fat goose and gifted it to Bob Cratchit.

Finally, we see that Dickens aims to pioneer his new morality in politics about social responsibility has finally found its place in Society because there were drastic changes in Victorian society after this. The Ghost's mission is done, its purpose to make Scrooge understand the future and adopt the path of generosity and social responsibility leading to happiness and well-being, and now the baton of redemption can be passed onto Scrooge.

CHRISTMAS SPIRIT

The theme of Christmas and the Christmas Spirit is prevalent in all five staves. Dickens makes the title of his novella the framework for his supernatural story of redemption – the musical notations in a carol is written on a stave comprising five horizontal lines and four spaces. So chapters are called staves, to make a connection with the traditional Christmas practice of singing joyous carols to promote the spirit of Christmas.

Dickens uses this theme to underpin the path of redemption through acts of kindness, generosity, and care for others which Scrooge or the reader must embrace to achieve a long, happy and content life.

In **Stave One**, Scrooge rebuffs the Christmas spirit of his nephew Fred who greets Scrooge with a cheerful voice:

"A merry Christmas, uncle! God save you!"

Scrooge replies with

"Bah! Humbug!"

Fred continues the altercation

"What right have you to be dismal? What reason have you to be morose? You're rich enough."

Scrooge is indignant and adamant,

"every idiot who goes about with 'Merry Christmas' on his lips, should be boiled with his own pudding, and buried with a stake of holly through his heart."

and continues,

"Nephew! Keep Christmas in your own way and let me keep it in mine."

In support, Bob Cratchit, the clerk, applauds Fred, but is chastised by Scrooge who threatens Bob,

"Let me hear another sound from you, and you'll keep your Christmas by losing your situation."

Fred departs without a word, but Bob inadvertently lets in two charity collectors who fail to extract any Christmas spirit from Scrooge. Scrooge retorts,

"Are there no prisons?"

Scrooge when asked "What shall I put you down for?", replies an anti-Christmas spirit, "Nothing!"

Justifying his sentiments by,

"I don't make merry myself at Christmas and I can't afford to make idle people merry."

With the exit of the charity collectors, the carol singer receives the same ant-Christmas treatment,

'Scrooge seized the ruler with such energy of action, that the singer fled in terror.'

Just before leaving the counting house, Scrooge exhibits more of his ant-Christmas spirit to do with Bob having Christmas Day as a paid day,

"A poor excuse for picking a man's pocket every twenty-fifth December!"

In **Stave Two**, the First Spirit declares,

"I am the Ghost of Christmas Past."

and takes Scrooge on a journey through his past life where sadness and solitude are intermingled with Christmas joy at Fezziwigs.

Distraught by his younger self not having said a word to stop his girlfriend Belle from releasing him from their relationship, Scrooge tells the First Spirit to show him no more. But the Spirit is determined to show Scrooge what might have been if he had embraced the Christmas Spirit by whisking him to a room where an older Belle is waiting with her children for

'a man laden with Christmas toys and presents.'

Scrooge observed the Christmas spirit in action,

'The shouts of wonder and delight with which the development of every package was received!'

Scrooge is regretful, that having not adopted a Christmas spirit, he has missed out on having the joy of a loving wife and a family due to his love of money.

In **Stave Three**, the Second Spirit's garb is embellished with the Christmas spirit,

'on its head it wore no other covering than a holly wreath, set here and there with shining icicles.'

So on Christmas morning, the Spirit takes Scrooge on a journey to many different places to experience the Christmas spirit as practiced by all classes of Victorian society.

In the City,

'people who were shovelling away on the house-tops were jovial and full of glee: calling out to one another from the parapets'

In the marketplace and shops,

'the customers were all so hurried and so eager in the hopeful promise of the day'

To church and chapel people came,

'flocking through the streets in their best clothes, and with their gayest of faces'.

To quell discontent, the Spirit would sprinkle a few drops of water on them to restore good humour, for the people said,

'it was a shame to quarrel upon Christmas Day'

Scrooge is inquisitive and tries to admonish Spirit for not providing a free dinner on the seventh day but only at Christmas on Christmas Day. But the Spirit rebuffs, reminding Scrooge that,

'There are some upon this earth of yours who lay claim to know us and all our kith and kin, who do their deeds of passion, pride, ill-will, hatred, envy, bigotry, and selfishness in our name'

However, they follow their own practices, not ours. It is not the Spirits that shut out dinner every seventh day, but people and their religion! It is up to people to provide for those most in need!

Having understood the argument,

'Scrooge promised that he would'

take it upon himself to provide for those in need, particularly at Christmas where their needs are greatest due to the cold weather!

Scrooge had made his first step towards redemption!

Next, they arrive at Bob Cratchit's house, where Mrs Cratchit and the children await, in anticipation, the arrival of Tiny Tim and Bob to celebrate and enjoy Christmas dinner. The only time of the year where Bob and his family would be together for the whole day, to enjoy the best dinner ever in the year.

Tiny Tim arrived on Bob's shoulder, having attended church with Bob, and he hoped that people who saw him as a cripple in the church would remember upon Christmas Day,

'who made lame beggars walk, and blind men see.'

Tiny Tim believes in the Christmas Spirit and hopes others do too.

Bob declared that

"There never was such a goose" and "Oh, a wonderful pudding!"

Scrooge having observed all, with an interest he had never felt before, said,

"Spirit, tell me if Tiny Tim will live."

In sombre reply, the Spirit answers,

"If these shadows remain unaltered by the Future, none other of my race will find him here" followed by "I see a vacant seat."

The Spirit quotes Scrooge's past anti-Christmas words about the poor,

"If he be like to die, he had better do it, and decrease the surplus population."

Scrooge realises that Tiny Tim belongs to the surplus population, so in shame,

'bent before the Ghost's rebuke, and trembling cast his eye upon the ground.'

Bob toasts Scrooge 'The Founder of the Feast' but is rebuked by Mrs Cratchit who has no Christmas spirit towards Scrooge. She retorts,

"It should be Christmas Day on which one drinks the health of such an odious, stingy, hard, unfeeling man as Mr Scrooge."

Bob reminds his wife that it is Christmas Day, and she relents but said,

"I'll drink his health for your sake and the Day's, not for his."

Again, Scrooge is exposed to the Christmas spirit of love and forgiveness.

Dickens makes the point, yet again, that even an entrenched attitude can be won over by the Christmas spirit.

The merriment continued with Tiny Tim with a plaintive little voice singing with others about a lost child travelling in the snow.

Dickens emphasises the Christmas spirit possessed by the poor when he states that the Cratchit family,

"were not a handsome family; they were not well dressed; their shoes were far from being water-proof; their clothes were scanty; Peter might have known the inside of a pawnbroker's. But they were happy, grateful, pleased with one another, and contented with the time."

The one attribute the poor had, Scrooge did not – the Christmas spirit.

Next, the Spirit continued the journey by taking Scrooge to far flung places to experience more of the Christmas spirit: along streets where

'children of the house were running out into the snow to meet their married sisters, brothers, cousins, uncles, aunts'

or the lamplighter,

'who was dressed to spend the evening somewhere' but 'had any company but Christmas!'

or the miners who labour in the bowels of the earth, upon a bleak and desert moor,

'a cheerful company assembled round a glowing fire'
or the two men who watched the light inside a solitary lighthouse built upon a dismal reef of sunken rocks, some league or so from shore,

'joining their horny hands over the rough table at which they sat, they wished each other Merry Christmas'

or on a ship on a black and heaving sea, where every man on board,

'hummed a Christmas tune, or had a Christmas thought, or spoke below his breath to his companion of some by-gone Christmas Day'

Next, the Spirit continued the journey by taking Scrooge to a place where to his great surprise he heard a hearty laugh which he recognised as belonging to his nephew's Fred, and where he was now to experience the Christmas spirit for himself through fun and games with Fred and his guests.

Scrooge discovers that apart from Fred, the guests consider Scrooge to have no Christmas spirit.

Scrooge enjoyed the fun and games so much, he begged the Spirit to let him stay until the guests had departed. The Spirit relented for one half hour because I was

'greatly pleased to find him in this mood'

Again, the Christmas spirit possessed the guest to toast Scrooge,

"Well! Uncle Scrooge!" they cried.

Dickens then describes Scrooge's euphoria and his participation in the Christmas spirit,

'Uncle Scrooge had imperceptibly become so gay and light of heart, that he would have pledged the unconscious company in return, and thanked them in an inaudible speech, if the Ghost had given him time.

Scrooge and the Spirit continued their travels to,

'sick beds, and they were cheerful'
'on foreign lands, they were close to home'
'by struggling men, and they were patient in their greater hope'
'by poverty, and it was rich'
'in almshouse, hospital and jail'
'in misery's every refuge, where vain men had barred the spirit out'

the Spirit left his blessing, and taught Scrooge his precepts that of the Christmas spirit!

In **Stave Four**, the Last of the Spirits takes Scrooge on a journey into the future or Christmas yet to come, where there is no Christmas spirit. A bleak future where those like Scrooge who are without humanity, suffer ignominy and an early death.

Scrooge is terrified when the Spirit points to Scrooge's gravestone, and he declares,

"I will honour Christmas in my heart, and try to keep it all the year"

In **Stave Five**, previous events make Scrooge realise and adopt the Christmas spirit. He now knows that there is a better way to experience life and cannot wait to put into action on Christmas Day.

'Best and happiest of all, the Time before him was his own, to make amends in!'

Scrooge declares enthusiastically,

"I am as light as a feather, I am happy as an angel, I am as merry as a schoolboy,
I am as giddy as a drunken man. A merry Christmas to everybody!"

From his window, Scrooge calls to a street boy to bring the Poulterer with a prize Turkey and gets the boy to take a cab and deliver it to the Cratchit's house. He generosity knew no bounds. Scrooge ventures on to the streets,

'walking with his hands behind him, regarded every one with a delighted smile'

He astounds the charity collector he met in his office the previous day when he whispers in his ear a generous donation.

Scrooge went to church and questioned beggars and found that everything could yield him pleasure.

In the afternoon he turned his steps towards his nephew's house and passed the door a dozen times before he had the courage to go up and knock. He was greeted with immense joy by Fred, his wife and guest. All were in harmony, as all present, including Scrooge, exuded the Christmas spirit.

The next day, Scrooge arrived early at his office, Bob arrived late. Scrooge could not resist feigning his displeasure at Bob's lateness before shocking Bob by wishing him 'A Merry Christmas', raising his salary, promising to assist his struggling family.

Scrooge had no further interaction with Spirits,

'he knew how to keep Christmas well, if any man alive possessed the knowledge'

The Supernatural theme is prevalent in the first four staves. Dickens like many Victorian writers believed in the power of the imagination to propel a story forward and capture the attention of the reader.

A Christmas Carol is set in locations familiar to the Victorian reader, with characters that the reader can identify with. This makes the novel convincing and understandable to the Victorian reader.

Dickens use of the supernatural allows him to distort time, so past, present, and future events can be compressed in one night.

In **Stave One**, Scrooge first encounters the supernatural when he arrives at the front door of his lodgings.

'Scrooge, having his key in the lock of the door, saw in the knocker, without its undergoing any intermediate process of change – not a knocker, but Marley's face'

Dickens builds tension and suspense by describing the knocker in a supernatural way.

'It was not angry or ferocious, but looked at Scrooge as Marley used to look with ghostly spectacles turned up on its ghostly forehead'

As he climbs the stairs,

'Scrooge thought he saw a locomotive hearse going on before him in the gloom'

Having checked his chambers,

'Quite satisfied he closed his door, and double-locked himself in, which was not his custom'

Dickens makes use of sound and loud noises to herald the approach of the supernatural

'The cellar-door flew open with a booming sound, and then he heard the noise much louder, on the floor below, then coming up the stairs, then coming straight towards his door'

Dickens gives a vivid description of Marley's Ghost as it passed through the heavy bolted door passing into the room before Scrooge's eyes,

'The chain he drew was clasped about his middle. It was long, and wound about him like a tail, and it was made of cash-boxes, keys, padlocks, ledgers, deeds, and heavy purses wrought in steel. His body was transparent, and looking through his waistcoat, could see the two buttons on his coat behind.'

Dickens makes the reader aware of the peculiarities associated with the supernatural. Scrooge

'didn't know whether a ghost so transparent might find himself in a condition to take a chair. But the ghost sat down on the opposite side of the fireplace, as if he were quite used to it.'

Dickens makes the conversation between Scrooge and Marley's Ghost as a reunion between old friends, where Marley's Ghost is intent on saving Scrooge from the miseries of purgatory.

Scrooge tries to comprehend why his formal partner now in front of him, should be punish so,

"But you were always a good man of business, Jacob"

Marley's Ghost cried

"Business! Mankind was my business. The dealings of my trade were but a drop of water in the comprehensive ocean of my business!"

Marley is trying to explain to Scrooge that Greed not Mankind was his true business. Marley concludes by informing Scrooge that he is to expect Three Spirits,

"Without their visits, you cannot hope to shun the path I tread."

Dickens exits Marley's Ghost through the window to floated out upon the bleak, dark night to join other phantoms.

'Every one of them wore chains like Marley's Ghost, some few were linked together, none were free. Many had been personally known to Scrooge in their lives.'

In **Stave Two**, Scrooge is perplexed at first about the hour and relieved when the First Spirit does not arrive on time. But suddenly, the hour bell sounded ONE,

'Light flashed up in the room upon the instant'

and the curtains of his bed were drawn aside by a hand to reveal,

'the unearthly visitor who drew them'

Dickens creates a bizarre entity with a contradictive appearance to baffle and stretch the imagination of the reader,

'It was a strange figure – like a child: yet not so like a child as like an old man'
'Its hair was white as if with age, and yet the face had not a wrinkle in it'
'The arms were very long and muscular, the hands the same'
'Its legs and feet, most delicately formed'
'It wore a tunic of the purest white, and round its waist was bound a lustrous belt'

Dickens continues with the contradictions,

'It held a branch of fresh green holly in its hand, and in singular contradiction of that winter emblem, had its dress trimmed with summer flowers'

Dickens continues the bizarre description,

'But the strangest things about it was, that from the crown of its head there sprung a bright clear jet of light, by which all this was visible'

And to extinguish the light,

'a great extinguisher for a cap, which it now held under its arm'

Dickens adds a chameleon element to it,

'For as its belt sparkled and glittered now in one part and now in another'
'what was light one instant, at another time was dark'
'being now a thing with one arm, now with one leg'
'now with twenty legs without a head, now a head without a body'
'of which dissolving parts, no outline would be visible'

Dickens concludes by reassembling the appearance of this dynamic spectre'

'And in the wonder of this, it would be itself again, distinct and clear as ever'

The First Spirit takes Scrooge on a journey into his past life, selecting times and places to get Scrooge himself to understand what led to him becoming a self-centred miser, without humanity.

This journey exposes Scrooge to himself as an unhappy schoolboy with no friends, a vibrant apprentice with few friends, a young man who rejects his fiancée Belle in favour of money, and finally what might have been had he acquiesced to Belle – his own children with a loving wife.

In a broken voice, Scrooges asks the First Spirit to remove him from Belle's apartment. The Spirit relies

"I told you these were shadows of the things that have been"
"they are what they are, do not blame me!"

Scrooge retorts,

"Leave me! Take me back. Haunt me no longer!"
Scrooge tries to extinguish the Spirit with its extinguisher cap.

'The Spirit dropped beneath it, so that the extinguisher covered its whole form'
'But he could not hide the light, which streamed from under it'

Scrooge, tired, now in his bed chamber, reels into bed, and sank into a heavy sleep.

In **Stave Three**, Scrooge wakes early ready to challenge the Second Spirit on the moment of its appearance, so as not to be surprised by it.

Dickens narrates that Scrooge

'was ready for a good broad field of strange appearances'

And that

'nothing between a baby and rhinoceros would have astonished him very much'

A blaze of ruddy light issuing from the adjoining room, and his name called by a strange voice to enter, introduces Scrooge to a new spectre.

Dickens creates a more traditional appearance for the Second Spirit, less bizarre, more in tune with the expectations of the Victorian reader.

Scrooge is confronted by a room filled with seasonal winter fruits, traditional Christmas meats made into a kind of throne on which there sat a Jolly Giant,

'glorious to see, who bore a glowing torch, in shape not unlike Plenty's horn'

Invited in, Scrooge observes the Second Spirit,

'clothed in one simple green robe, or mantle, bordered with white fur'

Dickens gives a detailed description of his attire and features:

'The Spirit's

'Garment hung so loosely on the figure, that its capacious breast was bare'
'on its head it wore no other covering than a holly wreath, set with shining icicles'
'Its dark brown curls were long and free, free as its genial face, its sparkling eyes'
'free as its open hand, its cheery voice, its unconstrained manner, and its joyful air'
'Girded round its middle was an antique scabbard, but no sword, its feet were bare'

Submissively Scrooge said,

"Spirit, conduct me where you will"

The Second Spirit takes Scrooge on a journey into the present to experience how ordinary people celebrated Christmas with love, joy, and kindness. They visit the city streets, the markets, where the Spirits shed a few drops of water on those who needed their good humour to be restored. At the Cratchits, Scrooge is confronted by the reality of poverty, the power of love, and the need to help the cripple Tiny Tim.

The Spirit takes Scrooge along street, into a mining community, onto a lighthouse, onto a ship, and finally to the nephew's house where Scrooge found joy observing and encouraging Fred and his guests in their Christmas party games, even though he could not be heard or seen.

Scrooge had his doubts about the long night. if it were only a night,

'the Christmas Holidays appeared to be condensed into the space of time they passed together'

Eventually, having visited many other places: foreign lands, the almshouse, the hospital, the jail; Scrooge found it strange that while he'

'remained unaltered in his outward form, the Ghost grew older, clearly older'

On standing together in an open space, the Spirit tells Scrooge,

"My life upon this globe is very brief. It ends tonight."

From beneath the foldings of the Spirit's robe, emerged a boy called Ignorance with Doom written on its brow and a girl called Want. Their appearance was,

'Yellow, meagre, ragged, scowling, wolfish, but prostrate, too, in their humility'

The Spirit tells Scrooge that,

"They are Man's' and they cling to me, appealing from their fathers"

Alarmed, Scrooge cried,

"Have they no refuge or resource?"

The Spirit turning to him for the last time reciting Scrooge's previous words,

"Are there no prisons?" – "Are there no workhouses?"

The bell struck TWELVE, Scrooge lifting his eyes, beheld the Last Spirit, a solemn Phantom, draped and hooded, coming like a mist along the ground, towards him.
In the **Stave Four**, Scrooge is in fear, and so bent down upon his knee before the Phantom which,

'seemed to scatter gloom and mystery'

Dickens now makes the last spectre more ominous than any of the previous ones. This is the spectre to deliver stark choices: ignominy and an early death, or happiness and a long life. Dickens make this spectre dark, gloomy and mysterious to instil foreboding into the novel – will Scrooge choose redemption or continue with his old ways?

Scrooge in trepidation exclaimed,

"I fear you more than any spectre I have seen"

The Spectre gave Scrooge no reply but pointed straight ahead.

Dickens makes use of this silent, finger pointing trait to impact the graveness in which Scrooge finds himself.

The Last Spirit takes Scrooge on a journey into the future to learn the awful truth and consequences of his continued actions. Without redemption, Scrooge is doomed.

The Spirit stopped and pointed towards a knot of business men discussing the funeral of a miser, which Scrooge listened to but received no explanation from the Spirit as to its relevance.

Next, the finger pointed to two persons meeting on the street, again, discussing the funeral of a miser, but yet again, he received no explanation. Scrooge is baffled by so trivial conversations,

'feeling assured that they must have some hidden purpose'

Nor could he think of any one immediately connected with himself, to whom he could apply them.

The subject of death, disrespect and mockery continues when the Phantom directs Scrooge to a low-browed, beetling shop, where the possessions of the death are traded illicitly.

The scene changed to a very dark room where Scrooge is fearful that the dead man in the shroud might be him. Again, the scene changed to another place and room by daylight where a mother receives the good news that the money lending is deceased. Next, in an overgrown churchyard, the Phantom finger pointed to a stone engraved with Scrooge's name.

Dickens dark robed, silent spectre is essential in propelling the supernatural element of the novel to a successful conclusion, laying the foundation to Scrooge's redemption in **Stave 5**, the final chapter.

SOLITUDE

The theme of solitude is woven into the novel to explain in part, why Ebenezer Scrooge drifted into the solitude business of money lending, and miserly practices.

In **Stave One**, Scrooge had no friends except his former now deceased partner Jacob Marley,

'Scrooge was his sole executor, his sole administrator, his sole friend, and sole mourner'

Dickens tells us that,

'there would be nothing more remarkable in his taking at stroll at night'

Scrooge was,

'self-contained, and as solitary as an oyster'

Scrooge's standing in the community was one of solitude,

'Nobody ever stopped him in the street'
'No beggars implored him bestow a trifle'
'No children asked him what it was o'clock'
'No man or woman ever inquired the way to such and such a place'

Dickens even extends this solitude to the blind men's dogs,

'when they saw him coming on, would tug their owners into doorways'

Dickens reveals that Scrooge was intoxicated with solitude,

'But what did Scrooge care! It was the very thing he liked. To edge his way along the crowded paths of life, warning all human sympathy to keep its distance'

This action to keep human sympathy at a distance is evident when Scrooge rejects his nephew's invite to Christmas dinner, offers no donation to the two charity collectors, chases the carol singer away with ruler in hand, and expects Bob Cratchit his clerk to work in the cold, in another part of the office away from him.

His solitude is extended to his place of residence, where apart from his chambers, all other rooms are let out as offices. Solitude is evident as he is by himself with no interference by other humans. He lived in rooms which had once belonged to his only friend and deceased business partner Jacob Marley. The yard was so dark that even Scrooge, who knew its every stone, was fain to grope with his hands. Solitude prevailed everywhere.

Scrooge is confronted first by the brief transfiguration of the door knocker into the face of his now deceased partner Jacob Marley, then by the image of a locomotive hearse going on before him as he climbed the stairs to bed chamber, resulting in the shocking appearance of Marley's Ghost, there to save his old friend Scrooge from damnation, by not distancing himself from human sympathy, but instead embracing it. The remedy, to break his solitude and his miserly ways was for Scrooge to be taken through time by different spirits so that when he returned on Christmas Day, his life could start anew.

In **Stave Two**, Scrooge travels back in time to his school days, to view his boyhood self, lonely, without friends, rejected by all. Dickens makes use of the word 'melancholy' repeatedly to emphasis the gloom and apathy within him. Solitude starts to take hold, and so he comforts himself with imaginary characters from books read, such as Ali Baba, others such as the Sultan's Groom turned upside down by the Genii, and others such as Robin Crusoe and man Friday, running for his life.

Scrooge becomes regretful,

'with a rapidity of transition very foreign to his usual character, he said, in pity for his former self, "Poor boy!" and cried again'

Scrooge is beginning to understand the unhappiness solitude creates, and rejects his actions the previous night when he with ruler in hand, chased away the carol singer,

"I should like to have given him something"

His boyhood solitude is eased when his sister Fan arrives to take him home from School, from the root of his solitude,

"I have come to bring you home, dear brother"
"never to come back here"
"we're to be together all the Christmas long"
"and have the merriest time in all the world"

In recognitions of her love, and her persistence to remove Scrooge from that dreadful school by convincing their father that Scrooge should return home, Scrooge agreed when the Spirit proclaimed,

"Always a delicate creature, but she had a large heart!"

Her only legacy was her son Fred, Scrooge's nephew, the antipathy of solitude.

Next the Spirit of Christmas past stopped at a warehouse, where Scrooge was once an apprentice to Fezziwig, and where gaiety, dancing, and friendship reigned, and where solitude was banished.

The Spirit observed,

"My time grows short, Quick!"

Within a flash, Scrooge is transport to a park bench where in the prime of his life he sat by the side of a fair young girl in a mourning dress, remonstrating to him about a new mistress, a golden one which has displaced love. The girl is Belle his fiancée, she departs with sadness, remarking,

"May you be happy in the life you have chosen!"

Scrooge is mortified, realising that by rejecting love in favour of money, he had accepted a life of solitude.

The Spirit is determined to continue and force Scrooge to observe the outcome, despite his cries,

"No more!" cried Scrooge. "No more. Show me no more!"

Without warning, Scrooge and the Spirit arrive,

'in another scene and place; a room, not very large or handsome, but full of comfort'

The husband arrives home to be greeted by his wife and children who scramble over him, eager to discover and open the Christmas toys and presents he had brought home.

The mention of Belle's name by the husband confirms what Scrooge thought initially when arriving in the room that it was Belle, and this might have been the scene with him as the husband had he not reject love in favour of money.

Dickens continues the agony created solitude hen the husband tells Belle that as he passed Scrooge's office window, he saw Scrooge

"there he sat alone. Quite alone in the world, I do believe"

with his partner, his only friend, upon the point of death.

Again, Scrooge is disturbed by events, asking the Spirit in a broken voice,

"Remove me from this place"

In response, the Spirit reminds Scrooge that events are his doing.

"I told you these were shadows of the things that been"
"That they are what they are, do not blame me!"
In frustration, and to remove this adversary, Scrooge

'turned upon the Ghost, and seeing that it looked upon him with a face, in which in some strange way there were fragments of all the faces it had shown him'

In the struggle, Scrooge seized the extinguisher cap, and by a sudden action pressed down it down upon the Spirit's head. The Spirit dropped beneath it, but the Spirit's light streamed from under it, in an unbroken flood upon the ground.

At last, exhausted, he reeled into bed, sank into a heavy sleep with solitude his bed fellow.

In **Stave Three**, the Second Spirit takes Scrooge on a journey where solitude is absent, where Christmas rulers supreme, where people celebrate together: the market traders and shoppers, the Cratchits, the children in the street, the lamplighter, the miners, the lighthouse keepers, the ship's crew, the guests at Fred's house party.

Enjoying the party games, learning to socialise, and not wishing to leave his newfound vocation in favour of solitude, Scrooge is suddenly confronted by the reality of Ignorance in the form of a boy, and Want, a girl. Social issues caused by society distancing itself from Humanity, promoting solitude between rich and poor.

In **Stave Four**, the moody changes, solitude rears its ugly head. The Last Spirit exposes Scrooge to the truth about solitude, and the future demise by it should he not rejects solitude in favour of Humane acts.

In the City, on the street, Scrooge listens to people talking about a miser's funeral, not sure if the miser talked about is himself.

At the beetling shop, the shop keeper Old Joe buys purloined items from a Charwoman, the Laundress Mrs Dilber, and an Undertaker's man. They are of the opinion that the dead man in his bed had no need of his possessions, but others do.

Mocking, laughing, deriding the dead man, they sought the best price for their ill gained goods. Solitude had resulted in the dead man losing his possessions to unknown scavengers. The charwoman removed bed-curtains, and even the shirt he was to be buried-in.

Scrooge, shuddering from head to foot, acknowledging,

"The case of this unhappy man might be my own"

Scrooge recoiled in terror, for the scene had changed, similar to that described by the charwoman, and now he

'almost touched a bed: a bare, uncurtained bed: on which, beneath a ragged sheet, there lay something covered up'

Beneath the ragged sheet, Scrooge suspects the dead man might be him. He could not bring himself to uncover the sheet, for fear of the truth.

Solitude had resulted in the man's demise, now

'a cat was tearing at the door, and there was a sound of gnawing rats beneath the heart-stone'

What they wanted in the room of death, and why they were so restless and disturbed, Scrooge did not dare to think.

Travelling on to other places, the climax is reached when the Spirit takes Scrooge to a churchyard,

"walled in by houses; overrun by grass and weeds, the growth of vegetation's death, not life; choked up with too much burying"

The Spirit's finger points to a neglected grave, engraved with 'EBENEZER SCROOGE'. The finger pointed back to Scrooge when he asked,

"Am I that man who lay upon the bed?"

Solitude had been the catalyst for this version of his future demise!

In **Stave Five**, Scrooge rejects Solitude in favour of participating in society and helping those less fortunate than himself. He had learnt the lessons taught to him by the three Spirits.

Dickens makes use of Solitude to mould Scrooge into the character described in **Stave One**,

"a tight-fisted hand at the grindstone"
"a squeezing, wrenching, grasping, scraping, clutching, covetous old skinner!"
"Hard and sharp as flint"
"secret, and self-contained"

And Dickens poignant epitaph,

"solitary as an oyster"

In the end, Solitude is defeated by the realisation that man is at his best when he helps his fellow man. Scrooge learnt this and redeemed himself by not only re-joining society but making a positive contribution.

As Dickens writes,

'Scrooge was better than his word. He did it all, and infinity more; and to Tiny Tim, who did NOT die, he was a second father.'

FAMILY

The theme of family is used as foil against solitude.

In **Stave One**, nephew Fred invites uncle Scrooge to dine with him and his family on Christmas Day.

"Don't be angry, uncle. Come! Dine with us tomorrow."

Scrooge is dismissive about the invitation, and his reaction as to why Fred married is indignant,

"Because you fell in love!" 'growled Scrooge, as if that were the only thing in the world more ridiculous than a merry Christmas'

Scrooge's preference for solitude rather than a family gathering is clear.

"I am sorry, with all my heart, to find you so resolute. So A Merry Christmas, uncle!"

Again, Scrooge's response is a stern,

"Good afternoon!"

Scrooge prefers is own solitude to that of family or anyone.

In **Stave Two**, as a schoolboy with no friends, Scrooge makes up his own imaginary family out of characters read in popular books. His feels abandon by his family; deposited at a boarding school by his unkind Father; lonely as an oyster; and in desperate need of love.

"there is was, alone again, when all the other boys had gone home for the jolly holidays"

On this occasion, who should dart in the school room but his younger sister Fan to relieve his solitude,

"Dear, dear brother"
"I have come to bring you home, dear brother!"
"Home for good and all, Home, for ever and ever"

Fan explains,

"Father is so much kinder than he used to be, that home's like Heaven!"
"He sent me in a coach to bring you"

The schoolboy Scrooge is overwhelmed, and exclaims,

"You are quite a woman, little Fan!"

Fan believed in the family. She was not afraid to ask their Father once more if Scrooge might come home. Scrooge acknowledges that she had a large heart.

The First Spirit reminds Scrooge that she had one child, his nephew Fred. Scrooge feels uneasy, because he realises that he does have an obligation to family in repayment for Fan's love to him.

"Scrooge seemed uneasy in his mind"

As a young apprentice at Fezziwigs, Scrooge becomes part of a new family where friendship, fun, and humour abound. At the Christmas, Mr and Mrs Fezziwig, their three daughters, his fellow apprentice Dick Wilkins, and others together with Scrooge would dance and make merry,

'There were more dances, and there were forfeits, and more dances, and there was cake, and there was Cold Roast, and there were mince-pies, and plenty of beer.'

Scrooge is overwhelmed at observing his former self enjoying everything within a family atmosphere. The First Spirit decides to play devil's advocate,

"A small matter to make these silly folks so full of gratitude"

Scrooge heated by the remark, speaking unconsciously like his former self,

"It isn't that Spirit. He has the power to render us happy or unhappy; to make our services light or burdensome; a pleasure or a toil"

Speaking again about Mr Fezziwig, Scrooge concludes,

"The happiness he gives, is quite as great as if it cost a fortune"

Scrooge recognises that he was part of Mr Fezziwig extended family.

In **Stave Three**, the Second Spirit takes Scrooge on a journey to observe the family of man where status in society is no barrier to people celebrating and enjoying Christmas together as one family.

'the people who were shovelling away on the house-tops were jovial and full of glee; calling out to one another from the parapets'

Dickens consolidates the theme of family by recounting how people came together,

'But soon the steeples called good people all, to church and chapel, and away they came, flocking through the streets in their best clothes, and with their gayest faces.

Next, at the Cratchit's dwelling, Scrooge observes the togetherness of the family.

'Mrs Cratchit made the gravy hissing hot'
'Master Peter mashed the potatoes with incredible vigour'
'Miss Belinda sweetened up the apple sauce'
'Martha dusted the hot plate'
'Bob took Tiny Tim beside him in a tiny corner at the table'
'the two young Cratchits set chairs for everybody'

The love and joy conveyed within the family is overwhelming, even though they possessed very little wealth,

'they were not a handsome family'
'they were not well dressed; their shoes were far from being-waterproof'
'their clothes were scanty; and Peter might have known the inside of a pawnbroker's'

But they were,

'happy, grateful, pleased with one another'

The First Spirit and Scrooge left the Cratchits with Tiny Tim singing about a lost child travelling in the snow. Getting dark and snowing heavily, Scrooge and the Spirit went along the streets,

'all the children of the house were running out into the snow to meet their married sisters, brothers, cousins, uncles, aunts, and be the first to greet them'

Next, without a word of warning, Scrooge and the Spirit stood upon a bleak and desert moor, where below a family of Miners live, who labour in the bowels of the earth. Passing through the wall of a mud and stone hut, they found

'a cheerful company assembled round a glowing fire'
'the old man was singing them a Christmas song'
'from time to time they all joined in the chorus'

Next, the Spirit and Scrooge arrived at a lighthouse, built upon a dismal reef of sunken rocks, some league or so from shore, where two lighthouse keepers act as a Christmas family of colleagues, 'joining their horny hands over the rough table, they wished each other Merry Christmas in their can of grog; struck up a sturdy song that was like a Gale in itself'

Again, they sped on, above the black and heaving sea, alighting onto a ship, where the crew act as a Christmas family of shipmates,

'every man on board, waking or sleeping, good or bad, had had a kinder word for another on that day in the year, and had; and had remembered those he cared for at a distance, and had know that they delighted to remember him'

Dickens completes his collection of families, by Scrooge arriving at his nephew's house. Scrooge having observed the connectiveness of families from different parts of society at Christmas, now gets to observe the family closes to him, and discovers that as with the other families they had visited on Christmas Day, joy and affection abounds. Scrooge particularly enjoyed the party games 'blind-man's bluff', 'How, When, Why, and begged the Spirit to stay for one-half hour, to play the game 'Yes and No',

"Here is a new game", said Scrooge, "One half hour, Spirit, only one!"

Next, the Spirit took Scrooge to visit others less fortunate or entrapped by society, the family of the poor,

'In almshouse, hospital and jail, in misery's every refuge, where vain man in his little brief authority had not made fast the door, and barred the Spirit out'

The Spirit left his blessings, and taught Scrooge his precepts.

The Spirit began to age, but underneath his robe emerged two children belonging to the family of man,

'They were a boy and girl. Yellow, meagre, ragged, scowling, wolfish; but prostrate, too, in their humility. This boy is Ignorance. This girl is Want.'

In **Stave Four**, Dickens juxtaposes the family against its absence, in essence solitude and loneliness, the consequences of which on death are mockery, loss of possessions to scavengers, and loss of money owed by debtors.

Dickens makes the funeral a scene where the deceased is mocked,

"Why what was the matter with him? I thought he'd never die."
"What has he done with his money? He hasn't let it to me."
"It's likely to be a very cheap funeral'
"I don't mind going if lunch is provided"

Dickens makes the loss of possessions a scene where the scavengers justified their gain and the deceased his loss,

"Who's the worse for the loss of a few things like these? Not a dead man"

Dickens makes the loss of money a scene where the debtors are overjoyed,

"We may sleep to-night with light hearts, Caroline!"

In **Stave Five**, Dickens resumes the theme of family, where Scrooge wishes to make amends and re-join the family of man, in particular, his nephew's family, the Cratchit family, and the family of charity towards others.

Dickens underlining theme in his novella 'A Christmas Carol' is the plight of the poor in Victorian society. Dickens creates a supernatural tale, set at Christmas, to act as a platform to make the upper echelons of society aware of the injustice visited upon the impoverished working class.

Dickens is not seeking a revolutionary solution as advocated by political theorists Marx and Engels, but by changes in working conditions, with employer treating their employees fairly and those with wealth contributing to charities.

Dickens makes the Cratchit family the face of the poor in his 'A Christmas Carol.

In **Stave One**, Scrooge the employer berates his clerk Bob Cratchit for the slightest infarction. He eye was always on Bob, so that what he paid Bob was accounted for.

'The door of Scrooge's counting-house was open that he might keep his eye upon his clerk, who in a dismal little cell beyond, a sort of tank, was copying letters'

For Bob, the working conditions were grim

'Scrooge had a very small fire, but the clerk's fire was so very much smaller that it looked like one coal. But he couldn't replenish it, for Scrooge kept the coal-box in his own room'

Otherwise, Scrooge the master threatened Bob the clerk with dismissal,

'so surely as the clerk came in with the shovel, the master predicted that it would be necessary for them to part'

Bob's failed solution was to

'put on his white comforter, and tried to warm himself at the candle'

Scrooge's nephew Fred tries to convince Scrooge that Christmas time is when

"men and woman seem by one consent to open their shut-up hearts freely, and to think of people below them as if they really were fellow passengers"

Scrooge is unmoved by Fred's appeal, but Bob applauded, resulting in a stern, authoritarian threat by his employer Scrooge,

"Let me hear another sound from you, and you'll keep your Christmas by losing your situation!"

As Fred departs, two charity collectors enter, intent on securing some slight provision for the Poor and destitute,

"Many thousands are in want of common necessaries; hundreds of thousand are in want of common comforts"

Scrooge is scornful, and asks one of the two charity collectors who entered,

"Are there no prisons?" - the collector answered "*Plenty of prisons*"
"And the Union workhouses? Are they still in operation?" - "*They are. Still*"
"The Treadmill and the Poor Law are in full vigour, then?" - "*Both very busy, sir*"

When asked by the Charity collector,

"What shall I put you down for?"

Scrooge replied "Nothing!"

Scrooge justifies his refusal,

"I help to support the establishments – they cost enough; and those who are badly off must go there"

The Charity collector responds,

"Many can't go there, and many would rather die"

Scrooge, more interested in money than people, counters,

"If they would rather die, they had better do it, and decrease the surplus population"

Dickens is alerting the Victorian reader to the harsh unsympathetic attitude of some employers like the fictional character Scrooge, to those outcasts in society.

Scrooge reveals his mean spirit when he tells Bob,

"you don't think me ill-used, when I pay a day's wages for no work"

Scrooge's attitude is clear, the employee must work to be paid at whatever rate the employer decides. Scrooge paid Bob a low wage, as did most employers with their employees making poverty more prevalent in Victorian society.

Dickens makes use of the supernatural element to draw the attention of the Victorian reader to poverty in society.

Marley's Ghost joined in the mournful dirge, floated out through Scrooge's bedroom window, upon the bleak, dark night to wander hither and thither with the other phantoms. Scrooge had been quite familiar with one old ghost, in a white waistcoat, with a monstrous iron safe attached to its ankle,

'who cried piteously at being unable to assist a wretched woman with an infant, whom it saw below, upon a door-step'

Dickens go on to infers that if society could not alleviate misery, then nor could the spirit world since spirits could only inform but not physically interact to save the destitute.

'The misery with them all was, clearly, that they sought to interfere, for good, in human matters, and had lost the power for ever.'

In **Stave Three**, Dickens draws the reader's attention to the bare-thread attire of the poverty stricken Cratchits.

'Mrs Cratchit dressed out but poorly in a twice-turned gown, but brave in ribbons, which are cheap and make a goodly show for sixpence'

'In came Bob, his threadbare clothe darned up and brushed'

Later, Dickens describes the Cratchits general situation,

'They were not a handsome family; they were not well dressed; their shoes were far from being water-proof; their clothes were scanty'

Although poor, their strength lay in their belief in each other, guided by Christian principles,

'they were happy, grateful, pleased with one another, and contented with time'

Poverty did not favour cripples, so Tiny Tim is not expected to live long. Dickens generates empathy by first making Scrooge curse those who are or become a drain on society, the so called 'surplus population' of which Tiny Tim is a member, then regretting his former words, now deeply concerned about those who are helpless and need society's aid.

'yet in the bright sprinklings of the Spirit's torch at parting, Scrooge had his eye upon them, and especially on Tiny Tim, until the last'

After the gaiety, and party games at Fred's House, the Spirit beings to age, and Scrooge obverse something strange emerging from the foldings of its robe,

'it brought two children, wretched, abject, frightful, hideous, miserable. They knelt down at its feet and clung upon the outside of its garment'

Instead of graceful youth, their features and appearance are akin to the face of Poverty,

'They were a boy and girl. Yellow, meagre, ragged, scowling, wolfish'
'a stale and shrivelled hand, like that of age, had pinched, and twisted them'
'where angels might have sat enthroned, devils lurked, and glared out menacing'

Dickens draws the reader into the horror by getting Scrooge to back away and ask the question,

"Spirit! Are they yours!"

The Spirit replies,

"They are man's, and they cling to me, appealing from their fathers"

Dickens builds up a picture as to why these children are to be feared, and why previous bias and prejudices held by Scrounge, harbour man's' demise unless action is taken to root out Poverty and cast it from the streets, the city and the earth.

"This boy is Ignorance"
"This girl is Want"
"Beware both, and all of their degree"
"But most of all beware this boy, on his brow is Doom, unless the writing be eased"

Scrooge is still convinced that there exist places for the Poor,

"Have they no refuge or resource?"

Knowing that existing institutions of prisons and workhouses will not alleviate Poverty, the Spirit answers Scrooge using Scrooge's previous words,

"Are there no prisons?"
"Are there no workhouses?"

to provoke awareness in Scrooge that these refuges are inadequate to remove Poverty whereas redistribution of wealth and a caring society are the keys, promoted by better Education.

In **Stave Four**, Dickens describes the squalor in the back streets of the city, away from the wealthy sector of town, where Scrooge had not been before and where Poverty reigns,

"The ways were foul and narrow; the shops and houses wretched"
"the people half-naked, drunken, slipshod, ugly"
"alleys and archways, like so many cesspools,
 disgorged their offences of smell, and dirt, and life, upon the straggling streets"
"and the whole quarter reeked with crime, with filth, and misery"

Dickens is very descriptive about poor areas to ram home the conditions poor people endure, and he goes on to describe how some make a living from the dead.

The Spirit and Scrooge arrive at a beetling shop, where scavengers of the dead have arrived, to trade goods scavenge from the recently deceased. Old Joe the shopkeeper entertains three prospective clients,

"Let the charwoman alone to be the first!"
"Let the laundress alone to be the second"
"Let the undertaker's man alone to be the third"

The charwoman is the cleaning lady who removed the deceased's bed curtains, blankets, and silk shirts, justifies her actions by,

"Every person has a right to care of themselves. He always did"

The laundress Mrs Dilber removed the deceased's sheets, towels, some clothing, silver teaspoons, a pair of sugar-tongs, and a few boots, justifies her actions by,

"Who's the worse for the loss of a few things like these, Not a dead man"

The undertaker's man had few things to impart, a seal or two, a pencil-case, a pair of sleeve-buttons, and a broach of no great value.

Scrooge observing all,

"viewed them with a detestation and disgust, which could hardly have been greater, though they had been obscene demons, marketing the corpse itself"

Debt was another issue that plunged people into poverty. Dickens experienced this within his own family. His father, John Dickens, was arrested for debt in 1824 and sent to the Marshalsea prison in Southwark, but eventually released on payment of the debt. It was an experience that Charles was never to forget.

Later, the Spirit and Scrooge arrive in a room, where a mother and her children were anxiously awaiting news from her husband who eventually arrives to tell Caroline that

"He is past relenting. He is dead!"

Caroline is relieved that the debt need not be paid at this pressing time.

Again, the deceased alluded to is Scrooge should he not change his ways and seek the path of redemption by embracing the milk of human kindness.

Without this change, Tiny Tim will not survive long, nor will Scrooge himself, both destined for an early grave.

Poverty is a crime visited on society by those with wealth and prestige who have abdicated their responsibility to create a society which cares for those with needs.

AVARICE [greed]

Dickens theme of money and avarice (greed) juxtaposes his theme of Christmas and the Christmas spirit. Scrooge is initially on the side of money and greed, but through the auspices of the supernatural redeems himself, and puts people before avarice.

In **Stave One**, hammers home Scrooge's relentless obsession with making money, and his thriftiness in spending it.

"Oh! But he was a tight-fisted hand at the grindstone, a squeezing, wrenching, grasping, scraping, clutching, covetous, old sinner!"

The sin was avarice, one of the seven deadly sins of Christian tradition.

He had learnt much from his deceased business partner Jacob Marley who he considered an excellent business man.

Dickens reveals the lengths to which Scrooge goes to save money,

'Scrooge had a very small fire, but the clerk's fire was so very much smaller that it looked like one coal'

To replenish it meant possible dismissal,

'Scrooge kept the coal-box in his own room; and so surely as the clerk came in with the shovel, the master predicted that it would be necessary for them to part'

Scrooge is dismissive of the money he pays his clerk, considering it more than generous, when in fact it is not sufficient at all to keep his Bob's family, and sarcastically remarks,

"my clerk, with fifteen shillings a week, and a wife and family, talking about a merry Christmas. I'll retire to Bedlam"

Scrooge is not amused when Bob inadvertently let in two charity collectors seeking a donation for the Poor and destitute, who suffer greatly at this present time. When asked "What shall I put down for?", Scrooge's reply is "Nothing!"

The Christmas carol singer fared no better,

"Scrooge seized the ruler with such energy of action, that the singer fled in terror"

Scrooge is not prepared to give money unless it is in his interest. Scrooge even attempts to justify why he should not pay Bob on Christmas Day,

"A poor excuse for picking a man's pocket every twenty-fifth of December"

At his lodgings, Scrooge although rich, sat by the fireplace with a bowl of gruel in hand, and a very low fire indeed.

Dickens now introduces the supernatural to guide Scrooge forward in his quest to redeem himself from Avarice, one of the seven deadly sins.

The Ghost of Jacob Marley passes into the room before Scrooge's eyes, who by now is petrified at the noise, the flames, and the sight of

'cash-boxes, keys, padlocks, ledgers, deeds, purses wrought in steel'

attached to a heavy chain clasped about his middle.

Marley's Ghost tells Scrooge that to prevent a similar fate, he must be guided by three spirits,

"without their visits, you cannot hope to shun the path I tread"

In **Stave Two**, Dickens introduces the antipathy of Avarice portrayed by Fezziwig who unlike Scrooge spends his wealth on his family and his employees. Scrooge as a young apprentice at Fezziwig was a beneficiary of this benevolent.

At Fezziwig, Scrooge enjoyed friendship, happiness, and entertainment unlike his days as a boy at school. Later, as a man in the prime of life,

'his face had not the harsh and rigid lines of later years, but it had begun to wear the signs of care and avarice'

Dickens continues by describing the path set for Scrooge by adopting the sin avarice

'There was an eager, greedy, restless motion in the eye, which showed the passion that had taken root, and where the shadow of the growing tree would fall'

Avarice is about to lose Scrooge his fiancée,

"a fair young girl in a mourning-dress, in whose eyes there were tears"

She admonished Scrooge

"It matters little to you, very little"
"Another idol has displaced me"
"if it can cheer and comfort you in time to come, I have no just cause to grieve"

Scrooge is anxious to know what idol, to which his fiancée replies "A golden one."

A discussion ensues on security through wealth or

"improve our worldly fortune by our patient industry"
Unable to convince Scrooge of her arguments, his former fiancée Belle departs, with a farewell remark,

"you will dismiss the recollection of it, gladly, as an unprofitable dream, from which it happened well that you awoke. May you be happy in the life you have chosen!"

Bewildered by this outcome, Scrooge continues his life of avarice towards the inevitable present-day events he now finds himself tethered to, under the auspices of the Spirits sent by Marley's Ghost to oversee his redemption. Love is the path of life, not avarice.

Dickens then presents the alternative outcome, whereby choosing love, Belle is happily married with children of her own, waiting patiently for her husband to arrive home with the Christmas presents.

Scrooge is distressed by this, realising that this is what is wanted in life, but took the wrong path, the path of avarice not that of love. Scrooge in a broken voice,

"Spirit! Remove me from this place. Remove me! I cannot bear it!"

In **Stave Four**, the Last Spirit in the form of a dark, ominous, menacing phantom, takes Scrooge into the future to observe the consequences and legacy of avarice, with the unknown deceased revealed later to Scrooge as himself.

The mockery and sarcasm visited on the deceased throughout the city and streets is testament to the distain city merchants, and debtors held the deceased,

"Why, what was the matter with him? I thought he'd never die"
"What has he done with his money? Left it to his company, perhaps"
"He hasn't left it to me. That's all I know."

This pleasantry was received with a general laugh.

"It's likely to be a very cheap funeral, for upon my life I don't know of anybody to go"
"I don't mind going if a lunch is provided, but I must be fed"
"Well, I am the most disinterested among you, but I'll offer to go, if anybody else will"

Finally, one of the merchants remarks in a nonchalant way,

"When I come to think of it, I'm not at all sure that I wasn't his most particular friend"

Dickens tells the reader that Avarice has no worthy friends, therefore no legacy for the person who embraces it.

The Phantom points his finger towards two men of business who Scrooge knew, perfectly, very wealthy, and of great importance,

"Old Scratch has got his own at last, hey?"
The reply was "So I am told"

That was their meeting, their conversation, and their parting.

Scrooge is surprised that the Spirit should attach importance as to a trivial, brief conservation unless it had some hidden purpose. Surely not Jacob Marley as the deceased because this was the providence of the First Spirit, not the Last Spirit he was with now.

In a taste of irony, Dickens is laying the ground for the reader to realise what Scrooge does not, that he is the deceased the Merchants and wealthy Business men are talking about. Later, Scrooge gradually becomes aware of this fact, and it is confirmed when the Phantom points his finger at the gravestone on which are engraved the words 'EBENEZER SCROOGE'.

Avarice is not just the providence of the wealthy. Poor people practised it when temptation and opportunity revealed themselves.

Arriving in an obscure part of town, where Scrooge had never penetrated before, and of bad repute, the Phantom points his finger at a Beetling Shop owned by Old Joe, a procurer of oddities such as possessions no longer needed by the departed.
Stolen possessions, easy pickings, no questions asked. Fertile ground for Avarice.

Old Joe tells the three scavengers,

"You couldn't have met in a better place, come into the parlour"

The charwoman threw her bundle of stolen possessions on the floor, looking with a bold defiance at the other two: Mrs Dilber, the laundress, and the undertaker's man.

"What odds then! What odds, Mrs Dilber?"
"Every person has a right to take care of themselves. He always did."

Mrs Dilber agrees,

"That's true, Indeed! No man more so."

The charwoman cried,

"Very well, then!"
"Who's the worse for the loss of a few things like these? Not a dead man, I suppose."

The charwoman justifies the theft by saying that if he wanted to keep 'em after he was dead, he should have married, and that

"It's no sin"

to help oneself when all was acquired by avarice in the first place.

The undertaker's man was the first to open his plunder, and then Mrs Dilber, and finally the charwoman.
The undertaker's man took few possessions, Mrs Dilber much more, and the charwoman even removed the Bed-curtains together with the expensive shirt the deceased was to be buried in. Sacrilege indeed!

"Putting it on him to be buried in, to be sure, replied the charwoman with a laugh."
Somebody was fool enough to do it, but I took it off again."

Scrooge is horrified, and even more so when Old Joe produces a bag with money in it, to pay the three scavengers,

"This is the end of it, you see!"
"He frightened every one away from him when he was alive,
to profit us when he was dead!"

Dickens is making the point that the ill-gotten gains acquired by avarice are relinquished to others who also have the same intent. The gains are always lost to others who lose to others unless Avarice is banished.

Scrooge is beginning to realise that it may be him who is the deceased man, on this journey into the future.

"Spirit!" said Scrooge, shuddering from head to foot,
"The case of this unhappy man might be my own. My life tends that way, now"

Dickens now increases the tension and dread, by placing Scrooge in a room where on the bed,

'plundered and bereft, unwatched, unwept, uncared for, was the body of this man'

Scrooge, reluctant to reveal the man's face beneath the shroud for fear it might be his future self, thought,

'if this man could be raised up now, what would be his foremost thoughts?'
Avarice, hard-dealing, griping cares? They have brought him to a rich end, truly!'

Scrooge seeking salvation, and quite agonised, asks the Phantom,

"If there is any person in the town, who feels emotion caused by this man's death,
Show that person to me, Spirit, I beseech you!"

The Phantom spread its dark robe like a wing to reveal a room by daylight, where a mother with her children, was expecting some one, and with anxious eagerness,

'for she walked up and down the room; glanced at the clock; tried, but in vain, to work with her needle; and could hardly bear the voices of the children in their play'

Dickens builds tension by describing how easily the mother is distracted.

Dickens then releases the tension when,

'At length the long-expected knock was heard. She hurried to the door, and met her husband; a man whose face was careworn and depressed, though he was young'

Dickens continues,

'There was a remarkable expression in it now, a kind of serious delight
of which he felt ashamed, and which he struggled to repress'

Caroline, his wife, is unsure what to make of it, but when her husband reveals that the man, they owe money to is dead, she is much relieved and thankful,

'she was thankful in her soul to hear it, and she said so, with clasped hands
she prayed forgiveness the next moment, and was sorry,
but the first was the emotion of her heart'

Dickens continues

'their hearts were lighter. The children's faces were brighter, and it was a happier house for this man's death!'

Dickens educates the reader in the plight awaiting those who borrow money from moneylenders. Force to borrow money to avoid catastrophe, poor people find themselves in deeper distress when avarice lenders such as Scrooge, charge such high interest to make it sometimes impossible to repay the debt. Death of the moneylender may bring permanent relief, but there is no guarantee that the debt may be transferred to another creditor.

Next, the Phantom and Scrooge arrive at Poor Bob Cratchit's house, where Scrooge is confronted with the distressing news that Tiny Tim is dead. Poverty had claimed another victim, as so often it did in Victorian society.

Next, the Phantom takes Scrooge to a churchyard, where the Phantom's finger points to a gravestone inscribed with the name 'EBENEZER SCROOGE'. The rewards of Avarice are loneliness and, in some case where miserly behaviour is prominent through not spending a penny on heat and food, such as with Scrooge, an early death. Scrooge is terrified, promising that he will redeem himself,

"I will honour Christmas in my heart"
"The Spirits of all Three shall strive within me"
"I will not shut out the lessons that they teach"

In **Stave Five**, Scrooge is true to his promise, and makes generous donations to the charity collectors, breaks his solitude by arriving at Fred's house for Christmas dinner, but most of all to take the Cratchit family out of Poverty's clutches, and become a second father to Tiny Tim. Scrooge has rejected Avarice and replaced it by 'patient industry', as advocated by Belle, his last vestige of love.

TIME

Time is used as a **motif** to aid the supernatural element of the novella.

In **Stave One**, Marley's Ghost sets the timeframe,

"Expect the first to-morrow, when the bell tolls ONE"
"Expect the second on the next night at the same hour"
"The third upon the next when the last stroke of TWELVE has ceased to vibrate"

A limited time window is evident in each of the staves.   Marley's Ghost is the first to tells Scrooge,

"Hear me! My **time** is nearly gone"

Dickens uses **Time** to impact the severity of the punishment that Marley's has had to endure over seven years, travelling constantly since his dead,

"No rest, no peace. Incessant torture of remorse. On the wings of the wind'

In **Stave Two**, Scrooge is astonished to hear the heavy bell as it went on,

'from SIX to SEVEN,
and from SEVEN to EIGHT,
and regularly up to TWELVE, then stopped'

Scrooge is confused,

'TWELVE! It was past TWO when he went to bed. The clock was wrong'

Scrooge concludes an icicle must have got into the work.

This fluctuation in time continued with Scrooge staying awake perplexed and confused, as if locked into a realm of supernatural time, until the hour bell sounded, which it now did with a deep, dull, hollow, melancholy ONE., heralding the arrival of the First Spirit – the Ghost of Christmas past,

In **Stave Three**, Scrooge awakes in readiness for the arrival of the Second Spirit again upon the stroke of ONE because he wished to challenge the Spirit on the moment of its appearance. The bell struck ONE but no Spirit. Eventually, Scrooge reasons that the blaze of ruddy light form the adjoining room, must be where the Second Spirit – the Ghost of Christmas present – resides.

The Spirit had taken Scrooge to many places in only a night. Scrooge is perplexed and had his doubts of this,

'because the Christmas Holidays appeared to be condensed into the space of time they passed together'

Also, Scrooge noticed that time had been distorted,

'while Scrooge remained unaltered in his outward form, the Ghost grew older'

Dickens uses **Time** as an instrument to separate the physical world from the spiritual one. Scrooge's **time** is controlled by the supernatural. The consequence of which is much can be fitted into the timeframe in only one night. Each Spirit is allotted a fix time to complete their mission, so when Scrooges asks,

"Are spirits' lives so short?"

To which the Spirit replied,

"My life upon this globe is very brief. It ends to-night. To-night at midnight"

The chimes were ringing the three quarters past eleven, and within the one quarter hour, the Spirit gone, replaced by the Last Spirit in form of a dark, menacing Phantom.

In **Stave Four**, Scrooge is transported into the future, where the Last Spirit –- the Ghost of Christmas yet to come –- reveals a bleak outcome, unless Scrooge recognises the errors of his ways, and reforms.

Scrooges learns that **time** is running out for Tiny Tim, as well as himself. Right from the start, the Phantom takes Scrooge to places where people are either talking about a deceased man or later to his actual death bed.

Arriving at the Cratchit's house, Scrooge observes the pain endured by the family members. Scrooge is conscience of **time**,

"Spectre, something informs me that our parting moment is at hand"
"I know it, but I know not how"

Scrooge continues,

"Tell me what man that was whom we saw lying dead?"

The Phantom takes Scrooge to a churchyard and points to his gravestone.

Time is the discriminator. Scrooge must be ready to act because Christmas will come and go. Scrooge **time** on earth is short, so is that of Tiny Tim, unless he acts.

In **Stave Five**, Scrooge does act,

"the **Time** before him was his own, to make amends in!"

On Christmas Day, Scrooge set in motion his redemption,

"Scrooge was better than his word. He did it all, and infinitely more, and to Tiny Tim, who did NOT die, he was a second father"

Scrooge had extended Time, for Tiny Tim, as well as himself!

DARKNESS

Darkness is used as a **motif** to aid the supernatural element of the novella, as well as mortality.

In **Stave One**, Scrooge encounters **darkness** in the form of Jacob Marley's funeral, then in the form of solitude,

'there would be nothing more remarkable in his taking a stroll at night'

Dickens endows Scrooge with a sinister **dark** aura, recognised by animals

'Even blind men's dogs would wag their tails as though they said, No eye at all is better than an evil eye, **dark** master!'

Dickens makes use of the time of year, where nights are long and days are short, to set the tale in **darkness**.

Scrooge arrived at his counting-house.

'The city clocks had only just gone three, but it was quite **dark** already'

Dickens continues the motif of **darkness** to emphasis the harshness of the conditions imposed by Scrooge to save money. Both Scrooge and his clerk work by candlelight, insufficient to make the working space but dismal.

Outside people and shops dispel the **darkness**,

'Meanwhile the fog and **darkness** thickened so, that people ran about with flaring links proffering their services to go before horses in carriages, to conduct them home

On closing the office, and making his way home, the **darkness** makes it almost impossible for Scrooge to find the front door of his chambers.

'the yard was so **dark** that even Scrooge, who knew its every stone, was fain to grope with his hands'

Scrooge describes the reshaped door knocker in the image of Marley's face,

'like a bad lobster in a **dark** cellar'

Scrooge prefers **darkness**, his walking companion, to people because, unlike people, there is no cost,

'**Darkness** is cheap, and Scrooge liked it'

Scrooge knows that **darkness** can be a menace, being an accomplice, harbinger of the supernatural.

Scrooge is disturbed when the quaint Dutch tiles illustrating the Scriptures, are swallowed up by the image of Marley's face,

'if each smooth tile had been a blank at first, there would have been a copy of old Marley's head on every one'

Throughout the novella, Dickens makes Scrooge's response to things he does agree with or understand as 'Humbug!' as in the case of the things supernatural.

On entry by Marley's Ghost, Scrooge fearful, is unsure if the Ghost is **darkness** in the form of damnation but learns that the Ghost is there to save his soul from the heavy chains of iniquity in the afterlife.

Dickens makes use of **darkness** as a tool of the supernatural,

'The spectre, after listening for a moment, joined in the mournful dirge, and floated out upon the bleak, dark night'

With the phantoms no more, **darkness** no more posed a threat to Scrooge,

'they and their spirit voices faded together; and the night became as it had been when he walked home'

In **Stave Two**, **darkness** is banished by the brilliant light emanating from the First Spirit.

At the start of **Stave Two**, before the arrival of the First Spirit, Scrooge wakes,

'it was so **dark**, that looking out of bed, he could scarcely distinguish the transparent window from the opaque walls of his chamber'

Dickens continues to set the scene by use of **darkness** to juxtapose the forthcoming light emanating from the First Spirit,

'He was endeavouring to pierce the **darkness** with his ferret eyes'

With the arrival of the First Spirit, their journey begins, passing through Scrooge's chamber wall, and standing upon an open country road, surrounded by open fields. **Darkness** is juxtaposed to white snow,

'The **darkness** and the mist had vanished it, for it was a clear, cold, winter day, with snow upon the ground'

In **Stave Three**, the Second Spirit takes Scrooge on a journey to observe the light of celebration within people on Christmas Day, but by the time they left the Cratchits, it was getting dark. **Darkness** is no barrier to the ongoing celebrations. People would shut out cold and **darkness**,

'deep red curtains, ready to be drawn to shut out cold and **darkness**'

Dickens continues the journey in the **darkness**, from the mining community, lighthouse keepers, seamen on the raging sea,

'while listening to the moaning of the wind, and thinking what a solemn thing it was to move on through the lonely **darkness** over an unknown abyss'

to their final destination at his nephew's residence.

In **Stave Four**, the Last Spirit's appearance is **darkness** personified,

'It was shrouded in a deep black garment. It would have been difficult to detach its figure from the night, and separate it from the **darkness** by which it was surrounded'

Dickens instils **darkness** in the Last Spirit to add weight to the consequences awaiting Scrooge should he not heed the lessons taught to him by all three Spirits.
The Phantom never speaks but only points with his figure.

The Phantom takes Scrooge into the future to teach him about the **darkness** of man. Businessmen mock and decry the practices of a recently deceased moneylender. Next, wealthy friends of Scrooge hardly say anything about the deceased, as if his death is of no consequence.

Scrooge is confused, not sure if the deceased might be his future self, but

'quiet and **dark**, beside him stood the Phantom, with its outstretched hand'

Next, they travel into an obscure part of the town, where **darkness** lurks in the guise,

'shops and houses wretched; people half-naked, drunken, slipshod; reeked with crime, with filth, and misery'

Onto a beetling shop, and the **dark** side of death, where solitude creates the opportunity for scavengers to steal possessions once belonging to the deceased.
Old Joe buys, the charwoman, laundress, and the undertaker's man sell.

Scrooge listened to their dialogue in horror, and viewed them

'with a detestation and disgust, which could hardly have been greater, though they had been obscene demons, marketing the corpse itself'

The charwoman, on collecting her money from Old Joe remarks,

"He frightened every one away from him when he was alive, to profit us when he was dead! Ha, ha, ha!"

Scrooge, shuddering from head to foot, realising that **darkness** has created these events, remarks

'the case of this unhappy man might be my own'

Scrooge recoiled in terror, for the scene had changed,

'The room was very **dark**, too **dark** to be observed with any accuracy'
'upon the bed plundered and bereft, unwatched, unwept, uncared for, was the body'

Next, at the Cratchit's dwellings, the scene of tenderness connected with a death, requested by Scrooge, shows the **darkness** within the family caused by the premature death of Tiny Tim. Mrs Cratchit and the children await Bob who is beside himself with grief, and relieves part of the darkness within himself by going upstairs and spending a few moments with his deceased son,

'Poor Bob sat down, and when he had thought a little and composed himself, he kissed the little face. He was reconciled to what

COLD

Cold, and its counterpart heat, is used as a **motif** to impact the very nature of Scrooge and his attitude and behaviour towards friends and outsiders, as well as his workplace and living quarters.

In **Stave One**, Scrooge is described as immune to heat and cold,

'External heat and **cold** had little influence on Scrooge.
No warmth could warm, nor wintry weather chill him.'

Scrooge made his counting-house **cold** to save money and as a conniving way to make Bob Cratchit shiver and generate his own body heat.

'Wherefore the clerk put on his white comforter, and tied to warm himself at the candle; in which effort, he failed'

Dickens describes the weather as

'piecing, searching, biting, **cold**'

And in the simile, Dickens describes the nose of the of the rebuked carol singer as

'gnawed and mumbled by the hungry **cold** as bones are gnawed by dogs'

Dickens continues the motif of **cold** in weather and in buildings to match Scrooge's persona. On his way home,

'The cold became intense'

In his living quarters,

'Scrooge had a cold in his head'

In **Stave Two**, Scrooge is transported by the First Spirit to an open country road, with fields on either side, on a

'clear, **cold**, winter day, with snow upon the ground'

Scrooge recognised the boys in the gigs and carts,

his **cold** eye glisten, and his heart leap up as they went past!

His childhood school, they found,

'poorly furnished, **cold**, and vast'

The motif of **cold** is melted by Fan, Scrooge's sister, and the flamboyant Mr Fezziwig, but re-emergence when Scrooge as a young man, his is spurned by his fiancée Belle in response to his cold-hearted nature and love of money.

In **Stave Three**, the Second Spirit shows Scrooge the warmth of the Christmas spirit where **cold** is dispelled by the milk of human kindness.

'deep red curtains, ready to be drawn, to shut out **cold** and darkness'

They went to all the coldest places on earth, the cold streets, the bleak and deserted moor, the miner's huts in the barren waste, the solitary lighthouse built upon a dismal reef of sunken rocks, the deck of a ship on a black heaving sea, onto his nephew's house, and finally, the cold street and his destiny with the coldness of the Third Spirit of doom.

In **Stave Four**, the Third Spirit takes Scrooge to listen to businessmen talking about the recent death of a man who they deride. Two men known to Scrooge, remark,

"Well!" said the first. "Old Scratch has got his own at last, hey?"
"So I am told" returned the second. "**Cold**, isn't it"

Scrooge starts to think with fear that maybe they are talking about his future death. Still perplexed, and not recognising his future self, standing in his accustomed corner at his usual time of day, and with the Phantom pointing his figure at him, this

'made him shudder and feel very **cold**'.

Next, at the beetling shop, the shopkeeper Old Joe welcomes with glee the three cold-hearted scavengers who desire to sell the dead man's property: the charwoman, the laundress Mrs Dilber, and the undertaker's man.

The charwoman having taken the dead man's bed curtains, and expensive calico burial shirt, mockingly justifies the taking of the dead man's blankets,

"He isn't likely to take **cold** without 'em, I dare say."

Suddenly, the scene changes, Scrooge is terrified to find himself standing next to the body of the dead man covered by a ragged sheet, lying in the bed uncurtained by the charwoman. Scrooge is too scared to uncover the face beneath the sheet, fearing that it might be his future self.   Instead, he addresses dreadful Death as,

'Oh **cold**, **cold**, rigid, dreadful Death, set up thine altar here'

in the hope that by redemption, his future demise would not be as **cold**, lonely, and uncaring as experienced by the dead man lying in the bed before him.

At the end of this journey, the Phantom's finger points to the coldness of the gravestone. No epitaph engraved except the words EBENEZER SCROOGE.

In **Stave Five**, Scrooge looking out of his window on Christmas morning exclaims,

'No fog, no mist; clear, bright, jovial, stirring, **cold**'

followed by

'**cold**, piping for the blood to dance to'

Perhaps, Dickens was revisiting his past, and thinking of the happy, snowy Christmas's at Fezziwig, where dance banished **cold**.

FOG

Fog is used as a **motif** to create a link with the supernatural world, and as a companion to Scrooge's blindness to the plight of the poor.

In **Stave One**, fog pervades and obscures all.

'The **fog** came pouring in at every chink and keyhole'

and preluding to forthcoming events,

'was so dense without, that although the court was of the narrowest, the houses opposite were mere phantoms'

Again, the fog immobilises all,

'**fog** and darkness thickened so, that people ran about with flaring links, proffering their services to go before horses in carriages, and conduct them on their way'

Dickens emphasises the loneliness created by the fog,

'the singer fled in terror, leaving the keyhole to the **fog**'

Even Scrooge is blinded by the fog

'The **fog** and frost hung about the black old gateway of the house'

The **fog** heralds the arrival of Jacob Marley's ghost, and his brethren phantoms.

In **Stave Five**, looking out of his window on Christmas morning, Scrooge exclaims

'No fog, no mist'

With the fog obscuring Christmas lifted, so too is the fog within Scrooge's own mind, that has prevented him from recognising his own responsibility to those less fortunate than himself!

SYMBOLS

MUSIC

Music is used as a **symbol** of shared values of tradition, happiness and kinship within communities, and is an indicator of Scrooge's annoyance and joy.

In **Stave One**, carol singers annoy Scrooge.

In **Stave Two**, at Fezziwigs, music enthrals Scrooge, and makes him dance.

In **Stave Three**, at the Cratchits residence, Scrooge is mesmerised by Tiny Tim's angelic voice. Next the voice of an old man singing a Christmas song to others in a miner's hut, and finally to the music and dance at his nephew's house, which Scrooge relates to, and enjoys.

In **Stave Five**, Scrooge cannot wait to get back to the music and dance once enjoyed at Fezziwigs.

MARLEY'S CHAINS

Marley's chains are the rewards of purgatory.

In **Stave One**, Marley's chains are the **symbol** of avarice and selfishness, which await Scrooge should he not embrace community and humanity.

SCROOGE'S BED

Scrooge's bed is the **symbol** of sanctuary, a private space where Scrooge is safe from the outside world, but not seemly from the supernatural world.

SCROOGE'S GRAVESTONE

Scrooge's gravestone is the **symbol** of oblivion where, as in life, so in death, isolation ensures no one mourns and weeds abound.

BOB'S PAY

Unlike Fezziwig, Scrooge is symbolic of a bad employer, who pays less than that needed for an employee to live and feed his family.

STAVE 1

Read this extract from Stave One of the Novella then answer the question that follows.

Scrooge and Bob Cratchit are in the counting house on Christmas Eve.

> Once upon a time -- of all the good days in the year, on Christmas Eve -- old Scrooge sat busy in his counting-house. It was cold, bleak, biting weather: foggy withal: and he could hear the people in the court outside, go wheezing up and down, beating their hands upon their breasts, and stamping their feet upon the pavement stones to warm them. The city clocks had only just gone three, but it was quite dark already: it had not been light all day: and candles were flaring in the windows of the neighbouring offices, like ruddy smears upon the palpable brown air. The fog came pouring in at every chink and keyhole, and was so dense without, that although the court was of the narrowest, the houses opposite were mere phantoms. To see the dingy cloud come drooping down, obscuring everything, one might have thought that Nature lived hard by, and was brewing on a large scale. The door of Scrooge's counting-house was open that he might keep his eye upon his clerk, who in a dismal little cell beyond, a sort of tank, was copying letters. Scrooge had a very small fire, but the clerk's fire was so very much smaller that it looked like one coal. But he couldn't replenish it, for Scrooge kept the coal-box in his own room; and so surely as the clerk came in with the shovel, the master predicted that it would be necessary for them to part. Wherefore the clerk put on his white comforter, and tried to warm himself at the candle; in which effort, not being a man of a strong imagination, he failed.

Starting with this extract, how does Dickens create atmosphere in A Christmas Carol?
Write about:
- How Dickens creates atmosphere in this extract
- How Dickens creates atmosphere in the novel as a whole.

Read the following extract from Stave One then answer the question that follows. Here, we are introduced to Ebenezer Scrooge.

Marley was dead: to begin with. There is no doubt whatever about that. The register of his burial was signed by the clergyman, the clerk, the undertaker, and the chief mourner. Scrooge signed it. And Scrooge's name was good upon 'Change, for anything he chose to put his hand to. Old Marley was as dead as a door-nail. Scrooge knew he was dead? Of course he did. How could it be otherwise? Scrooge and he were partners for I don't know how many years. Scrooge was his sole executor, his sole administrator, his sole assign, his sole residuary legatee, his sole friend, and sole mourner. And even Scrooge was not so dreadfully cut up by the sad event, but that he was an excellent man of business on the very day of the funeral, and solemnised it with an undoubted bargain. The mention of Marley's funeral brings me back to the point I started from. There is no doubt that Marley was dead. This must be distinctly understood, or nothing wonderful can come of the story I am going to relate. Scrooge never painted out Old Marley's name. There it stood, years afterwards, above the warehouse door: Scrooge and Marley. The firm was known as Scrooge and Marley. Sometimes people new to the business called Scrooge, and sometimes Marley, but he answered to both names. It was all the same to him. Oh! But he was a tight-fisted hand at the grind- stone, Scrooge! a squeezing, wrenching, grasping, scraping, clutching, covetous, old sinner! Hard and sharp as flint, from which no steel had ever struck out generous fire; secret, and self-contained, and solitary as an oyster. The cold within him froze his old features, nipped his pointed nose, shrivelled his cheek, stiffened his gait; made his eyes red, his thin lips blue; and spoke out shrewdly in his grating voice. A frosty rime was on his head, and on his eyebrows, and his wiry chin. He carried his own low temperature always about with him; he iced his office in the dogdays; and didn't thaw it one degree at Christmas. External heat and cold had little influence on Scrooge. No warmth could warm, no wintry weather chill him. No wind that blew was bitterer than he, no falling snow was more intent upon its purpose, no pelting rain less open to entreaty. Foul weather didn't know where to have him. The heaviest rain, and snow, and hail, and sleet, could boast of the advantage over him in only one respect. They often `came down' handsomely, and Scrooge never did. Nobody ever stopped him in the street to say, with gladsome looks, `My dear Scrooge, how are you? When will you come to see me?' No beggars implored him to bestow a trifle, no children asked him what it was o'clock, no man or woman ever once in all his life inquired the way to such and such a place, of Scrooge. Even the blind men's dogs appeared to know him; and when they saw him coming on, would tug their owners into doorways and up courts; and then would wag their tails as though they said, `No eye at all is better than an evil eye, dark master!' But what did Scrooge care! It was the very thing he liked. To edge his way along the crowded paths of life, warning all human sympathy to keep its distance, was what the knowing ones call 'nuts' to Scrooge.

Starting with this extract, how is Scrooge presented in A Christmas Carol?
Write about:
- How Scrooge is presented in this extract
- How Scrooge is presented in the novel as a whole

Read the following extract from Stave One of A Christmas Carol.
It is Christmas Eve and two portly gentlemen have arrived collecting for charity for the poor and homeless.

"At this festive season of the year, Mr Scrooge," said the gentleman, taking up a pen, ``it is more than usually desirable that we should make some slight provision for the Poor and destitute, who suffer greatly at the present time. Many thousands are in want of common necessaries; hundreds of thousands are in want of common comforts, sir."

"Are there no prisons?" asked Scrooge.

"Plenty of prisons," said the gentleman, laying down the pen again.

"And the Union workhouses?" demanded Scrooge. "Are they still in operation?"

"They are. Still," returned the gentleman, "I wish I could say they were not."

"The Treadmill and the Poor Law are in full vigour, then?" said Scrooge.

"Both very busy, sir."

"Oh! I was afraid, from what you said at first, that something had occurred to stop them in their useful course," said Scrooge. "I'm very glad to hear it."

"Under the impression that they scarcely furnish Christian cheer of mind or body to the multitude," returned the gentleman, "a few of us are endeavouring to raise a fund to buy the Poor some meat and drink, and means of warmth. We choose this time, because it is a time, of all others, when Want is keenly felt, and Abundance rejoices. What shall I put you down for?"

"Nothing!" Scrooge replied.

"You wish to be anonymous?"

"I wish to be left alone," said Scrooge. "Since you ask me what I wish, gentlemen, that is my answer. I don't make merry myself at Christmas and I can't afford to make idle people merry. I help to support the establishments I have mentioned: they cost enough: and those who are badly off must go there."

"Many can't go there; and many would rather die."

"If they would rather die," said Scrooge, "they had better do it, and decrease the surplus population. Besides -- excuse me -- I don't know that. "

Starting with this extract, how does Dickens present attitudes towards poverty in A Christmas Carol?
Write about:
- How Dickens presents attitudes towards poverty in this extract
- How Dickens presents attitudes towards poverty in the novel as a whole.

Read this extract from Stave Two of the novella then answer the question that follows.

The Ghost of Christmas Past has just appeared to Scrooge whilst he was bed

It was a strange figure -- like a child: yet not so like a child as like an old man, viewed through some supernatural medium, which gave him the appearance of having receded from the view, and being diminished to a child's proportions. Its hair, which hung about its neck and down its back, was white as if with age; and yet the face had not a wrinkle in it, and the tenderest bloom was on the skin. The arms were very long and muscular; the hands the same, as if its hold were of uncommon strength. Its legs and feet, most delicately formed, were, like those upper members, bare. It wore a tunic of the purest white and round its waist was bound a lustrous belt, the sheen of which was beautiful. It held a branch of fresh green holly in its hand; and, in singular contradiction of that wintry emblem, had its dress trimmed with summer flowers. But the strangest thing about it was, that from the crown of its head there sprung a bright clear jet of light, by which all this was visible; and which was doubtless the occasion of its using, in its duller moments, a great extinguisher for a cap, which it now held under its arm.

Starting with this extract, how does Dickens present the supernatural in A Christmas Carol? Write about:
- How Dickens presents the supernatural in this extract
- How Dickens presents the supernatural in the novel as a whole.

STAVE 2

Read this extract from Stave Two of the novella then answer the question that follows.

In this extract, Scrooge is watching his former self as an apprentice for his previous employer, Mr. Fezziwig. Accompanied by the ghost of Christmas Past, he observes the celebrations and becomes caught up in the excitement.

There were more dances, and there were forfeits, and more dances, and there was cake, and there was Negus, and there was a great piece of Cold Roast, and there was a great piece of Cold Boiled, and there were mince-pies, and plenty of beer. But the great effect of the evening came after the Roast and Boiled, when the fiddler (an artful dog, mind! The sort of man who knew his business better than you or I could have told it him!) struck up 'Sir Roger de Coverley'. Then old Fezziwig stood out to dance with Mrs. Fezziwig. Top couple, too; with a good stiff piece of work cut out for them; three or four and twenty pair of partners; people who were not to be trifled with; people who would dance and had no notion of walking.

But if they had been twice as many — ah, four times — old Fezziwig would have been a match for them, and so would Mrs. Fezziwig. As to her, she was worthy to be his partner in every sense of the term. If that's not high praise, tell me higher, and I'll use it. A positive light appeared to issue from Fezziwig's calves. They shone in every part of the dance like moons. You couldn't have predicted, at any given time, what would become of them next. And when old Fezziwig and Mrs. Fezziwig had gone all through the dance; advance and retire, both hands to your partner, bow and curtsy, corkscrew, thread-the-needle, and back again to your place: Fezziwig 'cut' — cut so deftly, that he appeared to wink with his legs, and came upon his feet again without a stagger.

Starting with this extract, how does Dickens create an atmosphere of celebration? Write about:
* How Dickens presents a celebratory atmosphere in this extract
* How Dickens presents a celebratory atmosphere in the novel as a whole.

STAVE 2

Read this extract from Stave Two of the novella then answer the question that follows.

Here, the Ghost of Christmas Past has taken Scrooge to see himself as a boy.

"The school is not quite deserted," said the Ghost. "A solitary child, neglected by his friends, is left there still."

Scrooge said he knew it. And he sobbed.

They left the high-road, by a well-remembered lane, and soon approached a mansion of dull red brick, with a little weathercock-surmounted cupola, on the roof, and a bell hanging in it. It was a large house, but one of broken fortunes; for the spacious offices were little used, their walls were damp and mossy, their windows broken, and their gates decayed. Fowls clucked and strutted in the stables; and the coach-houses and sheds were over-run with grass. Nor was it more retentive of its ancient state, within; for entering the dreary hall, and glancing through the open doors of many rooms, they found them poorly furnished, cold, and vast. There was an earthy savour in the air, a chilly bareness in the place, which associated itself somehow with too much getting up by candle-light, and not too much to eat.

They went, the Ghost and Scrooge, across the hall, to a door at the back of the house. It opened before them, and disclosed a long, bare, melancholy room, made barer still by lines of plain deal forms and desks. At one of these a lonely boy was reading near a feeble fire; and Scrooge sat down upon a form and wept to see his poor forgotten self as he used to be.

Not a latent echo in the house, not a squeak and scuffle from the mice behind the paneling, not a drip from the half-thawed waterspout in the dull yard behind, not a sigh among the leafless boughs of one despondent poplar, not the idle swinging of an empty store-house door, no, not a clicking in the fire, but fell upon the heart of Scrooge with a softening influence and gave a freer passage to his tears.

Starting with this extract, to what extent do you think that Dickens presents Scrooge as a sympathetic character?

Write about:

- How Dickens presents Scrooge in this extract
- How Dickens presents Scrooge in the novel as a whole.

Read this extract from Stave Two of the novella then answer the question that follows.

Scrooge and the Ghost of Christmas Past watch as Belle releases Scrooge from their engagement.

> This was not addressed to Scrooge, or to any one whom he could see, but it produced an immediate effect. For again Scrooge saw himself. He was older now, a man in the prime of life. His face had not the harsh and rigid lines of later years; but it had begun to wear the signs of care and avarice. There was an eager, greedy, restless motion in the eye, which showed the passion that had taken root, and where the shadow of the growing tree would fall.
>
> He was not alone but sat by the side of a fair young girl in a mourning-dress: in whose eyes there were tears, which sparkled in the light that shone out of the Ghost of Christmas Past.
>
> "It matters little," she said, softly. "To you, very little. Another idol has displaced me; and if it can cheer and comfort you in time to come, as I would have tried to do, I have no just cause to grieve."
>
> "What Idol has displaced you?" he rejoined.
>
> "A golden one."
>
> "This is the even-handed dealing of the world!" he said. "There is nothing on which it is so hard as poverty; and there is nothing it professes to condemn with such severity as the pursuit of wealth!"
>
> "You fear the world too much," she answered, gently. "All your other hopes have merged into the hope of being beyond the chance of its sordid reproach. I have seen your nobler aspirations fall off one by one, until the master-passion, Gain, engrosses you. Have I not?"
>
> "What then?" he retorted. "Even if I have grown so much wiser, what then? I am not changed towards you."
>
> She shook her head.
>
> "Am I?"
>
> "Our contract is an old one. It was made when we were both poor and content to be so, until, in good season, we could improve our worldly fortune by our patient industry. You are changed. When it was made, you were another man."
>
> "I was a boy," he said impatiently.

Starting with this extract, explain how Dickens writes about how Scrooge changes from boyhood up to the death of Marley.

Write about:

- How Dickens presents Scrooge in this extract
- How Dickens presents Scrooge in the novel as a whole.

STAVE 3

Read this extract from Stave Three of the novella then answer the question that follows.

Scrooge is woken to find the Ghost of Christmas Present in his living room.

It was his own room. There was no doubt about that. But it had undergone a surprising transformation. The walls and ceiling were so hung with living green, that it looked a perfect grove; from every part of which, bright gleaming berries glistened. The crisp leaves of holly, mistletoe, and ivy reflected back the light, as if so many little mirrors had been scattered there; and such a mighty blaze went roaring up the chimney, as that dull petrification of a hearth had never known in Scrooge's time, or Marley's, or for many and many a winter season gone. Heaped up on the floor, to form a kind of throne, were turkeys, geese, game, poultry, brawn, great joints of meat, sucking-pigs, long wreaths of sausages, mince-pies, plum-puddings, barrels of oysters, red-hot chestnuts, cherry-cheeked apples, juicy oranges, luscious pears, immense twelfth-cakes, and seething bowls of punch, that made the chamber dim with their delicious steam. In easy state upon this couch, there sat a jolly Giant, glorious to see, who bore a glowing torch, in shape not unlike Plenty's horn, and held it up, high up, to shed its light on Scrooge, as he came peeping round the door.

"Come in!" exclaimed the Ghost. "Come in. and know me better, man!"

Scrooge entered timidly and hung his head before this Spirit. He was not the dogged Scrooge he had been and though the Spirit's eyes were clear and kind, he did not like to meet them.

"I am the Ghost of Christmas Present," said the Spirit. "Look upon me!"

Starting with this extract, how does Dickens present Christmas?
Write about:
- How Dickens presents Christmas in this extract
- How Dickens presents Christmas in the novel as a whole.

Read this extract from Stave Three of the novella then answer the question that follows.

In this extract, Scrooge is observing the Cratchit family during Christmas dinner, accompanied by the Ghost of Christmas Present.

Martha, who was a poor apprentice at a milliner's, then told them what kind of work she had to do, and how many hours she worked at a stretch, and how she meant to lie a-bed to-morrow morning for a good long rest; to-morrow being a holiday she passed at home. Also, how she had seen a countess and a lord some days before, and how the lord ``was much about as tall as Peter;" at which Peter pulled up his collars so high that you couldn't have seen his head if you had been there. All this time the chestnuts and the jug went round and round, and bye and bye they had a song, about a lost child travelling in the snow, from Tiny Tim; who had a plaintive little voice, and sang it very well indeed. There was nothing of high mark in this.

They were not a handsome family; they were not well dressed; their shoes were far from being water-proof; their clothes were scanty; and Peter might have known, and very likely did, the inside of a pawnbroker's. But they were happy, grateful, pleased with one another, and contented with the time; and when they faded, and looked happier yet in the bright sprinklings of the Spirit's torch at parting, Scrooge had his eye upon them, and especially on Tiny Tim, until the last.

Starting with this extract, how does Dickens present family?
Write about:
- How Dickens presents family in this extract
- How Dickens presents family in the novel as a whole.

STAVE 3

Read this extract from Stave Three of the novella then answer the question that follows.

Here, the Ghost of Christmas Present shows Scrooge how different groups of people celebrate Christmas.

"What place is this?" asked Scrooge.

"A place where Miners live, who labour in the bowels of the earth," returned the Spirit. "But they know me. See."

A light shone from the window of a hut, and swiftly they advanced towards it. Passing through the wall of mud and stone, they found a cheerful company assembled round a glowing fire. An old, old man and woman, with their children and their children's children, and another generation beyond that, all decked out gaily in their holiday attire. The old man, in a voice that seldom rose above the howling of the wind upon the barren waste, was singing them a Christmas song – it had been a very old song when he was a boy – and from time to time they all joined in the chorus. So surely as they raised their voices, the old man got quite blithe and loud; and so surely as they stopped, his vigour sank again.

The Spirit did not tarry here, but bade Scrooge hold his robe, and passing on above the moor, sped – whither. Not to sea? To sea. To Scrooge's horror, looking back, he saw the last of the land, a frightful range of rocks, behind them; and his ears were deafened by the thundering of water, as it rolled and roared, and raged among the dreadful caverns it had worn, and fiercely tried to undermine the earth.

Built upon a dismal reef of sunken rocks, some league or so from shore, on which the waters chafed and dashed, the wild year through, there stood a solitary lighthouse. Great heaps of sea-weed clung to its base, and storm-birds – born of the wind one might suppose, as sea-weed of the water – rose and fell about it, like the waves they skimmed. But even here, two men who watched the light had made a fire, that through the loophole in the thick stone wall shed out a ray of brightness on the awful sea. Joining their horny hands over the rough table at which they sat, they wished each other Merry Christmas in their can of grog; and one of them: the elder, too, with his face all damaged and scarred with hard weather, as the figure-head of an old ship might be: struck up a sturdy song that was like a Gale in itself.

Starting with this extract, explain what is meant by the spirit of Christmas and how Dickens writes about it.

Write about:

- How Dickens writes about the spirit of Christmas in the extract
- How Dickens about the spirit of Christmas in the novel as a whole.

Read this extract from Stave Three of the novella then answer the question that follows.

Scrooge has come to the end of his journey with The Ghost of Christmas Present when he notices something beneath the spirit's robes.

"Oh, Man! look here. Look, look, down here!" exclaimed the Ghost.

They were a boy and girl. Yellow, meagre, ragged, scowling, wolfish; but prostrate, too, in their humility. Where graceful youth should have filled their features out, and touched them with its freshest tints, a stale and shrivelled hand, like that of age, had pinched, and twisted them, and pulled them into shreds. Where angels might have sat enthroned, devils lurked, and glared out menacing. No change, no degradation, no perversion of humanity, in any grade, through all the mysteries of wonderful creation, has monsters half so horrible and dread.

Scrooge started back, appalled. Having them shown to him in this way, he tried to say they were fine children, but the words choked themselves, rather than be parties to a lie of such enormous magnitude.

"Spirit! are they yours?" Scrooge could say no more.

"They are Man's," said the Spirit, looking down upon them. "And they cling to me, appealing from their fathers. This boy is Ignorance. This girl is Want. Beware them both, and all of their degree, but most of all beware this boy, for on his brow I see that written which is Doom, unless the writing be erased. Deny it!" cried the Spirit, stretching out its hand towards the city. "Slander those who tell it ye! Admit it for your factious purposes and make it worse! And bide the end!"

"Have they no refuge or resource?" cried Scrooge. "Are there no prisons?" said the Spirit, turning on him for the last time with his own words. "Are there no workhouses?"

The bell struck twelve.

Starting with this extract, how does Dickens present social injustice in A Christmas Carol?
Write about:
- How Dickens presents social injustice in this extract
- How Dickens presents social injustice in the novel as a whole.

Read this extract from Stave Three of the novella then answer the question that follows.

In this extract, the Ghost of Christmas Present shows Scrooge the Cratchit family's Christmas celebrations.

Oh, a wonderful pudding! Bob Cratchit said, and calmly too, that he regarded it as the greatest success achieved by Mrs. Cratchit since their marriage. Mrs. Cratchit said that now the weight was off her mind, she would confess she had had her doubts about the quantity of flour. Everybody had something to say about it, but nobody said or thought it was at all a small pudding for a large family. It would have been flat heresy to do so. Any Cratchit would have blushed to hint at such a thing. At last, the dinner was all done, the cloth was cleared, the hearth swept, and the fire made up. The compound in the jug being tasted, and considered perfect, apples and oranges were put upon the table, and a shovel-full of chestnuts on the fire. Then all the Cratchit family drew round the hearth, in what Bob Cratchit called a circle, meaning half a one; and at Bob Cratchit's elbow stood the family display of glass. Two tumblers, and a custard-cup without a handle. These held the hot stuff from the jug, however, as well as golden goblets would have done; and Bob served it out with beaming looks, while the chestnuts on the fire sputtered and cracked noisily. Then Bob proposed: "A Merry Christmas to us all, my dears. God bless us!" Which all the family re-echoed. "God bless us every one!" said Tiny Tim, the last of all. He sat very close to his father's side upon his little stool. Bob held his withered little hand in his, as if he loved the child, and wished to keep him by his side, and dreaded that he might be taken from him.

Starting with this extract, explore how Dickens uses the Cratchit family to show the struggles of the poor
Write about:
- How Dickens presents the Cratchit family in this extract
- How Dickens uses the Cratchit family to show the struggles of the poor in the novel as a whole.

Read this extract from Stave Four of the novella then answer the question that follows.

The Ghost of Christmas Yet to Come has appeared before Scrooge.

The Phantom slowly, gravely, silently approached. When it came, Scrooge bent down upon his knee; for in the very air through which this Spirit moved it seemed to scatter gloom and mystery.

It was shrouded in a deep black garment, which concealed its head, its face, its form, and left nothing of it visible save one outstretched hand. But for this it would have been difficult to detach its figure from the night and separate it from the darkness by which it was surrounded.

He felt that it was tall and stately when it came beside him, and that its mysterious presence filled him with a solemn dread. He knew no more, for the Spirit neither spoke nor moved.

"I am in the presence of the Ghost of Christmas Yet To Come?" said Scrooge.

The Spirit answered not but pointed onward with its hand.

"You are about to show me shadows of the things that have not happened, but will happen in the time before us," Scrooge pursued. "Is that so, Spirit?"

Starting with this extract, how does Dickens use the supernatural to create atmosphere?
Write about:
- How Dickens uses the supernatural in this extract
- How Dickens uses the supernatural in the novel as a whole.

Read this extract from Stave Four of the novella then answer the question that follows.

The Ghost of Christmas Yet to Come takes Scrooge to the Royal Exchange.

The Spirit stopped beside one little knot of business men. Observing that the hand was pointed to them, Scrooge advanced to listen to their talk.

"No," said a great fat man with a monstrous chin, "I don't know much about it, either way. I only know he's dead."

"When did he die?" inquired another.

"Last night, I believe."

"Why, what was the matter with him?" asked a third, taking a vast quantity of snuff out of a very large snuff-box. "I thought he'd never die."

"God knows," said the first, with a yawn.

"What has he done with his money?" asked a red-faced gentleman with a pendulous excrescence on the end of his nose, that shook like the gills of a turkey-cock.

"I haven't heard," said the man with the large chin, yawning again. "Left it to his Company, perhaps. He hasn't left it to me. That's all I know."

This pleasantry was received with a general laugh.

"It's likely to be a very cheap funeral," said the same speaker; "for upon my life I don't know of anybody to go to it. Suppose we make up a party and volunteer?"

"I don't mind going if a lunch is provided," observed the gentleman with the excrescence on his nose. "But I must be fed, if I make one."

Another laugh.

"Well, I am the most disinterested among you, after all," said the first speaker, "for I never wear black gloves, and I never eat lunch. But I'll offer to go, if anybody else will. When I come to think of it, I'm not at all sure that I wasn't his most particular friend; for we used to stop and speak whenever we met. Bye, bye!"

Starting with this extract, how does Dickens present business and commerce in A Christmas Carol?

Write about:

- How Dickens presents business and commerce in this extract
- How Dickens presents business and commerce in the novel as a whole.

Read this extract from Stave Four of the novella then answer the question that follows.

The Ghost of Christmas Yet to Come shows Scrooge a vision of the Cratchit's in the future. They have been discussing how Scrooge's nephew, Fred, has helped the family and is likely to secure a job for their son, Peter.

"But however and whenever we part from one another, I am sure we shall none of us forget poor Tiny Tim -- shall we -- or this first parting that there was among us?"

"Never, father!" cried they all.

"And I know," said Bob, "I know, my dears, that when we recollect how patient and how mild he was; although he was a little, little child; we shall not quarrel easily among ourselves, and forget poor Tiny Tim in doing it."

"No, never, father!" they all cried again.

"I am very happy," said little Bob, "I am very happy!"

Mrs Cratchit kissed him, his daughters kissed him, the two young Cratchits kissed him, and Peter and himself shok hands. Spirit of Tiny Tim, thy childish essence was from God!

"Spectre," said Scrooge, "something informs me that our parting moment is at hand. I know it, but I know not how. Tell me what man that was whom we saw lying dead?"

Starting with this extract, how does Dickens present death in A Christmas Carol? Write about:
- How Dickens presents death in this extract
- How Dickens presents death in the novel as a whole.

Read this extract from Stave Four of the novella then answer the question that follows.

Here, the Cratchits are mourning the death of Tiny Tim.

They drew about the fire and talked; the girls and mother working still. Bob told them of the extraordinary kindness of Mr Scrooge's nephew, whom he had scarcely seen but once, and who, meeting him in the street that day, and seeing that he looked a little – "just a little down you know," said Bob, inquired what had happened to distress him. "On which," said Bob, "for he is the pleasantest-spoken gentleman you ever heard, I told him. 'I am heartily sorry for it, Mr Cratchit,' he said, 'and heartily sorry for your good wife.' By the bye, how he ever knew that I don't know."

"Knew what, my dear?"

"Why, that you were a good wife," replied Bob.

"Everybody knows that", said Peter.

"Very well observed, my boy!" cried Bob. "I hope they do. 'Heartily sorry,' he said, 'for your good wife. If I can be of service to you in any way,' he said, giving me his card, 'that's where I live. Pray come to me.' Now, it wasn't," cried Bob," for the sake of anything he might be able to do for us, so much as for his kind way, that this was quite delightful. It really seemed as if he had known our Tiny Tim and felt with us."

"I'm sure he's a good soul," said Mrs Cratchit.

"You would be surer of it, my dear," returned Bob, "if you saw and spoke to him. I shouldn't be at all surprised mark what I say, if he got Peter a better situation."

"Only hear that, Peter," said Mrs Cratchit.

"And then," cried one of the girls, "Peter will be keeping company with someone, and setting up for himself."

"Get along with you!" retorted Peter, grinning.

"It's just as likely as not," said Bob, "one of these days; though there's plenty of time for that, my dear. But however, and whenever we part from one another, I am sure we shall none of us forget poor Tiny Tim – shall we – or this first parting that there was among us."

"Never, father!" cried they all.

Starting with this extract, how does Dickens present death in A Christmas Carol? Write about:
- How Dickens presents the Cratchit family in this extract
- How Dickens presents the Cratchit family in the novel as a whole.

STAVE 5

Read the following extract from Stave Five then answer the question that follows.

Here, we are told about Scrooge at the end of the novel.

> In the afternoon he turned his steps towards his nephew's house.
> He passed the door a dozen times, before he had the courage to go up and knock. But he made a dash, and did it:
> "Is your master at home, my dear?" said Scrooge to the girl. Nice girl! Very.
> "Yes, sir."
> "Where is he, my love?" said Scrooge.
> "He's in the dining-room, sir, along with mistress. I'll show you up-stairs, if you please."
> "Thank'ee. He knows me," said Scrooge, with his hand already on the dining-room lock. "I'll go in here, my dear."
> He turned it gently, and sidled his face in, round the door. They were looking at the table (which was spread out in great array); for these young housekeepers are always nervous on such points and like to see that everything is right.
> "Fred!" said Scrooge.
> Dear heart alive, how his niece by marriage started! Scrooge had forgotten, for the moment, about her sitting in the corner with the footstool, or he wouldn't have done it, on any account.
> "Why, bless my soul!" cried Fred, "who's that?"
> "It's I. Your uncle Scrooge. I have come to dinner. Will you let me in, Fred?"
> Let him in! It is a mercy he didn't shake his arm off. He was at home in five minutes. Nothing could be heartier.

Starting with this extract, how is Scrooge presented in A Christmas Carol?
Write about:
- How Scrooge is presented in this extract
- How Scrooge is presented in the novel as a whole

STAVE 5

Read the following extract from Stave Five then answer the question that follows.

In this extract, Scrooge visits his nephew, Fred.

Scrooge was better than his word. He did it all, and infinitely more; and to Tiny Tim, who did not die, he was a second father. He became as good a friend, as good a master, and as good a man, as the good old city knew, or any other good old city, town, or borough, in the good old world. Some people laughed to see the alteration in him, but he let them laugh, and little heeded them; for he was wise enough to know that nothing ever happened on this globe, for good, at which some people did not have their fill of laughter in the outset; and knowing that such as these would be blind anyway, he thought it quite as well that they should wrinkle up their eyes in grins, as have the malady in less attractive forms. His own heart laughed: and that was quite enough for him. He had no further intercourse with Spirits, but lived upon the Total Abstinence Principle, ever afterwards; and it was always said of him, that he knew how to keep Christmas well, if any man alive possessed the knowledge. May that be truly said of us, and all of us! And so, as Tiny Tim observed, God bless Us, Every One!

Starting with this extract, how does Dickens present attitudes to family?
Write about:
- How Dickens presents attitudes to family in this extract
- How Dickens present attitudes to family in the novel as a whole

STAVE 5

Read the following extract from Stave Five then answer the question that follows.

It is the day after Christmas day and Scrooge is at his counting house.

But he was early at the office next morning. Oh, he was early there. If he could only be there first, and catch Bob Cratchit coming late! That was the thing he had set his heart upon.

And he did it; yes, he did. The clock struck nine. No Bob. A quarter past. No Bob. He was full eighteen minutes and a half behind his time. Scrooge sat with his door wide open, that he might see him come into the Tank.

His hat was off, before he opened the door his comforter too. He was on his stool in a jiffy; driving away with his pen, as if he were trying to overtake nine o'clock.

"Hallo," growled Scrooge, in his accustomed voice, as near as he could feign it. "What do you mean by coming here at this time of day?"

"I'm very sorry, sir," said Bob. "I am behind my time."

"You are?" repeated Scrooge. "Yes. I think you are. Step this way, if you please."

"It's only once a year, sir," pleaded Bob, appearing from the Tank. "It shall not be repeated. I was making rather merry yesterday, sir."

"Now, I'll tell you what, my friend," said Scrooge, "I am not going to stand this sort of thing any longer. And therefore," he continued, leaping from his stool, and giving Bob such a dig in the waistcoat that he staggered back into the Tank again; "and therefore I am about to raise your salary."

Starting with this extract, how does Dickens present the transformation of Scrooge in A Christmas Carol?

Write about:

- How Dickens presents the transformation of Scrooge in this extract
- How Dickens presents the transformation of Scrooge in the novel as a whole

Q1   Discuss how Dickens presents the character of Scrooge in the book.

[Total 40 marks]

Q2   Discuss the relationship between Scrooge and nephew Fred in the book.

[Total 40 marks]

Q3   Discuss how Dickens presents the First Spirit in the book.

[Total 40 marks]

Q4   Discuss how Dickens presents the Second Spirit in the book.

[Total 40 marks]

Q5   Discuss how Dickens presents the Last Spirit in the book.

[Total 40 marks]

Q6   Discuss the relationship between Scrooge and his clerk Bob Cratchit.

[Total 40 marks]

Q7   Discuss the relationship between Bob Cratchit and his wife and children.

[Total 40 marks]

Q8   Discuss the relationship between Scrooge and the First Spirit.

[Total 40 marks]

Q9   Discuss the relationship between Scrooge and the Second Spirit.

[Total 40 marks]

Q10   Discuss the relationship between Scrooge and the Last Spirit.

[Total 40 marks]

Q11   Discuss the relationship between Old Joe and his clients.

[Total 40 marks]

Q12   Discuss the relationship between Scrooge and outsiders such as charity collectors, carol singers, ordinary town folk and in particular his debtors.

[Total 40 marks]

Q13   Discuss the theme of 'Christmas Spirit' in the book.

[Total 40 marks]

Q14   Discuss the theme of 'the Supernatural' in the book.

[Total 40 marks]

Q15 Discuss the theme of 'Isolation' in the book, with particular reference to Dickens use of the phrase 'solitary as an oyster'.

[Total 40 marks]

Q16 Discuss the theme of 'Money and Avarice' in the book.

[Total 40 marks]

Q17 Discuss the theme of 'Poverty' in the book.

[Total 40 marks]

Q18 Discuss the theme of 'Ignorance and Want' in the book.

[Total 40 marks]

Q19 Discuss the theme of 'Family' in the book.

[Total 40 marks]

Q20 Discuss the theme of 'Motifs and Symbols' in the book.

[Total 40 marks]

Q21 Discuss the theme of 'Social Responsibility' in the book.

[Total 40 marks]

Q22 Discuss the theme of 'Redemption' in the book.

[Total 40 marks]

Q23 Describe and evaluate Scrooge's journey to redemption.

[Total 40 marks]

Q24 How does Dickens use motifs of time, darkness, and cold in the storyline.

[Total 40 marks]

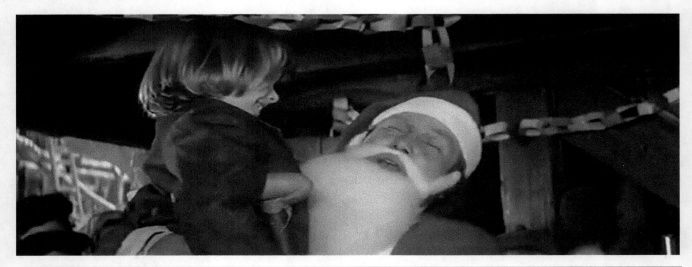

AUTHOR

Evelyn Samuel was born in South Africa, educated at the University of Durban-Westville, gaining a BA in English, Speech and Drama. She then went on to gain a Higher Education Diploma at the University of South Africa, and then onto the UK where her knowledge and skills were applied in educating students to achieve top grades in English Language and Literature up to A-level. Evelyn gained her Qualified Teacher Status in 2006, but in her pursuit to explore new horizons, continued her education gaining Diplomas in teaching English as a Foreign Language' to International Students, 'Writing Stories for Children', and most recently, gaining a Diploma in 'Travel Journalism'. Apart from teaching and writing, Evelyn's interests include travel to exotic places, cycling, dance, cuisine, and exploring new horizons.

www.EveSuperEasyBooks.com
EveSuperEasyBooks@gmail.com

STUDY GUIDE

Evelyn provides an in depth **SUPER SUPER EASY** interpretation of one of Dickens' most popular poignant moralistic novels, first published just prior to Christmas 1843. This guide is a must for those students determined to achieve a top grade in English Literature at any level from Key Stage 3 to GCSE to A-level.

STORY LINE

A Christmas Carol is the story of Ebenezer Scrooge, a wealthy old miser who is set in his ways with no love except for money until he is confronted by the Ghost of his former business partner Jacob Marley who out of concern for Scrooge's mortal soul, has arranged for three Spirits in turn visit and put Scrooge on the road to redemption.

The First Spirit takes Scrooge on a journey through his past life, reliving his unhappy childhood, contrasting with his happiness as an apprenticeship at Fezziwigs, then his rejection of love in favour of money, concluding with his miserly ways as a money lender.

The Second Spirit takes Scrooge on a journey through the streets of the City where Scrooge discovers the Christmas spirit in the marketplace, at dinner at the Cratchits, at the miners' community, at a lighthouse, on a ship, and at his nephew's house, after which the Spirit reveals from underneath his robe a bedraggled boy named Ignorance and a girl named Want.

The Last Spirit takes Scrooge into the future, where Scrooge experiences two possible outcomes: disregard for misers and their monetary ways, scavengers taking the possessions of the dead and Scrooge's early death. Else, redemption resulting in a long life, and the saving of Bob Cratchit's crippled son Tiny Tim from an early death.

Printed in the USA
CPSIA information can be obtained
at www.ICGtesting.com
LVHW071409251123
764796LV00019B/1813

9 781739 998134